MANKIND BEHAVING:
Human Needs and Material Culture

MANKIND BEHAVING:

Human Needs and Material Culture

By

JAMES K. FEIBLEMAN

Department of Philosophy
Tulane University

and

Department of Psychiatry
School of Medicine
Louisiana State University

CHARLES C THOMAS · PUBLISHER
Springfield · Illinois · U.S.A.

Published and Distributed Throughout the World by
CHARLES C THOMAS • PUBLISHER
BANNERSTONE HOUSE
301-327 East Lawrence Avenue, Springfield, Illinois, U.S.A.

Library of Congress Catalog Card Number: 63-16801

With THOMAS BOOKS careful attention is given to all details of manufacturing and design. It is the Publisher's desire to present books that are satisfactory as to their physical qualities and artistic possibilities and appropriate for their particular use. THOMAS BOOKS will be true to those laws of quality that assure a good name and good will.

Printed in the United States of America
H-2

PREFACE

My aim in this work has been to seek an understanding of individual human behavior. I have tried to examine social behavior in *The Institutions of Society* (1956) and cultural behavior in *The Theory of Human Culture* (1946). The three books together constitute a study of social organization; they belong together logically in the reverse of the order in which they have been written and published.

If, as Donne said and Hemingway made popular, no man is an island, neither is a book. While the central thesis and the organization of the present work is my own, the rest is the contribution of my predecessors and contemporaries in such fields as biology, psychology, the social sciences and philosophy. Their ideas support my own if I am right, but if I am wrong their ideas are not to be condemned along with mine, since more than one particular synthesis is possible. Nor would they necessarily agree with the use which has been made here of what they have accomplished. Anyone who endeavors to account for the entire man in terms not only of his principal needs but also of the culture he has produced out of the materials available to him in his environment must lay his work open to some of the charges of inadequacy which no doubt will be levelled against this book if indeed it is considered at all. I can only hope in such a case that I may then have given impetus to an inquiry even though it had been by contributing to a fairly new field a theory which was not entirely supported in it.

Special obligations which are more important than others will be listed in the early chapters. Here I wish to add only that the debt is broader than it will seem. One learns to recognize the larger borrowings but often the smaller escape notice; no doubt

I owe more than I know. A greater number are carried by the specific references.

A word of thanks is here recorded to a silent partner who has done so much to make my intellectual labors possible. She has other and more significant ways of being heard.

J.K.F.

New Orleans

CONTENTS

MANKIND BEHAVING:
Human Needs and Material Culture

Chapter 1

THE PROBLEMS OF HUMAN BEHAVIOR

It seems now to be generally agreed that much of animal behavior can be accounted for in terms of the efforts to reduce the pressure of basic tissue-needs. Human individuals, whatever else they may be, are animals, and they share the needs of animals. Among the more exigent of the animal needs are those for food and a mate, hunger and sexual desire being recognized as the driving forces. These have been studied separately. The psychology of animal behavior on objective grounds was formally initiated in the last half of the nineteenth century by the physiologists, Bernard, DuBois-Reymond, Sechenov, and particularly by Pavlov (3). It was developed by Sherrington (4), Thorndike (6, 7) and Hull (1), and is continuing today with Skinner (5) and others, as usual with the assistance of the physiologists. Most of Pavlov's laboratory experiments on dogs were conducted with the alimentary reflex. Most of Freud's clinical interpretations were based on the sexual reflex. Both reflexes are to be found in the sub-human animal and the human individual alike, they are very powerful and very pervasive. But they are not the only ones.

The reflexes (or responses) to be studied here are those which in the sub-human animal have been called the investigatory and defense reflexes. We shall examine them in the human individual in whom they have been considerably transformed and developed. The investigatory reflex becomes in the human individual the need to know, the need for knowledge, while the defense reflex becomes the need to continue to be, the need for survival or security.

How intense is the need to know about the nature of things,

or the need for ultimate surival? All animal needs may be considered special cases of the need to be active and to dominate the environment. Each drive has selected some part. The need to dominate the environment, in its candid and unspecified form, is the drive to do. It has not received the kind of concentrated examination that Freud has given to the sex drive or Pavlov to the hunger drive, for instance. Such needs can best be apprehended at the point where they issue in behavior. What does the human individual do to obtain need-reduction?

Human behavior, like all animal behavior, is a function of the central nervous system and the endocrine system. A structure is what it is as a result of what it does, and a function does what it must because of what it is. We have learned that structure and function are intimately related. A structure is a standing function and a function is a moving structure. Thus central nervous system and higher nervous activity are interdependent.

Yet each can be studied in quasi-isolation from the other. The study of the central nervous system must be left to the neurophysiologist, while the psychologist deals with overt behavior. Human behavior is more complex than the behavior of other animals, and so specialists may have to be called in from time to time to contribute to the knowledge of different aspects, the anthropologist, for instance, and even the philosopher.

Human behavior is also a function of the material environment. In addition to the highly complex internal structures and functions there are inter-relations and inter-changes with the external world which are equally complex. The extent of the alterations in the matter and energy of environing objects which result from human action must be taken into the account, as must also the extent of the effects upon the human individual of the alterations in those objects.

The attempt will be made, then, to study the stereotypic and adaptive responses in the human individual as mediated by the central nervous system and endocrine system together with the important addition of the material products of those responses and their counter-effects upon the individual as provided by the ecological mechanism of the re-entrant circuit.

The work has other and subsidiary aims which, however, are

also important. If we wish to discover the relevance of psychology to other areas of inquiry it becomes necessary to abstract the content of mental events in order to determine which is and which is not psychological. It would seem that error is peculiar to the mind, while truth has other origins. Obviously, everything known has a psychological aspect, but usually we do not behave as though what is known depends for its existence upon being known, whatever theory of knowledge we explicitly hold. What, then, happens to the theory of abstract relations and of religious knowledge? In a fundamental way, what is the human individual after, and how does he go about finding what he wants?

A still further distinction in the subsidiary aims of this work is to be found in the corollary effects of the chief aim if the main thesis can be established. For instance one result would be to effect a kind of Galilean transformation of the theory of knowledge and to support the claims of philosophy by imbedding it in an appropriate context of individual endeavor. Philosophy, it would have been shown, exists not only in the thoughts of men but also in their feelings and behavior, as elicited by them from external material objects.

Philosophy has often been employed to explain human behavior but not as often human behavior to explain philosophy. The result has been that only certain philosophies could be validated while others had to be left unexplained. The case of religion was even worse than that of philosophy, for religion was not explained at all, it was explained away, and this in the face of all the evidence from the many world religions. The present undertaking seeks to account for human behavior in such areas as philosophy and religion without making value judgments involving preference, desirability or efficacy. Only the reasons for their existence are suggested.

A word should be said, perhaps, about the method to be employed here. My theory is to some degree an extension of the findings of the laboratory experiments conducted on sub-human animals, in particular by Pavlov and Hull and their followers. If it cannot be supported in the same way as theirs has been, at least there are reasons. In the first place, human individuals cannot be tested while standing in harness in a laboratory after submitting to a minor operation in which the salivary duct is transplanted from the mucous membrane of the mouth to the outside of the cheek or chin. In the second place, the results of human behavior necessary to its understanding consist in the construction of institutions, such as universities or world religions, or the destruction of societies by means of war, none of which can be brought into the laboratory for purposes of controlled experimentation. It is possible to conduct some types of experiments with free individuals, but societies are too large to lend themselves to such manipulation.

Thus the study of the behavior of human individuals is not a laboratory science in the conventional sense in which psychology has sought to follow the procedure of physics and chemistry. But this does not mean that such a study cannot be a science. Laboratory experiment is not the only kind of scientific research. Any science which takes as its field of investigation large-scale objects must limit itself to the method of testing hypotheses by means of very exact observations. The study of human behavior must share this method with some branches of astronomy. The analogy can be carried a little further. For just as astronomy supports its findings by the more rigorous investigations of experimental physics, so the study of human behavior does by means of the classical experiments in animal physiology.

The comparison of the psychological theory set forth in the following pages with the science of astronomy as both dealing with large-scale objects not amenable to laboratory treatment, and the comparison of sciences of this sort with the more traditional experimental sciences of physics and chemistry, together lead to an abstract conclusion. The distinction between explanation and description so often made by those who theorize about science is not tenable. A proper analysis produces both, an improper analysis neither. Accurate explanations also include descriptions, accurate descriptions may also be explanations. If we can offer a sufficient description in depth of the workings of human behavior, we can be said to have explained it, at least to some extent.

I have conducted no experiments to support my hypotheses,

but I argue that they do allow for the deduction of consequences capable of being compared with experience. Elementary studies on lower animals are basic and without them applications of the theory of behavior to human behavior would not have been possible. But the problems in the case of human behavior are far more complicated. There is a tremendous elaboration of the preparatory responses in terms of material objects altered through human agency, and for the more sophisticated needs, such as inquiry, activity and survival, the drives are positive rather than negative, and they are greatly extended. In addition, for the human, there are complex skills and technologies. The current conception of the animal faculties will have to be greatly revised and extended if we are to explicate human behavior, since the human animal is in many ways a peculiar type. For the understanding of human behavior, the use of signs has had to be added to the use of tools and the interview method employed as a supplement.

Recent comparisons between the computer and the brain have been highly illuminating without necessarily carrying the implication that the brain is no more complex than the computer. It is important to remember that man can be an animal very high in the scale and still be an animal; and he can be an immensely complex machine, one whose control device, the cortex, alone is estimated to contain something of the order of nine billion neurons, and still be a machine (2, 8, 9).

The application of the mechanistic principles of the scientific method to human behavior are helpful. They would be too limiting only if we were to suppose that all machines are inherently simple. While it is true that the conditioned reflex seems to employ the connection between the interoceptive and the exteroceptive pathways, reflexes will never be entirely automatic so long as there are moods and insightful learning. The human individual considered as a machine is more complex than any other, and the mechanism of human behavior will require intensive and prolonged analysis.

Of course no number of such descriptions will exhaust the explanation of human behavior, but this can be said for every finding in every science. Descriptions may be of many sorts, and one sort is capable of constituting explanation. It is the sort that seeks to describe observations in terms of causes. But what is true of nature is equally true of every segment of nature, namely, that what actually exists always exceeds our powers of understanding, no matter how penetrating these may be. When in science it proves difficult to take the big step it is useful to remember that the little step will take us farther forward than no step at all.

The claim that there is no basic distinction between explanation and description must meet the contention that to the contrary there is one in behavioristic psychology. Skinner for instance distinguishes between respondent and operant behavior, where by respondent behavior is meant behavior with the stimulus present and observable, and by operant behavior behavior with no stimulus present and observable but only the frequency of occurrence (5, pp. 19-21).

The point is particularly important in a work which proposes to explain human behavior on the basis of both operant and respondent behavior. Actually, Skinner himself provides a way of escape from the absoluteness of the distinction when he suggests that in the case of operant behavior it cannot be said that there is no stimulus but only that no stimulus can be detected by observation (5, p. 21).

The issue hangs upon the origin of the memory trace. In so-called spontaneous behavior, behavior which is emitted by rather than elicited from the organism, the environmental source may no longer exist. It once did and made an impression, but it remains now only as an engram. The contention that operant behavior differs from respondent behavior in any way which the scientist should consider seriously must contain the insistence that what issued from the environment in the past is not environmental because it does not issue from the environment in the present. It is fair to conclude that while respondent behavior depends upon stimuli from the environment, operant behavior depends upon the memory of past stimuli from the environment, a distinction which makes no fundamental difference to the study of behavior.

To assume that the behavior of organisms can be explained

as an isolated phenomenon in no way dependent upon events taking place in the central nervous system leaves such behavior as a system of separate data unlike any other in the scientific purview. It ignores the general connections of the integrative levels and seems more like the parallelism of the Cartesians who denied interaction between thought and extension. So long as it is possible to control behavior from the chemical level, for example by means of tranquilizers like chlorpromazine and energizers like iproniazid, it will not be legitimate to speak of isolating behavior at the psychological level as a phenomenon having no connections with lower levels. Science eventually seeks a knowledge of causes even though there may be some preliminary work to be done first, and causes are explanatory rather than descriptive. An independent science of behavior need not be a wholly separate science of behavior. Structure and function cannot be that completely divorced. Pavlov inferred some physiological properties by controlling behavior, and of course Skinner himself thinks the study of behavior can be of assistance to neurology.

The investigator who, like Skinner, limits himself to description will nevertheless add the knowledge of one more level to the integrative levels. Animal behavior is assuredly not without a cause. And lower integrative levels from the point of view of behavior take the investigator into the study of the central nervous system. The CNS has its own functions and it is also responsible for overt behavior. As Sherrington pointed out, there is behavior connected with the autonomic nervous system as well as overt behavior on the part of the whole organism, both connected to the structure of the CNS. It is possible to add now another behavior-controlling mechanism: the endocrine system.

Below that, of course, there are still deeper levels determining behavior. Genetics is a flourishing science, and studies of the genotype abound. The effects of the genotype on the phenotype are profound and extensive, but they lie well beyond the considerations of the present work. I am attempting to treat here, not of the evolution of successive generations of *Homo sapiens*, but only of the behavior of single generations and where specifically possible, of the individual. The technique of learned behavior is transmitted through tools and symbols. Man has become specialized for culture as apes for brachiation, and it is that aspect which is the subject-matter here. Thus, this book is not an evolutionary treatment, but a study of the structure of human behavior. Where interaction with the material objects in the environment and their alteration is held accountable for changes in human behavior, it is an external inheritance which is intended. Darwin and Mendel and their followers have undertaken to describe the internal genetic inheritance. What Lamarck should have been talking about was external: the inheritance of acquired characters is that of artifacts with which human individuals interact. Thus, human behavior is explicable chiefly on the basis of the interactions between phenotype and the appropriate material objects in the available environment. It does not take the form of a study of the evolution of the species but rather of the effects on chain learned behavior of the external inheritance as this affects the drives to reduce the basic tissue needs.

I take it that psychology is the study of the behavior of the organism which is intact, while physiology is the study of the organism which is not. Thus psychology can go so far as conditioning experiments while physiology can work with the decorticate animal or with one in which there are chronically implanted electrodes. Behaviorism in psychology studies the behavior over which the animal exercises some measure of control, physiology the behavior over which it both does and does not exercise such control. Not all valid scientific evidence is directly observable, some is indirect, and this is true in every experimental science, it is true in physics and chemistry as well as in biology and psychology. Conspicuousness can hardly be taken seriously as a criterion, and the action of the glands and smooth muscle is also behavior. Overt behavior is simply the only part of animal behavior visible to the unaided observer, the only part, so to speak, that shows above the surface.

We may conclude that the physiology of animal behavior has two broad subdivisions, one called neurophysiology concerned with the activity of the central nervous system, and the other called psychophysiology concerned with overt behavior.

Thus the subject-matter of this book is in large part the psychophysiology of the human individual.

Yet this is not the whole story. There is another part which has not been conventionally represented in psychology. Animal behavior affects the environment, and human behavior drastically so. It will be necessary to study in a way which has not been customary the alterations brought about in some of the material objects of the environment and their reaction upon subsequent animal behavior. We know more about matter now than we did when materialism first became prominent as a philosophy. Matter is no longer considered a simple, inert stuff which resists analysis and has to be reckoned with only in the round, but has become recognized instead as a highly dynamic agent capable of sustaining the most complex activities. Matter, in other words, is a substance which can be analyzed into the most intricate forms. Let us note quickly how it affects organisms, for this will be the major theme of this book.

The contention that all animal behavior consists in a series of responses to stimulations from the environment can be defended successfully by means of elaboration. Not all the responses are immediate, and the mediating processes may be exceedingly complex. In the case of some animal behavior and almost all human behavior, both stimulants and respondents modify each other in a cumulative fashion which alters both of them, often in a productive way. The modifications of the stimulant may be in complex constructions, either in sign-systems such as a language or a philosophy, or in tool-systems, such as a cathedral or a high-speed computer, or in the products of their multiplication and combination, such as a capital city or a whole civilization. The modifications of the respondent may be in behavorial capacities. Both by the exercise of his faculties and from the storage of information, the human individual may gain in the repertory of response resources requisite for reacting to the alterations in the material objects which his actions had brought about previously.

We shall find that the individual is generally a member of a society of one of two types: those in which no appreciable change occurs, and those in which change is prominent. In the second type the emphasis is on the production of material tools and signs to which adaptation is necessary. In the first type, such adjustments are final, but in the second they are required again and again. The result is that in the first type adaptation is accomplished once for all, while in the second adaptation is continual. The first will be called 'stereotyped' behavior and the second 'adaptive.'

The theory which is set forth here enables a number of contemporary movements to meet, even though in the process they are considerably revised: realism, existentialism, behaviorism, together with recent developments in neurophysiology and psychiatry. A great many lines of inquiry are suggested. If there is any merit in them it might be worth while investigating for example the strength and intensity of the peculiarly human (here called secondary) drives, the nature of artifacts as self-conditioning devices, and the nature of institutions in relation to needs.

PART ONE
STEREOTYPED BEHAVIOR

Chapter 2

GENERAL THEORY OF HUMAN BEHAVIOR

IF WE ADHERE to the decisions of the vertebrate paleontologists then man is the last in a development of the order of primates, the *Hominidae.* Adjacent to but descending in a separate family from the *Pongidae,* the apes, monkeys and lemurs, the family of man is a continuous line from the Australopithicines through Pithecantropus to the Neanderthallers and so to *Homo sapiens.* He is generically the latest of such arrivals on the geological time scale, having made his appearance as a tool-using animal during the later Pliocene some 1,750,000 years ago (1), and so it will be instructive to examine human behavior from the animal point of view. But first we shall have to set forth that theory of animal behavior we can expect to find the most helpful.

ANIMAL BEHAVIOR

By 'behavior' here will be meant the movement of organisms so far as it has any pattern or structure, and by 'animal behavior' any movement aimed at reducing a need. The standard account of animal behavior is rendered in terms of a stimulus-reflex cycle. In the account to be relied upon here, this cycle will have to be enlarged and its center somewhat shifted. The account will be enlarged by the addition of the concepts of tropism, cue, taxis, and releaser; and the center will be shifted to the material object in the animal's environment. The result will be to suppose a reverberating feedback circuit, in which each of the elements above named takes its proper place.

An animal is an organism immersed in an environment to the stimulations from which it responds in certain fixed ways. The organism is a material system possessing a high degree of plasticity of response. Certain material objects in the environment serve as cues to the animal. Within the energy-field of such an object, the animal is compelled to an orienting movement in the direction of the stimulus (tropism) and then, with focusing, to a movement toward it (taxis). What enables it to do this is the possession by the animal of a generalized drive of aggression, here defined as the drive to dominate the environment (11). The aim of life is the preservation of life, as Pavlov observed (10, vol. i, p. 277), and this becomes more likely as greater portions of the environment can be compelled to cooperate. The drive to dominate is more developed in some animals than in others, more developed, for instance, in the lion than the deer, but fully developed only in the human, in whom it appears as the will to power. The drive of aggression is usually manifested as one of a number of basic tissue-needs or drives. A 'need' or 'tissue-need' is what a material object can supply to an animal which is necessary for its or its species' survival. There are many needs but we will deal chiefly with six: thirst, hunger, sex, approach-and-exploration (curiosity), activity, and the avoidance of pain (survival). For each need there is an appropriate organ: for instance the kidney for thirst, the stomach for food, and the gonads for sex. We shall be concerned in the case of the animal primarily with the first three, called here the primary drives, and in the case of the human individual primarily with the last three, called here the secondary drives. The stimulus evokes in the animal the appropriate response, for instance a female in estrus producing sexual excitation in the male. The stimulus has its effect through a cue, in our example perhaps the receptive posture or odor of the female. Whenever the stimulus and the response occur together and there is drive reduction, then the connections are strengthened. Whether all animal behavior is motivated or not is irrelevant to the purposes of the present thesis. Much is, and what is it is important to understand.

Somewhere in the central nervous system there is a mechanism of instincts which are innate and released on cue. The instincts are inborn patterns of behavior which are inherited, such as the nest-building instinct of birds. One prevalent instinct is that manifested in cooperative behavior, group participation to obtain need-reductions not possible for the solitary individual, such as group attacks on a prey, for instance the piranha of the Brazilian rivers feeding on human beings. When the instincts are triggered, the animal makes a preparatory reflex. Good examples are courtship or hunting practices, preening before a mate, or stalking a prey. Often there occurs at this point the displacement behavior prompted by surplus or inadequate motivation, for example nesting movements in the fighting gull. The preparatory reflex is followed by the consummatory reflex: eating or mating. The reward is the reduction of the need or the termination of the drive.

The stimulus-reflex cycle extends, then, from tropism to reward, from a property in the material object to the consumption or alteration of that object by the animal. There is a regular cycle of changes in the rhythm of attainment and quiescence (10, vol. i, p. 278). But now we suppose that this cycle is repeated an indefinite number of times, then there will be results not evident in a single operation of the cycle. The repetition of the cycle turns it into a reverberating feedback circuit, for there will be interactions between material object and animal which were present neither in the original object nor in the unprovoked animal. There will be also alterations in the material object and adaptations in the animal.

The alterations in the material object are extremely important in the understanding of animal, and especially of human, behavior. They may be of a destructive or a constructive nature. A beaver, for example, may kill a squirrel or build a dam. In the case of destruction the material object which furnished the stimulus disappears as an object having any connection with that stimulus, but in the case of construction at each stage it is able to furnish a new set of stimuli and has itself become a compound conditioned stimulus.

The adaptations in the animal have, then, to be made in terms of such a stimulus. The adaptation itself is a primary reinforcement, a strengthening consequent upon following the conditioned stimulus with the unconditioned stimulus in the reduction of need. Secondary reinforcement is furnished by another stimulus which has been closely associated with need reduction.

The behavior of animals is a result of the effects of the environment. As the animal is stimulated to react by objects in his environment, he exercises an effect upon those objects, and changes them. The effects of the changed object upon the animal are different from those of the original object, and as a consequence he reacts differently, adapting his behavior continually to the changing object. An artificial object thus might be said to be an indirect method taken by the animal to stimulate himself in ways not otherwise possible. Certainly the beaver's behavior will not be the same when he is confronted with a completed dam as it was with a dam under construction, nor will he behave toward a dead squirrel as he did toward a live one.

HUMAN BEHAVIOR

So much for the acount of animal behavior. Let us now turn to human behavior, with its similarities and differences. Although the progress made by man toward that of the other animals is enormous, a great deal is still to be learned about human behavior by considering it to be an advanced type of animal behavior. Much of human behavior can be explained on the model of the primate with added properties.

There is one peculiar feature of human behavior which is the source of drastic effects on the character of human life. Let us call it instrumental self-conditioning. In order to understand the term it will be necessary to contrast it with classical and instrumental conditioning in animal behavior experiments.

According to the law of effect in psychology, learning takes place only when there is a reward or punishment. In the classical conditioning of Pavlov, the animal learns to respond to a conditioned stimulus. A dog confronted with food will salivate in anticipation of being given it to eat. If now a bell is rung every time the animal is fed and this is repeated a sufficient number of times, then when the bell is sounded without feeding, the animal will salivate. In the modification of this experiment known as instrumental conditioning and introduced by Skinner, the animal is first isolated by being placed in a box which is empty except for a lever and a nearby trough. In the course of its exploration it will accidentally depress the lever which is wired to a food container in such a way that a food pellet is delivered to the trough. The animal eats the pellet and soon learns to press the lever when it wants another food pellet.

In the case of the animal experiment, someone else—a psychologist—provides the box. In the case of human behavior the situation is somewhat different. The peculiar feature of human behavior is that man himself builds the instrument he wishes to be the source of the stimuli to which he can respond. Moreover, what in the case of the animal was an experiment, in the case of man is a way of life! For the fact is that almost any sequence of human activity would serve equally well as an example. For instance, man builds a restaurant to which he can repair with gustatory reward, or he paints a picture to which he can then respond with aesthetic enjoyment. In this sense, he is the engineer of his own fate. But not entirely. For with each new type of construction he produces in himself altered responses, and among these altered responses are still newer types of construction, so that the process becomes a semi-automatic and cumulatively self-perpetuating one.

We shall, however, need to account chiefly for that portion of human behavior which is exclusively human, and we shall attempt to do so in several ways. The first way will be by means of the transformation of the animal drives. For the human individual by extension maintains intact the first three of the animal drives, thirst, hunger and sex, only with greatly expanded preparatory responses; while the last three, curiosity, activity and the avoidance of pain are transformed in peculiarly human fashion.

In addition to the needs mentioned, there are literally dozens of other and in many cases subordinate needs too numerous to treat here, needs such as for authority, prestige, belonging, virtue, comfort and self-esteem, but also for air, for infant toilet training, for some kind of calendar, for some form of weather-control, for some form of lawfulness, some form of greeting, of joking, of medicine (8, p. 124). Man is in many respects still a stimulus-bound animal, only in his case the stimuli are much more complex and are more often than not those of his own devising. The most elementary form of human behavior is here termed 'stereotyped behavior,' the behavior of individuals in primitive cultures.

The primary drives, thirst, hunger and sex, are similar in man and the other animals, but in the human individual they are reduced only through the channels provided by an elaborate series of preparatory responses. There are always table manners and courting practices which must precede eating and mating, however much such practices may vary from society to society. Not so with the secondary drives of approach-and-exploration (curiosity), activity, and the avoidance of pain (self-preservation). Curiosity becomes in man an extended need to know, the search for complete knowledge. Activity, which in the animal is spontaneous and without a goal-object, becomes in man the need to do, the need for achievement. And the avoidance of pain which in the animal is negative becomes in man the positive need to continue to be, the search for personal security. These are the human, or secondary, drives, and they, like the primary, are tissue-needs. For the need to know there is again an appropriate organ: the brain. Even the need to be has a special organ: the skin, and is a need which surrounds the whole organism.

The second way in which we shall attempt to account for that portion of human behavior which is exclusively human will be by means of the material objects with which human individuals interact. What human individuals make is to that extent human; it is also natural. "Artificial," then, will mean human-natural, and not an area almost outside nature and opposed to it, as is so often meant now.

In both the primary and secondary drives, human behavior is characterized by the activity of the will. The will is the human capacity for sustained response. The type of response called out by long-term projects, and especially by the use of artifacts, is not a single impulse but a continuous series of reactions. The sequence of actions necessary to prepare a dinner or to drive an automobile cannot be reduced to a single stimulus-response reaction. To plan and then execute a series of connected movements means to possess the capacity for long-range interactions, often lasting for days, years or even decades.

The task of understanding human behavior, then, cannot be accomplished by analyzing the organism alone. Although many of the other animals employ tools, man is *sui generis* the tool-using animal (2, 4-7, 9, 12). Not only does man make tools but in a certain sense the tools also make him. All that man is capable of experiencing is his own set of reactions. The repertory is a wide one, and some may be sharpened by use and others dulled by disuse. But ordinarily the external world determines this. Man is, as Sherrington said, "a puppet moved by the external world in which it is immersed" (11, p. 353), except in so far as he can anticipate by planning his future reactions. The technology for this consists in constructing artifacts of both the tool and sign varieties, to which he will react as he wishes and as he knows from similar previous experiences he can be expected to do. A considerable portion of human behavior can be accounted for by considering it as consisting in the responses of individuals to the stimuli issuing from altered material objects, and this is no less true because the individuals were themselves responsible for the alterations.

Human behavior is conditioned by artifacts. By 'artifacts' is meant material objects altered through human agency. The use of the term 'artifact' here needs to be distinguished from the biological use of the term in which it denotes material faults in experimental technique, and also from the archaeological use in which it is reserved for the material objects found in the unearthing of past cultures. There are two kinds of artifacts: tools and signs. A tool is a material object employed to move other material objects. A sign is a material object employed to refer to other material objects. A symbol is a quality attached to a sign. Artifacts trigger immediate responses in the reflex arc of stimulus and response. In the sense intended throughout this book, the living person is profusely surrounded by the artifacts of a present culture. It is by means of artifacts that human experience is rendered cumulative and the individual advanced beyond the point at which his predecessors had perforce to begin.

Of the three secondary drives, which are for knowledge, activity and security, it is perhaps the first which will be most easily recognized. The need to know has its origin in the subhuman animal need to approach and explore. In man, the need to know is the need for knowledge, a craving for the assimilation of naturally occurring relations exhibiting recurrence. Childish curiosity is well known, even extending to knowledge where there is no practical motive. The second of the three secondary drives, the need to do, is the need for activity, manifested in play, in construction and destruction, and indeed in all aggressive behavior. In man, as in the other animals, there is a deep necessity to keep on the move. Life is work for the healthy man. The third of the three secondary drives, the need to be, is the positive aspect of the sub-human animal need to avoid threats and escape from pain. In man, the need to be is the need for ultimate security, manifested by an identification with material objects exhibiting persistence.

The six tissue-needs may now be considered together. All six are grounded in the central nervous system and all are indicated by the behavior they call out, an effort to dominate completely both biotic and abiotic factors in the environment. Each enjoys the same kind of autonomy as the others. Each has its own kind of learning; for instance, there is a need to know about feeding and breeding opportunities as well as about naturally occurring relations and persistent material objects. The need to be affords a kind of protection to the others; man is the animal that knows about death, and there is in him an innate need for survival. Thus the secondary needs are based on the primary.

The needs are ranked one way for importunateness and another for importance. The rank order of importunateness runs: thirst, hunger, mating, knowing, acting, surviving. The rank order of importance runs: surviving, acting, knowing, mating, hunger, thirst. The distinction is made between the needs *by* which satisfactions are sought and the needs *for* which satisfactions are sought. Feeding and breeding needs are reduced through the aid of economic enterprises and the family, respectively. Knowing and surviving needs are reduced by means of philosophies and religions. In all five cases, man can do no more than alter the shape and position of material objects by means of interchanges with them on or near the surface of the earth, or within reach by means of his instruments, which are also material objects.

Animal behavior has been discussed in terms of stimulus and *reflex. Human* behavior will be discussed in terms of stimulus and *response.* The usage of the terms, *reflex* and *response,* is far from uniform in behavioristic psychology. The convention adopted here is purely to indicate in human behavior a slightly more complex reaction.

It will be necessary for the development of the theory of human behavior to discuss the secondary needs one at a time, beginning with the need to know.

THE NEED TO KNOW

The need to know does not have as its aim a material object but instead the naturally occurring relations between material objects, and beyond: the relations between such relations. For man, the tropistic attraction issues from abstract relations, as a result of the similarities among material objects. C. S. Peirce was one of the first to recognize the biological nature of knowing (3, 2.754). The need, he insisted, had developed from an animal instinct.

The tropism of knowledge will be called 'gnoseotropism.' Gnoseotropistic behavior is sign-behavior: logical connectives between classes having material objects as members and between classes having classes as members, leading to the discovery and verification (or falsification) of the existence of causal chains. Later we shall see that C. S. Peirce was also one of the first to recognize the compulsion exerted by signs; communication cannot be refused. Such compulsions are not as insistent as the primary needs, but with the latter effectively reduced they come to the fore.

The name for those changes made by the environment in the individual which make it possible for the individual to change the environment is 'learning': acquiring from responses the capacity to respond. The abstract relation cannot be manipulated like food or a mate; it can be engaged like them, but, unlike them, is not changed in the process. Learning is not always conscious or deliberate, but it is possible to know that one has learned. Learning, in the case of the kind of content referred to here, may come to involve knowing, as the process of abstraction rises from particulars to generals by means first of a comparison of sense impressions and then of a comparison of ideas. Mental operations include apprehending true ideas by discovering relations between them; they also include the inadvertent invention of false ideas.

Preparatory response in the human is planning for action—in the case of knowledge, learning—for which as we have already noted there are well-worn socially prescribed channels. Almost the whole of human culture is constructed of preparatory responses whereby the individual anticipates and plans the reception of the impressions from his environment. A custom, like a work of art, is a preparatory response. Plans may be made of course for reasoning, feeling or acting.

The consummatory response to knowledge is eventually lodged in the memory trace. Retention occurs at various levels within the somatic organism as records of events are recorded in the brain, and in this case the more primitive the level the more powerful the effect of the knowledge. The incorporation of knowledge tends to shut off further inquiry. The abstract relations function as distal variables only if there exist the intermediate processes of a reverberating circuit.

The reward of knowing is the pleasure of understanding. The conviction that lawfulness is a world-condition reinforces the feeling of security. The mechanism in this case is the discovery that there are hitherto unknown relations cutting across the causal chains which knowledge has apprehended. The more general the knowledge, the more secure the feeling; universals are the most dependable and provide the greatest comfort, the securing of some permanence by identification with recurrent things.

Belief is the feeling that a proposition is true. It is not always entirely conscious. Every thought, feeling or action involves a belief about some segment of the world. Belief hooks up with action, but the hookup may be mediated by decision. Action alters material objects, but belief may have to await recall by relevant events before such alteration occurs.

The resumption of inquiry is occasioned by intractable material objects which resist alteration, or by the disclosures of false knowledge. The cycle is repeated in the reverberating circuit of inquiry: knowing, philosophy, inadequacy, curiosity. Frustrated attempts at consummation trigger the drive and reconstitute inquiry as the fear of ignorance becomes transformed into the threat of insecurity.

So much for the need to know. We turn now to the need to do.

THE NEED TO DO

The need to do is the need for aggression *sui generis.* The need for activity is the need to make changes in the environment. Every other need contains activity as a component, but here we are considering activity on its own ground. The tropism of doing will be called prattotropism, and the appropriate behavior of doing or making prattotropistic behavior.

The possession of an organ involves the drive to the reduction of a need. In the case of the need to do, the organ is the musculature. Healthy animals are active animals, healthy men are men who are active in the effort to achieve something. A material object is to be changed, which is to say constructed or destroyed. In every one of the needs it is necessary to move among the material objects and engage in encounters with them, whether it is to obtain water, food, a mate, information or survival. It is from action that man learns how the existence of things corresponds with their appearances; and if not always, then usually.

The impulse to activity comes from material things which present themselves to the perspective of the individual as a challenge: a mountain to be climbed, a house to be built or an enemy to be destroyed. Acquisitiveness is a variety of the need to do, whether the drive be turned on real estate, money, women or works of art. The aim in all cases is at achievement, if possible of something permanent: a building that will stand, a conquered enemy who will remain subservient.

The need to do is primitive and under deprivation takes precedence over all other needs. Any element in the environment which presents the appearance of resistance acts as a releaser for the need to do. Opposition is a necessary component—there must be something to be overcome.

In man, the need-reductions of the need to do are planned occasions. There are anticipations of the occasions which will bring the individual into relation with the stimulus and so precipitate the proper response. In such a case tools are designed and sign employed. Even the musculature is trained in anticipation, as in learning certain special techniques; how to do certain exercises, for instance. In cooperative activity, there is displacement of the need to do, otherwise mutual destruction would result as being the more direct of the expressions of aggression.

The consummatory response of the need to do consists in struggle. Success is secondary. The most primitive kind of consummatory response, therefore, is play, which is sheer spontaneity of activity. Play is an end in itself, and represents actions carried out for their own sake. A more advanced phase of the consummatory response of the need to do consists in achievement.

An important part of the need to do in man is the need to say. Verbal behavior is a variety of prattotropistic behavior. Speech and writing are activities. In the practice of the scientific method we can see clearly how the need to do becomes sophisticated: there is speech, perhaps also writing, and certainly always planned and skilled movements intended to interfere with material objects, perhaps even to destroy them, in order to learn more about them. Thus the activities resulting from the need to do may be gentle or violent, constructive or destructive, but in many cases sustained and so exhibiting the kind of plasticity which we have come to consider human.

The cycle of doing begins with activity and moves to construction (or destruction); the achievement is a source of satisfaction, but with the satisfaction there is an end to the activity. Thus the need to do is not reduced until there is a resumption of activity and so the initiation of a fresh cycle. Thus the series of cycles build a circuit which preserves the rhythm of activity initiated and terminated.

THE NEED TO BE

The need to (continue to) be is the need for ultimate security. The human individual manifests the same avoidance response to danger as the sub-human animals, only where they do so negatively he does so both negatively and positively. His negative response is the same as theirs. His positive response is the active pursuit of permanence through association or identification with persistent material objects. Security means survival in this world; ultimate security means survival in the next: immortality.

The tropism of being will be called sositropism, a compulsory movement toward opportunities of security in a domain containing both safety and danger. The tropistic object of the need to be is the persistent far-away object: a mountain, a planet, the cosmos. This is the movement-producing stimulus, the sositropistic object which attracts the human individual by its seeming immobility. He will form an attachment to it, dedicate himself to it or work for it by association or identification. There are not apt to exist any small but persistent material objects. Persistent material objects which are large or, by the same token, far away, release in the individual the craving for transcendentals, the mystical need for infinity. Abstract structures derived from the naturally recurring relations of material objects—universal propositions, for instance—are those which represent absent as well as present objects. Absent objects include objects which are far away. Thus since abstract structures represent absent objects they must also represent far-away objects. If far-away objects release in man the craving for transcendentals, systems of philosophy, which are more general than any other abstract structures, will have the same effect. That is why philosophies have their place in the reduction of the need to be, and why religions contain philosophies (in this case called theologies) as well as persistent material objects.

Religious ritual belongs to the preparatory response phase of need-reduction. The need for being is a posture of the entire man. The preparatory response ranges all the way from plans for seeking duration, through the commitment by reason to a security system centered on a persistent object, to the adoption by faith of a religion.

The exercise of ritual observance belongs to the consummatory response phase. Ritual reinforces belief, and with belief there is a termination of the need. But for the first time in the case of tissue-needs there is a reversal of roles; the animal dedicates himself to his goal-object and tends to immerse himself in it. Need-reduction for the individual becomes a matter of his taking a part, however small, in the whole. Ego-involvement is the same here as attainment. Such attainment is symbolic rather than material; identification is a matter of sign-behavior rather than of overt behavior.

The reward for the reduction of the need to be is faith, salvation exchanged for current behavior with its conformity to liturgy. The way the individual lives seems in all its aspects to be true; action appears as evidence for the assumptions from which it follows. Religions, with their security systems, bring an end to doubt; they begin as revelations and end as traditions.

But the acceptance of a security system shuts off inquiry. When being has been found, why look for being? The reinforcement which results from observance limits the individual's availability for inquiry into other security systems. The individuality of the human individual is extinguished in his identification with the system which so to speak closes in around him.

The periodicity of events has an effect on the interaction between animal and environment. The security system is not impervious to penetration by environmental variables. While the individual surrenders to it through his full adherence, the system itself suffers from its encounters with non-systematic elements and eventually fails. The individual is set free only to be exposed to his own tissue-needs and anxieties. Curiosity compels the behavior of approach-and-exploration in the presence of sositropistic objects. The cycle is repeated in the reverberating circuit: belief, security, observance, failure, doubt, inquiry. But the very repetition of the cycle insures that the circuit will break down. The monotony of repetition produces only fatigue. Unless there is a construction, there will be a repetition of the cycle. Thus the cycle can account for the construction of a religion but not for its continuance under conditions which do not allow for the revival of inquiry.

STRUCTURE OF THE CIRCUITS

Adaptive equipment is the name for the special structures by means of which the human individual sets about obtaining the reduction of his needs. The structure ordinarily assumed to be responsible for human interaction with the environment is the central nervous system. No doubt it is; but in addition to the central nervous system a number of processes are at work which together account for the organic integrity of the ordinarily alert animal. These processes are silent and do not manifest themselves separately unless there is a malfunction. The endocrine system is a good example. Thus Grave's disease results from a thyroid deficiency, and Cushing's syndrome from a pituitary excess. In addition to the neuroendocrine interactions there are many others. But for the sake of economy of presentation—and of paucity of information—we shall confine our investigation to the central nervous system. Since the human individual is in a state of continuous interaction with artifacts, it will be necessary to describe the alterations which such interactions bring about in the central nervous system and in the artifacts.

It will be assumed here that there are broadly speaking three distinct reverberating circuits within the human organism. These will be called: the neurophysiological circuit, the psychological circuit, and the cultural circuit. Before discussing the interrelations between these it will be necessary to say a word about each of them separately.

First, then, the neurophysiological circuit. To the Pavlovian stimulus-response cycle has been added the ascending and descending projections from the brain stem reticular formation controlling input, wakefulness and perhaps the entire nervous system, and it is this same reticular formation which makes possible the immediate connections with the material object as well as with the simple conditioned response variety of learning.

The chief feature of the psychological circuit in neurophysiological terms is the internuncial conduction path and the intermediate processes. In psychological terms it is the appearance of consciousness. The individual acquires control over his own responses the resources of which have at the same time increased. There is some displacement activity, and there is the motor level of thought: direct attempts at problem-solving and the operation of learned responses.

The cultural circuit is made possible by longer pathways, the diffused conduction of impulses, and the involvement of the association cortex. Speech areas are also in evidence, and there is the appearance of sign-communication. Full self-consciousness belongs to this circuit: the awareness of perception. Skills, verbal behavior, recall, and anticipation of the probabilities of need-reduction by means of the interposition of a considerable time interval between stimulus and response.

All three sets of re-entrant circuits lie together within the central nervous system, and there are interconnecting paths between them. Thus the account provides for both parallel and diffused conduction. The hierarchy of need-relationships is made possible by such close connections that to terminate one by a consummatory response touches off another. This means of course that between the laminated integrative levels, circuits allow for the activity in one to open and close another.

The joint operation of facilitation and inhibition of the network makes possible many combinations. The ensuing graded response is indicative of plasticity of behavior, but is made in terms of wholes rather than parts. Such plasticity is required if the individual is to deal with complex artifacts over any extended period of time. Instinctive behavior is quite sufficient for bee hives and bird nests which are always the same but not for the continually improved models of human artifacts, not for books or computers, for instance. It is the properties of the artifacts which force continuity of behavior upon the human individual. But with equilibrium supported by such complex mechanisms, disorder can easily occur. Below the highest integrative level there are opposed drives leading to behavioral oscillation. At the highest integrative level, over-determined drives become their own goal-objects, and circuits operate with lessened or absent drives.

EMERGENCE OF THE ARTIFACT

We have noted the alterations effected in the central nervous system by the interaction of the human individual with material objects. We shall now have to note the alterations which such interactions bring about in the material object itself to produce the artifact.

Human individuals, like all animals, live in a world in which there are diverse varieties of material objects and of other organisms. Some of these aid him, others are a threat, some exist for a short while, some longer. They are not dependent upon him but he is upon them, therefore whenever he can he alters them to suit his own needs. He must deal with a variety of stimuli, either in different objects or more often in the same object (compound conditioned stimuli). The material object possesses these properties independently, even though they may have come about as the result of his efforts. Such objects are flexible: they may exchange their properties for others in a wide range of variability.

Interactions between these material objects and human individuals require that the individual react in prescribed ways. He has secured his survival but only by becoming dependent upon the procedures called for by the objects. He does not exist as long as the object does in most cases, but leaves generations of successors to follow his behavior. Thus the object which he has fashioned in order to facilitate the reduction of his needs become permanent conditions of such need-reductions. A couple of examples might be in order. For the primary needs, instruments and customs help to organize agriculture and the family. For the secondary needs, concrete philosophies are embodied in universities and religions.

The material object which has been altered through human agency, looked at from psychology, is a compound conditioned stimulus; looked at from anthropology, an artifact. An artifact is an element of culture developed as a compound conditioned stimulus in a single planned material object. Anthropology in the end is the study of the kinds of constructions human behavior has been able to effect with artifacts. Human behavior is human making essentially, *Homo sapiens* become *Homo faber.*

Both kinds of artifacts: tools and signs, were probably accidental discoveries, tools when men first threw pebbles at wild beasts, signs when men first practiced naming. But the development of artifacts has come a long way, and now complex artifacts both select the individual who will operate them and dictate the terms of the requisite learned behavior. The immediate human environment is composed to an increasingly large extent of complex artifacts, with the result that the dimensions of the immediate environment are constantly being extended.

The whole of human culture, the range of civilization, is the result of the development of artifacts. These come to have persistence in their own right. What they are, they have become only through the agency of human behavior; but what they have become, that they are thereafter, independently of such behavior. They are not as dependent upon the interactions with human individuals as the individuals themselves are. But individuals and artifacts together seem to be working toward an evolutionary goal that neither has yet recognized. It lies in the general direction taken by society.

ADAPTIVE BEHAVIOR

We are now ready to move closer to an examination of the peculiarities of human behavior. Elementary forms of behavior were called 'stereotyped behavior.' The more advanced type of behavior characteristic of the human individual will here be called adaptive behavior. By 'adaptive behavior' is meant continuously revised self-conditioning. The self-conditioning takes place of course in the effort to obtain need-reduction: meeting or producing modifications in the special ways in which man sets about obtaining the reduction of the needs which he shares with the animals and the complex ways necessary for obtaining the reduction of those additional needs which exist in versions peculiar to him. Continuously revised self-conditioning is said to be human because none of the other animals practice it in the same way. For other organisms adaptation is always accomplished in some fixed pattern. There are no annual models or other types of improvements in the beaver's dam, the bee's hive, the spider's web, the bird's nest or the ant's hill. For man, adaptive behavior includes the capacity for revisions in the process of making.

Adaptive knowing consists in the special ways in which man sets about adapting himself to the knowledge he has acquired. Knowing affects learning, and so conditions further knowings. Thus there arise plans respecting additions to knowledge.

Through the acquisition of empirical insights, learning accelerates. The result is a personal philosophy capable of serving as the directive of a set of behavior-patterns. Language, in other words, provides the mechanism for the development of a security system, leading to cooperative activity. The need to know is reduced, but only temporarily. The accumulation of small amounts of adherence leads to a reactive inhibition; the awareness of ignorance rises and with it the painful state of doubt. Knowledge is never complete and its acquisition is rhythmic: inhibition is followed by oscillation, and oscillation by response evocation.

Adaptive doing consists in the special ways in which man sets about adapting himself to his own aggressiveness. Doing overcomes resistance and such overcoming conditions further efforts at transforming material objects. Thus there arise plans for further aggressions, and in this way doing accelerates. The result is a personal achievement of either construction or destruction. Artifacts are combined under sustained effort until something is erected which is capable of standing at least for a while. Or there is a systematic destruction of the artifacts of others. The need to do is reduced, but only temporarily. The accumulation of small amounts of residual effort unemployed lead to a reactive inhibition. The awareness of inertia arises, and with it the painful feeling of inactivity. Construction is never complete and all attempts at its completion rhythmic: inhibition is followed by the oscillation of exertion and rest, and then by the renewed sustaining effort through response evocation.

Adaptive being consists in the special ways in which man sets about adapting himself to the methods he has acquired for insuring his own ultimate survival. His reactions to the world are prompted by feelings, and his feelings are changed by his reactions to the world. Ritual is called out to reinforce the results of the encounter with religion conceived as an absolute security system, and theology as an absolute philosophy to reinforce faith. The need to be is reduced, but only temporarily. The acceptance of a religion leads to deterioration but there is no disposition to die. Ultimate security systems are never ultimately secure, the individual cannot accept any part of his forthcoming extinction. Acting out a security system leaves in its wake a held-over drive, and there is the latency period of rest followed by the recovery of inquiry. There is an oscillation of approach-and-avoidance: heaven and hell, and the response evocation of aggression ending with the surrender to a surrogate successive generation.

The most sophisticated form of adaptive behavior is the adaptive control of behavior. Sequences of behavior of which the human individual remains unaware flow through his consciousness. The most advanced degree of adaptive control consists in rendering unconscious adaptive processes conscious. Adaptive control means that the individual can calculate and plan the effects of artifacts upon him before they are constructed and employed. It means also that he can calculate and plan the effects of denotative language, much as literary artists plan the effects of connotative language. Lastly, it means that the human individual can calculate and plan both his contribution to society and its consequent effects upon him. Adaptive control is in the last analysis learning. The needs may conflict and so require the proper subordination, with adaptive knowing, doing and being able to supply it. Degrees of feeling must be adjusted to make possible the elimination of primary considerations for the short-range self and a nearby God. Death must be understood not as an arrangement of non-being but rather as a state of positive otherness.

Chapter 3

THE ANIMAL MODEL

INTRODUCTION

WE HAVE ALREADY noted that human beings are animals and that human behavior is part of animal behavior. In order to examine what is peculiarly human, it will be necessary first to set forth the principal features of animal behavior as exemplified by the behavior of animals other than man, and then to describe what it is necessary to add to it. It is the plan here, then, to account not for all of the behavior of animals but merely for that part of animal behavior which will aid in the explanation of human behavior.

To that end it will be necessary to offer a proposal for reconstructing behavior theory as it now stands. The concepts for this task are fortunately ready at hand. It may be best to begin by enumerating them before attempting to fit them into the proposed framework.

THE PSYCHOLOGICAL ELEMENTS

Let us look in slightly more detail at the record of some of the early work in behaviorism and at recent investigations in neurophysiology. Viewed in the light of this tradition, it becomes clear that the present thesis is little more than an extended version of behaviorism which brings together some of its hitherto more disparate elements.

As early as 1866, Sechenov had inferred from his experiments with frogs that mental activity is reflexive in nature; and in 1907 Bechterev had published his *Objective Psychology* in which he had attempted to discover how far psychology could be developed by purely external observations of behavior. In 1912 Loeb published *The Mechanistic Conception of Life* in which he argued that the psychic life of man is entirely explicable by means of physics and chemistry, a conception which is now taken for granted in many departments of investigation (13). Loeb, together with others of his time, dreamed of finding the forces which determine the movement of animals and discovering the laws according to which they act (13, p. 36). There are of course more recent accounts, but Pavlov's, Sherrington's, Hull's and Skinner's seem the most fully developed and will therefore be the ones utilized here, although with liberal borrowings from other versions. The theory of behaviorism will be revised by enlarging the stimulus-reflex mechanism with a reverberating circuit extended to the environment, as discovered by recent workers in neurophysiology, notably by Magoun and his group (20, p. 64, cf. also p. 68; 11).

A contribution to the present work is the theory of aggression as a generalized drive possessed in more or less developed form by all animals. The drive to dominate the environment is less strong in the rabbit, say, than in the tiger. But it is manifested in all animals as the source of the six basic drives. The elements necessary for need-reduction: water, food, a mate, construction, information, and the elements necessary for survival, all are material objects or properties of material objects existing in the environment, and may be obtained only by behavior aimed at dominating them in some way or other. Drinking water, killing for food, mounting a female, constructing an artifact, exploring an unknown territory, and defeating an enemy, are equally varieties of behavior in which domination prevails.

The structure of a reverberating nervous network has been studied since the work of McCullough and Pitts (17, 18, 19). Magoun and his colleagues are responsible for the identification of an ascending and descending projection system centered on the brain stem (10, pp. 319-331). According to Magoun, "It now seems clear that ascending reticular influences upon the cerebral hemispheres are importantly, and probably essentially, concerned with initiating, maintaining and modifying such states as wakefulness, attention or arousal" (20). And also, according to Dell:

"The way in which we apprehend the outside world depends on the actual balance of our internal milieu and its repercussions on the brain stem reticular activity" (5, p. 378). Finally, Jasper says, "The ascending reticular system, that portion intimately related to the cerebral cortex, seems to be the most closely associated with what we generally recognize as conscious behavior" (5, p. 58). Whether the reticular formation is responsible or not, certainly it is true that the "perceptions are made possible by the ever-changing integrative activity of the brain" (24, p. 39).

From these last quotations it might seem possible to make an entirely subjective interpretation. But the brain stem reticular formation operates not only to control perception but also to influence behavior. There is evidently a hook-up of the central nervous system with some segments of the environment; as Wiener put it, "a human link in the chain of the transmission and return of information" (32). The functioning of such a loop was described by McCullough as follows: The "close cortical coupling of each sensory input to output affecting that sensory input by moving the organ of sense is a mode of functional organization whose circuit leaves and returns to the body" (19). For, as MacLean has pointed out, "There is not only this multiple-interaction, multiple-connected system within the nervous system, but, of course, these loops extend to the environment, too." And he speaks of a "closed environmental loop" (16). Behavior cannot be specified without externality, since it means changing the relationships among material objects in the immediate environment, but even perception involves an external world. According to Gibson, "Experiences generally have a specific relationship to the stimuli which arouse them, as indeed they must if the experiencer is to adapt his behavior to his environment," and he also insists that "the image is a projection of the world" and not the converse (4). There is a continuous interaction between macrocosmic objects, such as artifacts, on the one hand, and microcosmic neurons within the central nervous system, on the other. Animal behavior is an ecological function.

To the theories of behaviorism and the reverberating circuit it is proposed here to add the concept of tropism (12). Loeb and his followers, notably Bethe and von Uexküll as early as 1899 anticipated the attempt of behaviorism to explain all animal behavior in mechanistic terms. Loeb's theory of tropisms was promulgated in 1896. More recently the theory has received support from Crozier and Hoagland (2). A tropism is a movement-producing stimulus, more specifically, the effect of external forces on the structure of animals, a movement taxically orienting an animal in the direction of an external agent. Tropism and taxis are overlapping terms. Loeb argued from the heliotropic effect of light on plants to the effect of light on lower animals, and predicted that the psychic life of man would eventually be explained in terms of physical and chemical data.

Finally, we have to add the concept of the releaser (15). As Lorenz and Tinbergen use the term, a releaser is a material object or sign in another member of the same species which has the effect of putting in operation an instinctive pattern of behavior. Releasers are, as Lorenz says, "differentiations which have developed solely in the service of a single function: they emit key stimuli to which [the innate mechanism in] another animal responds" (14, p. 292). Examples are: the feeding responses of young gulls as released by the red patch on the adult bill, and the zigzag courting dance of the male stickleback without which the female does not respond, both studied by Tinbergen (30, pp. 30, 192).

THE STIMULUS-REFLEX CYCLE

It is generally conceded that the physical world existed for a very long time before the emergence of organisms. When life appeared, it did so under conditions dictated by the environment. The phylogenetic development of animals occurred toward the end of an exceedingly long evolutionary process and is continuing today. Activity is a prerequisite of animal survival, but such activity must be aimed at adaptation to the environment. The nervous equipment of the animal is constructed to deal with the environment; all its activity is initiated by material objects and terminated by them. The influence of environmental factors operates now just as it has done in the past, the behavior of animals can be understood only as a response to stimuli from the external world.

Behavior theory, then, is a child of evolution (8, p. 17). If there were no sound waves there would have been no cochlea of the inner ear; if there had been no light waves, there would have been no rods and cones in the retina of the eye. In every case, the external factor existed first, and the animal organ was developed to detect it and take account of it. Thus there is considerable precedent for the assumption that in every psychological event involving an interaction between organism and environment the environment furnishes the stimulus to the organism, and the organism reacts with an appropriate response.

Behaviorism began as a reaction to the extreme subjectivism of introspective psychology. It undertook to study the behavior of animals objectively, but it considered the object to which the animal reacted only as an undiscriminated and unaffected stimulus. The simplest model is the stimulus-reflex model, patterned after the Cartesian conception of the sub-human animals. All animal behavior is a series of responses to stimuli. An external stimulus initiating the response can be identified in many cases, and the external stimulus always is a material object or its properties. The objectivity of behaviorism is increased if the center of emphasis be shifted from the animal to the environment.

The animal is a product of the environment and remains within its control. The environment of the intact animal in its natural state consists in a number of material objects of various sorts, all of which are capable of furnishing stimuli. The discrimination between stimuli is determined by the animal on the basis of the fact that the objects are not equally attractive. The neurophysiologists have pointed out that indiscriminate arousal reactions alone are insupportable, since the animal is incapable of adjusting either to chaotic input (10, pp. 319-331) or zero input (31, p. 378). The profuse abundance of orders in the external world would certainly appear collectively to the unprovoked animal as a chaos. Its discriminations are made on the basis of a hierarchy of basic tissue-needs.

Animals all have sets of tissue-needs or drives, collections of cells of the same kind bound together and performing a common function. By 'need' or 'tissue-need' is meant here a lack on the part of an animal of some component a material object can supply which is necessary to survival (8, p. 17). A 'drive' is the dynamic factor of a need, the "strength of behavior" (26, p. 368). It is currently accepted by most psychologists that there exists such tissue-needs, or drives, the reduction of which is necessary (33).

Probably a great many more needs exist than we know about or plan to consider here, such as the need for activity or the need to sleep. Hebb has collected some which have been neglected. A complete list of the drives would have to include maternity, sleep, anxiety, success, power, and many others (5, p. 459). We shall be dealing in this book primarily with six, namely, thirst, hunger, sex, activity, approach-and-exploration, and the avoidance of pain. These are the "unconditioned reflexes," and they seem more basic than the others. In this chapter we shall confine our attention to the first three. Just as all of the drives derive from the generalized drive of aggression, so they all serve the last of the drives, the drive for survival. Thirst and hunger aid the survival of the individual by means of the assimilation of the object; mating aids the survival of the species by means of the transformation of the object. Activity aids the survival of the individual by producing constructions useful to the primary drives. Approach-and-exploration aids the survival of the individual by locating material objects which are able to provide feeding and mating opportunities, though often extending beyond these. The avoidance of pain aids survival by protecting the individual from destruction—often by the absence of a material object, brought about by means of escape and defense reflexes (25, p. 239).

The last three needs rather than the first three are those which will be most extensively treated in the remainder of the book which is devoted to the description of human behavior, and so another word may be said about them here.

The possession of an organ is a commitment to its use. The existence of the musculature insures that under normal circumstances there shall be a need of activity. This can take the form of construction in the operation on artifacts, but it can also take the form of destruction when activity is thwarted or threatened (23, p. 182). Here it appears as naked aggression, destruction for its own sake. The most primitive form is the need of activity, which could be of a random sort, while the most developed involves elaborate constructions in reduction of the need for achievement.

Curiosity is what Pavlov called the "investigatory reflex" (23, pp. 12, 112) and Hebb the "exploratory-investigatory-manipulatory drive" (5, p. 458). It has not yet received the attention which has been accorded to hunger and sex, and very little research has been done on it. The manipulation of material objects in the immediate environment seems to satisfy a need to know, and may be composed of generalized efforts to discover objects capable of bringing about need-reduction in the case of the more basic drives of hunger and sex, but elements of play are no doubt also involved, activities which are their own reward.

The avoidance of pain is loosely associated in Pavlov's version with four others which are no doubt subvarieties: the "reflex of self-preservation" (23, p. 31), the "freedom reflex" (19, p. 11), the "defense reflex" (23, pp. 17, 31), and the "reflex of caution and restraint" (23, p. 312). All four of these presumably serve the need to survive. The avoidance of pain is the generic description of many species of behavior. Rapid escape reactions, concealment from predators, and often even aggression, are examples of the avoidance reflex. The survival of the animal often necessitates the escape from or the evasion of adverse influences in the environment.

The needs are recognized; the drives to satisfy the needs are unobservables, intervening variables; but it is in terms of them that it is possible to account for subsequent behavior. The drives are supported by instincts, as illustrated, for example, by nest building and migration. Evidence of a connection between the drives and such innate behavior patterns are beginning to appear (1). External stimuli call out the operation of instincts when they activate the unitary drives. A tropism which affects an instinct is an unconditioned stimulus. This kind of agreement between organism and environment is probably hereditary and may even date back to preneural changes. Instinctive behavior is species-predictable and involves the whole organism (7, pp. 110ff., 125).

The analysis of behavior begins, then, with the material object. So far as the animal is concerned, the object can be eaten, drunk or mated. Each of these needs belongs to a particular organ and activates a particular drive. Hunger-reward and sex-reward systems are localized in the brain as well as in specific organs (22). If the organ is not supplied with the material it needs it tends to deteriorate. If it is so supplied there is a periodicity to the drive. The kidney is not ordinarily considered as having a drive, but if we use the term "tissue-need" the case becomes clearer. Kidney tissues require water and can survive only a short time without it. Given a constant source of supply, however, the animal does not drink steadily but in bursts.

All behavior is taxis-controlled. That is to say, there is movement in the direction of the stimulus. The environment contains material objects which from the perspective occupied by the animal exhibit the phenomenon of tropism. By 'tropism' is meant a compulsory movement toward an object, "an impulse which the animal cannot resist" (13, pp. 26-7). Every material object is surrounded by the energy field of its tropism. The effect of a tropism on an animal which has moved into the field of energy of the tropism depends upon the degree of pressure exerted by the animal's particular need. For every instance of behavior there is an application of incentive, an orienting reaction to a source of external stimulation, a tropism. Many more tropisms exist potentially than are exercised on animals. For a tropism to be effective, an animal must move into the field of the tropism. This can be negative as well as positive: a negative tropism is an object of threat, of fear or danger, calling out an avoidance reflex or an aggression.

At the outset of every stimulus-reflex cycle there is a material object and in its environment an animal with drives. All behavior begins with the confrontation of an animal with a material object. If the material object has for the animal tropistic properties, then when there is a confrontation the tropism excites the animal to a certain behavior. 'Tropism' is the name for a drive seen from the object, and 'drive' the name for a tropism seen from the animal. From the point of view of the tropistic object, the behavior of the animal is elicited; from the point of view of the animal possessing the drive, such behavior is emitted. The monkey will reach for a banana when he sees one in the cage, and not when he does not. The banana is the occasion for the reaching; the cause of the reaching would have to be accounted for in neurophysiological terms.

The object in which a reward is sensed is the source of the stimulus; it holds out to the animal by its very presence the promise of need-reduction. The stimulus insures that the relevant need shall be selected in the animal and that the appropriate energy change shall excite the receptor. Thresholds determine the amount of stimulus necessary to elicit a response. Unstimulated drives are random, such as the nest building of birds in the absence of material. In discussing the stimulus, we are looking at the material object in its effect on the animal, the animal's behavior accounted for from without. The stimulus is, in short, the occasion when an object impinges on an animal in a specific way. It is the arousal of a drive by a tropism.

The cue is a secondary stimulus, usually a faint sign by which a stimulus is recognized. The cue source is that aspect of the object which enables the animal to identify the tropism as specific to the arousal of the drive. The tropism may involve a combination of interlocking stimuli, thus giving rise to a great variety of cues. The function of the cue is selective; in its presence irrelevant behavior is less likely to occur. Cues are the selected stimuli from the complicated patterns of objects, leading to response and reward. It is not the bare sensory stimuli but the meaning of those stimuli that provide the cues (5, p. 42). As Deutsch points out, a rat running a maze toward a goal of food will find the cues or "landmarks" in the maze attractive only if it is hungry (3, pp. 35, 39), but when it is then the tropisms involved are activated and the animal becomes excited.

We have been speaking of behavior from the aspect of the material object which prompts it. Now we must turn to observe the effect on the animal. It is at this point that the sensory analyzers, olfactory, acoustical, thermal and tactile, come into play. We may assume that the stimulus has impinged on a receptor in strengths sufficient to overcome threshold inertia and there been transformed into neural activity. The key perhaps to the initiation of a psychological event involving an animal with a material object—that is to say, evoking a drive by a tropism—is the "releaser." The term is used here in a more primitive, and therefore broader, connection than was intended by Lorenz, its inventor (30, pp. 55-56). By 'releaser,' as we have noted, Lorenz and Tinbergen mean 'social releaser': a feature of some other members of the same species to which an animal reacts. The term 'releaser' here will be widened to include that feature of any material object to which an animal reacts (including of course those material objects which are the animal members of the same species).

The animal possesses a number of innate releasing mechanisms which are triggered by cues, singly or in combination. It is supposed that such mechanisms exist somewhere within the receptor apparatus of the central nervous system. Called instincts, they indicate the presence in the organism of the behavior pattern of a drive. Instincts are complicated patterns of inherited reflexes. Lorenz and Tinbergen were active also in the revival of this concept (15; 30, pp. 30, 192), and Tinbergen has pointed out in the example of the reproductive instinct how large the normal repertory of such instincts can be (30, p. 104). Fixing the nature of instincts is difficult, but they resemble chains of conditioned reflexes.

Two examples of instinctive behavior may be given. Cooperative behavior and the maternal instinct are different techniques which have become instinctive because they proved useful for so long in aiding survival.

Cooperative behavior is characteristic of many animals. It involves participation in group action to obtain need reductions not possible to the individual alone (30, p. 168ff.). Examples are to be found in group assaults on a prey or on an enemy too large to attack singly, as for instance when a wolf pack attacks a man; and in the cooperative protection against predators, as for instance when cattle huddle in defense against attack by a lion or tiger. Although cooperative behavior means group participation, it always serves individual needs. Fighting for a goal is, in short, an attempt by the individual to obtain victories not obtainable through his isolated and unaided efforts.

The maternal instinct is essential to the survival of the species. It can be highly specific, as studies on releasing mechanisms have shown (30, pp. 182-83). From incubation to the final departure of the young at the beginning of their independent adult life, complex behavior is invoked on the part of the mother. Many types of behavior seem instinctive, such as those involved in protection, feeding and training.

Instincts can be released by appropriate cues. The releaser itself is a material object possessing a tropism and having the effect of a stimulus-emitter on the animal. As demonstrated in experiments performed by Lorenz and Tinbergen employing dummies, the cues must be both simple and conspicuous. The cue may not actually do anything, but its presence attracts the animal, on whom it acts as a releaser. The particular drive selected is chosen by a lack in the animal. In a field of potentially desirable objects, the one to which the animal reacts is the one which appears able to supply the most pressing need, and so singles out one reflex among the animal's repertory of need-terminating reflexes. Tendencies are inborn in animals, and stimuli exist potentially in objects, but it is the releaser which connects them by eliciting a drive in an animal aimed at the object as a goal essential to the consummation of the drive. But while individual cues may be simple, the tropism-stimulus and releaser-reflex are far from simple. A certain amount of learning is required in some cases to activate innate behavior patterns. There is no doubt a kind of animal logic, a recognition of similarities and differences, implicit in unconditioned reflexes. Behavior resulting from innate releasing mechanisms is not rigidly mechanical but possesses a certain plasticity.

The effect of the releaser is the activation of the preparatory reflex. The preparatory reflex, first distinguished by Sherrington (25), is the activity of the animal leading to the consummatory reflex. Anticipatory salivation at the sight of food is a preparatory reflex, as is erection and titillation. The distance-receptors play a large role in the preparatory response, thus showing its immense dependence upon the environment (25, p. 326). The preparatory reflex is a preliminary stage, making possible a consummatory reflex. It takes the animal from the selection of a goal through the progress toward it and into the goal-region. The mere physical approach to a material object from which a consummatory reflex is sought is therefore a preparatory reflex.

The consummatory reflex is designed to end the need or terminate the drive. It consists in the satisfaction of basic tissue-needs or drives by means of activities, such as eating, drinking or mating. There is now contact between the material object and the animal. According to Deutsch, the stimulus produced by a tissue-need does not elicit a reflex but terminates it; eating stops when food enters the stomach (3). Reducing a drive means removing the source of irritation, the lack or pain caused by the tissue-need of an organ. The nociceptive reaction is also consummatory, as Sherrington pointed out (25, p. 330). Reflex action, such as the knee-jerk or pupillary reflex, apart, the consummatory reflexes in the case of food or sex are all-or-nothing reflexes; but whether the animal makes the reflex to the stimulus depends upon the strength of the need: how hungry he has become, or how sex-deprived. Loeb held that the chief distinction between a reflex and an instinct is that the reflex is organic whereas the instinct is systematic: the reflex involves a part while the instinct involves the whole (13, p. 70). In any case, the drive results in ontogenetic and phylogenetic maintenance: the survival of the individual and of the species, hunger and thirst for the former and sex for the latter.

Inappropriate motivation may lead to activity which is misdirected: a conflict between the powerful antagonistic drives or a strong drive in the absence of adequate stimuli: conflicting motivation or surplus motivation. The latter is more common than the former, and is what Lorenz and Tinbergen call "displacement behavior" (14), the overflow from an activity serving a drive to another which does not, such as a fighting cock which abruptly pecks the ground as though feeding or a fighting heron which suddenly engages in preening.

The consummatory act is the reward for the drive; rewards are tangible material things associated with need-reduction, reflexes as the satisfaction of drives. Water, food or a mate is rewarding. Thus rewards act directly to strengthen the connections with stimuli and cues. Rewarding a reflex always strengthens it and makes it easier for a similar stimulus to be followed by a similar reflex the next time. Rewards spread in time, i.e., to the next reflex situation; they spread also in space: the effect of rewarding a reflex is to strengthen similar connections in the neighborhood (29).

Reinforcement is defined as the strengthening of a conditioned reflex. To its operation the repetition is essential. It would appear to be connected with the temporal lobes (21, p. 180). In reinforcement the conditioned stimulus is regularly followed by the unconditioned stimulus, until the animal learns to associate the two, the sight of food with the sound of a bell, to use Pavlov's example. The process may be generalized to an additional conditioned stimulus similar to the first, and by properly conditioned discrimination the first omitted yet the second retained. Reinforcement gradients indicate the time that can elapse between stimulus and response before the stimulus fails to elicit a reflex. At set intervals of time, on the other hand, periodic reconditioning can be effective.

The effector activities of the animal alter the material object. Such alteration may involve the destruction of the object or its transformation. Water and food are consumed, or the mated animal is made pregnant. In some cases, a structure is erected from 'raw' materials, and the altered material object then becomes a beaver dam, a spider web, a bee hive or an ant hill.

Thus with the altered material object we come to the end of the behavior cycle of stimulus and reflex. A new kind of situation arises in which the stimulus is compounded and conditioned and the behavior is repeated but each time with a slight alteration; what Hull has called the "pure stimulus act," when a reflex provides the stimulus for further acts (9).

THE REVERBERATING CIRCUIT

There is no doubt that in any sufficiently broad conception of the stimulus-reflex cycle a certain degree of flexibility is provided for. Interferences from the immediately environing circumstances have been known to exist since Pavlov's experiments with dogs in laboratory harness, and it is equally well known that the animal's physiological condition and psychological mood must also be taken into the account of any supposedly isolated situation (11). However, the model's shortcomings are greater than those just mentioned.

The limitations of the stimulus-reflex cycle are inherent in the conception of its repetition. It is not the intact animal but the decorticate specimen which is the pure stimulus-reflex mechanism, as Sherrington pointed out (25, pp. x-xiii). He thought that the difference could be accounted for by habit, but as we shall presently note it belongs to repetition plus novelty. A greater role is played by mediating processes, internuncial neurones, frontal lobes. It is true that habit makes the difference in the type of behavior induced by the conditioned reflex, but there are other types of stimulation, the type in which there is continual alteration rather than exact repetition, for example, and the latter type of stimulus-reflex cycle is not the proper model. It is necessary at this point to set up the model for the reverberating circuit.

The theory of the reverberating circuit is already present implicitly in behavior theory. Good definitions of animal behavior always include the effect of the action of the organism on the outside world (26, p. 6). But it is often forgotten that such action is a reaction, even in the case of memory, and that it results in further action of the outside world on the organism. The repetitions called for by primary reinforcement (8, p. 71) contain the necessary elements, but the configuration and its consequences have been never fully drawn in this connection. The flow of continuous behavior consists in a series of reflexes and stimuli, where a reflex provokes a new stimulation in such a way as to constitute a circuit similar to the feedback loops in servomechanisms.

If the stimulus-reflex cycle be repeated a sufficient number of times, then the effect of the animal on the material object as well as the effect of the object on the animal becomes cumulative and must be taken into consideration *as must the cycle itself*. Thus the last extension of behaviorism will be to suppose that the repetition of the cycle constitutes a reverberating circuit which begins with a material object stimulating an animal and ends with the animal's reflex in its effect upon the object. It has been pointed out that a good analogy to animal behavior when the control issues from the artifact is the servomechanism in which the behavior of a mechanism is controlled by the object toward which it is moving, such as the guided missile which may be directed by sound, light or heat waves from the target.

The functioning of intervening variables is continuous in the reverberating circuit, which is a matter of receptor and effector activities and includes the source of the energy acting on the receptors and the recipient of the energy resulting from the activity of effectors. When receptor and effector activities occur in quick temporal succession, reflex strength increases, particularly when there is need-reduction (primary reinforcement) and mediation by a stimulus closely associated with need-reduction (secondary reinforcement). This is perhaps the essential step in Hull's account. The drives function at their most powerful when there are patterns of behavior to be called out, the greater the proximity to need-reduction the more powerful. Reaction potentials are determined by the mutual effects of reflex strength and drive.

However, this is not the the whole story; for with the continual operation of the reverberating circuit, the interaction of animal and environment changes the environment as well as the animal. Behaviorism has not adequately described the effect of animal behavior on the material object which is the recipient of effector activities as a result of having been originally responsible for the stimulation of the receptors. Off-hand, it would seem as though a study of physiological processes would not need to include any object which was not a living organism. But when an organism is involved with material objects in a determinative fashion, and is changed as the result of changes in them, then the analysis will have to take a different turn. The novelty in the present account of the reverberating circuit is the emphasis on the inclusion within it of alterations in that sector of the environment—the material object—which is involved with it.

The material object was the source of the stimulation of sensory end organs; it is the recipient of the reflex action of the muscles, so that it both initiates and concludes a cycle. But it has been altered in the process, and the altered material object constitutes a slightly different stimulus upon each subsequent occasion, and this alteration and its altered reflex is repeated until there is a series of cycles or reverberating circuit. Where there was only one stimulus and one reflex, the cycle could be concluded without a second reference to the material object; but in some types of behavior there is more than one; specifically, there is more than one when the animal is making something, a construction.

The last point is perhaps crucial. It is characteristic of at least one type of animal behavior in relation to abiotic factors in the environment that it results in a construction. If psychology is to account for all of the significant features of animal behavior, then it will have to include not only feeding and breeding, but also making. The intricate behavior patterns thus revealed are not learned but innate. The complex bee dance indicating the direction and distance at which honey is to be found, and the elaborate behavior disclosed by the paper-building wasp which erects nests from reconstituted wood fiber, are no doubt of this character. Repeated operations of the reverberating circuit, altered slightly for every feedback cycle, results in a cumulative construction as a result of planned alterations in the material object. Good examples are to be found in the behavior of certain of the insects and animals already mentioned; for instance ants in making ant hills, spiders in weaving webs, bees in building bee hives, and beavers in constructing beaver dams. The nest building of birds should no doubt also be included. Ants, spiders, bees, beavers and birds may be described as tool-using organisms. Many animals in fact make some kind of construction, usually in connection with a primary drive: food storage, rearing the young, etc. Muskrats build winter shelters in stagnant water. The Norway rat digs a tunnel at the end of which it builds a nest.

Repeated activation of the circuit involves alteration of the material object, on the one hand, and adaptation of the animal organism on the other. One piece of evidence for the existence of the circuit as something different from the merely repeated cycle of stimulus and reflex is the summation method of surmounting a limen. In one cycle the excitation of the stimulus may be insufficient to elicit a reflex, but when the cycle is repeated the excitation is cumulative and the sum may be sufficient to overcome the inertia and so pass into action. There is little doubt that in some cases at least animal behavior is conditioned by artifacts. Nest-building behavior has been observed in the absence of suitable materials. The account of the effect of the reverberating circuit on the animal has already been given in the classical account of Pavlov, Hull and others, of primary and secondary (and higher) reinforcement. If the source of the original stimulus does not change, then the receptor-effector connections established by reinforcement constitute habits and the adaptation of the animal is measured in habit-strengths.

But the adaptation is more complex because there is more than one circuit. From the point of view of behavior, an animal is a whole acting through its parts, the organization of many interacting circuits which operate together to constitute its adaptiveness. For some biologists, adaptiveness is the key concept in living as compared with non-living systems (27). Reverberating circuits tend to spread: reflex generalizations extend outward to the material object in the environment, inward to other reflexes in the animal (8, p. 183). Both stimulus and reflex are terribly involved affairs; each on its own side, and through the other on the other side. And so animal behavior, at least of this sort, can be explained neither from within the organism alone nor with the material object considered merely as an initial stimulus, but only on the basis of a reverberating circuit. What we have instead of a single cycle is a closed system of conduction capable of indefinite repetition.

The notion of a reverberating circuit at the psychological level raises certain physiological questions. For instance, since there is a high degree of psychological plasticity of behavior to be accounted for, can this be done physiologically in terms of the now classic picture of fiber conduction (6)? Some additional mode of physiological plasticity seems almost required. There are phylogenetic reasons for supposing that evolutionary selection has operated in favor of circuit connections that are the most functionally adaptive. In the course of organic evolution, from endoskeletal weakness to tool-making, an increase in the plasticity of responses has gradually appeared. The plasticity of embryonic development has been retained in the functional specificity of the adult; in this case, an ontogenetic process extended into phylogenetic inheritance. There is evidence of plasticity, too, in the interchangeability of neuronal connections in the full functional regeneration which has sometimes occurred after ablation (28).

By means of what concepts, then, is such a structure to be analyzed? For this task, a new model is needed, and a new mathematics. The model will have to be drawn along the lines of a resonating physical system; there are glimpses of the possibility of constructing non-linear models defined by the relations existing between their elements. Also there will have to be a mathematics to deal with qualities and with multiple causes and multiple effects, and to provide for the breadth that there is to some concepts. These problems may have to be solved before it will be feasible to analyze nervous nets and reverberating circuits.

There are of course exceptions to the structure of the circuit in animal behavior. For such reactions as fear, rage, avoidance or escape, the stimulus-reflex mechanism must be retained in explanation. These negative reactions are often abortive in the animal, and we shall see in a later chapter how the human individual has organized them. Reaction potentials are limited by the range of the activities of the animal in effecting such alterations. The animal may destroy the object by drinking it, he may destroy it by eating it, or he may copulate with it. And, as in the case of monkey curiosity, he may destroy it by examining it. But in any case, whether the effect of the animal's reactions is to destroy the object or make constructions with it, drive consummations cannot be other than the effects of actions on material objects to alter them.

Thus reinforcement requires that the conditioning process be repeated again and again, that the material object exhibit features which function tropistically, that it act as a stimulus with cues, and that the releaser in the animal lead to a preparatory reflex and a consummatory reflex, with subsequent reward and reinforcement making possible the repetition of the process. But it should be noted that we have come a long way from the simple picture of the stimulus-reflex mechanism; for in making a repetition of the process essential we have allowed for the introduction of other elements and hence opened the way to an enormous increase in complexity, including of course an enormously increased role played by the environment. The repetition involves a greater organization, in which the incremental and decremental factors alone are not to be counted by qualitatively different structures brought into play. Such a circuit implies a modified stimulus-reflex model in which the emphasis is shifted to the stimulus produced by an altered material object and to the reflex made by an altered individual. A large part of the account of animal behavior will have to be supplied by the description of changes in the environing material objects which take place as a result of the interaction with animals.

Thus the conditioned reflex alone does not take into account all of the behavior of animals. It is to be expected that every time there is an alteration in the stimulus-producing material object, instead of the strengthening of existing connections, new receptor-effector connections would be set up. For there are naturally occurring psychological events in which the material object providing the stimulus is not shifted to a different one; instead, it is altered, and the altered material object provides another stimulus. The reaction situation now includes a compound conditioned stimulus (CCS) as well as a conditioned reflex (23, p. 141). In order to understand what is meant here by a compound conditioned stimulus, let us suppose a sequence of stimulus-reflex cycles in which the stimulus in a first cycle is called the original stimulus and the stimulus in an immediately subsequent cycle is called the new stimulus. Then a CCS is a new stimulus elicited by a previous reflex which by altering the original stimulus makes of it a biologically adequate substitute. Thus any material object which has been altered repeatedly through animal agency is a CCS (or artifact). The reflex, at least in its simplest overt terms of mechanical movement and change, must be altered in response to the tropisms of the altered material object.

And so now we have a circuit which is open at both ends: as the stimulus is changed, it changes, and so does the reflex. We are thus able to include in our account of animal behavior the cumulative effects of artificial construction. In a later chapter we will be prepared to deal with human responses of this character but on a larger scale.

TABLE 1

ANIMAL BEHAVIOR

The Stimulus-Reflex Cycle

Original Material Object
- stimulus
- tropism
- cue

Original Animal
- releaser
- preparatory reflex
- consummatory reflex
- reward

The Reverberating Circuit

Alteration of the Material Object
- construction-destruction
- compound conditioned stimulus

Adaptation of the Animal
- primary reinforcement
- secondary reinforcement

SUMMARY

We began by listing the elements involved in psychological events. These were, starting from the material object: tropism, stimulus and cue; and from the animal: releaser, preparatory reflex, consummatory reflex, reward and reinforcement; and finally, back to the material object with alterations to it. In a single operation, these are the elements of the stimulus-reflex cycle. Now when the cycle is considered to be in continuous operation so that it becomes an ingredient of the functioning, then there appears the phenomenon of the reverberating circuit. In Table 1 it can be seen how the stimulus-reflex cycle is repeated in the reverberating circuit, including all of the steps from the tropism of the original material object and its consequent operation as a CCS to the adaptation of the animal.

The fundamental principles of the reverberating circuit may be briefly stated. First, let it be assumed that in a typical circuit the stimuli are to be furnished by a material object and the reflexes by an animal. Then the circuit is activated when a drive is stimulated by an animal wandering into the energy field of a tropism, and the tropistic object is altered by the consummatory reflex. According to a second principle, the more the reflex alters the stimulus, the more the stimulus will alter the reflex. The differentiation of reflex is determined by the changing material object which was altered by the last reflex and which now stimulates a new one.

Both the organic nature of the drives, centers for which now can be located within the central nervous system, and the reverberating circuit itself extended to the environment from the reticular formation of the brain stem, are supported by recent findings in neurophysiology. It suffices only to complete the attempts of Sechenov and Pavlov, of Hull and Skinner, to objectify the phenomenon of animal behavior by considering the interaction with the environment as an essential factor in the functioning of the central nervous system.

It was an assumption in this chapter that everything exists in the external world which is capable of stimulating arousal reactions in animals, and it will be an assumption in the next chapter that included in the external world are all those things to which man alone responds. Human beings are animals, too, but they are animals whose complex organization of higher nervous activity supports drives which are superimposed upon the ones we have already studied. To an examination of the peculiarly human drives we must next turn our attention.

Chapter 4

THE HUMAN VERSION

INTRODUCTION

IF BEHAVIOR THEORY is correct in its essentials—and its staunchest advocates have claimed no more for it than that—then on the grounds that man is an animal and behavior theory an attempt to account for animal behavior, it ought to be possible to extend the theory of sub-human animal behavior to account for the behavior of man. The term 'sub-human' as employed here is a neutral one and refers merely to the animals other than man, even though the preponderance of superior abilities—intelligence, for instance—is, despite such exceptions as the ability of dogs to hear and of birds to see, on the human side. Those who have studied the sub-human animals remind us that there is in man himself an enormous phylogenetic inheritance. It is not the sub-human animals which resemble us but rather we who resemble them (11, p. 152).

If we suppose, then, that what is true of animal behavior is true of human behavior also, man, too, being an animal, we are left with the necessity of accounting for that portion of human behavior which is peculiarly or exclusively human.

The present work rests on the assumption that the extension of the theory of behaviorism to the behavior of man involves the generalized drives of aggression, manifested in the same basic sets of needs or drives as have been found in other animals. The sum of the hungers is sufficient to endow all of the animals with an aggressive posture. There is an element of aggression in every drive and not merely in the sexual. Action is always required, and there is no such thing as action that excludes force altogether. The characteristic behavior of the animal is a disturbance of the immediate environment in pursuit of the reduction of some one of his needs. Primary and secondary needs are sometimes identified as biological and psychological respectively (8, p. 23). It will be assumed here that the psychological needs are a subset of the biological. This will enable us to deal with the similarities which exist among them. We have noted in an earlier chapter that the analysis of all behavior properly begins with a drive to dominate the environment starting from the tropism of the material object: it arrests attention, and if attractive is to be drunk, eaten, mated, investigated, altered, and, if repulsive, avoided. Corresponding to these tropisms there are the six basic tissue-needs or drives already referred to: thirst, hunger, sex, curiosity, action, and the avoidance of pain. It will be our task first to examine the similarities between animal and human in the behavior called out by these drives; and, secondly, to examine the differences. There are important traces of other needs or drives in the human as evidenced by his behavior, but the discussion of these will have to be postponed to a later chapter.

THE SIMILARITIES OF HUMAN AND ANIMAL BEHAVIOR

There are many ways in which the human betrays a kinship with the animal. Possession of the generalized drive of aggression is one of the most prominent. Aggression is here defined, it will be remembered, as the drive to dominate the environment. It usually takes the form of one of the six specific drives aforementioned: the primary drives to drink, eat and mate, and the secondary drives to know, do, and survive.

The secondary needs like the primary are grounded in the central nervous system. The development of the human brain, and in particular of the frontal lobes, offers evidence from the standpoint of physiological structure. According to Olds, the needs of the animal differentially affect particular areas of the brain, as does the consequent behavior (5, p. 259). Pavlov thought that there is in animals a "self-preservation reflex" or "reflex of passive self-protection" (13, pp. 31, 410). Information can evidently be stored in the neurons in such a way as to allow for deliberate recall. Long ago Loeb suggested that the acceptance of certain ideas might affect chemical changes in the body, "increasing the sensitiveness to certain stimuli to such an unusual degree that such people become slaves to certain stimuli [i.e., ideas] just as the copepods become slaves to the light when carbon dioxide is added to the water" (10, p. 62).

The human drives to know and survive are responses as innate as the primary drives to eat and mate. They exist in some form roughly analogous to the printed circuit. There may be some kind of genetically transmitted programming, for it is evident that capacities at least are innate even though they can be elicited and rounded out by the acquisition of the contents of experience, through learning. Children even more than adults exhibit eager curiosity about everything and although lacking in experience are capable of tremendous fear. The drive for knowledge and survival does not have to be instilled in them but only directed, it does not have to be aroused but only cultivated. And with the adult the drive can be even more intense. Knowledge is often sought at the risk of life, as when scientists conduct dangerous laboratory research using themselves as experimental animals.

The needs or drives we are considering are to drink and to eat, to copulate, to know, to do and to survive. The aims of these drives, or their satisfactions as needs, are water and food, a mate, activity, knowledge, and ultimate security. For each need or drive there is a corresponding organ: kidney, stomach, gonads, brain, musculature, skin. Just as we saw in the last chapter that kidney tissue will deteriorate without water, so brain tissues will not develop without knowledge. The latter is not so obvious, yet it has been demonstrated that ground lost in children who have not been taught anything cannot be made up in later years, and they remain, if they live at all, mentally well below normal (12). The musculature is the organ for the need to do. Muscles work the skeleton to move material objects in the environment or to build tools that will move them more effectively.

In the recognition of goal-objects for the primary drives, the animals exhibit a rudimentary decision theory and a knowledge of class distinctions involving the use of similarity and difference. This is good to eat, or not, that is a friend, or an enemy. From such elementary beginnings, it is clear that an organism is a mechanism, but it is a mechanism not at the physico-chemical level merely, but instead one at the biological level, which is to say, a mechanism with an elaborate built-in set of controls which make a certain measure of self-direction possible. Tool-using is not yet developed, except with some animals, and sign-using is even less so.

Again, knowledge and security serve different needs in man but needs that enjoy the same autonomy as the others. The basic tissue-need of curiosity calls for the satisfaction of knowledge; the basic tissue-need for survival calls for the satisfaction of security. The specificity of these needs, like the primary ones, is made manifest by the variety of behavior they call out. The search for knowledge is no more like the search for food than the search for security is like the search for a mate. Each is peculiar in its own domain. In the following chapters we shall examine knowing and being as basic tissue-needs, and we shall consider them on the same basis as hunger and sex needs: animal drives peculiar to man and fundamental to his nature.

The needs are ordered and possess a certain rank. A clue is to be found perhaps in the phenomenon of inhibition (13, pp. 46-47). Of the two needs that one is more primitive which can inhibit the other. Hunger can inhibit sex, and as we have noted earlier in this chapter curiosity can inhibit survival. Importunateness in one direction and importance in another are the rank order criteria. The rank order of importunateness runs: thirst, hunger, mating, knowing, survival. The rank order of importance runs in the opposite direction: survival, knowing, mating, hunger, thirst. By importunateness is meant that need *by* which the satisfaction of the others is sought. By importance is meant that need *for* which the satisfaction of the others is sought. Roughly, the rank order of importunateness corresponds to means, and of importance to ends. The rank order of importunateness is common to all animals, that of importance is peculiar to man.

The arrangement of the primary and secondary drives in a rank order is to enable the former to prepare the way for the latter. The conductility of the stimulus-response circuit is a factor. The speed with which a single cycle is traversed within the circuit slows down from hunger to sex within the primary drives, from primary to secondary drives, and finally from curiosity to security within the secondary drives. In the primary drives, the basic gradient of reinforcement is short; but in the secondary drives it is comparatively long. Evidently, the longer the time between drive and consummation, the stronger the subsequent effects of reward and reinforcement. The reduction of the primary tissue-needs and the anticipation of and provision for their reduction in the future gives man temporarily a resting place, and allows him the time and energy to seek a greater knowledge and permanence. His plans for behavior cannot be rigid, however. The other animals are certain, and their expectations absolute. Man must have available a certain plasticity of behavior, be able to shift and change in his aims as his information is revised and the material objects with which he has been dealing altered. The attempt to arrive at need-reduction is no different in the case of the secondary drives than in that of the primary. For all four it is true that man like the other animals can do no more than alter the shape and position of material objects within reach of himself or his instruments on or near the surface of planet earth. This holds true of animals hunting or engaging in sexual intercourse. And it holds true also of changing the minds of men, of killing men in war, of painting on the walls of a cave, of worshipping a stone, and of performing certain ritual movements (15, p. 178).

The tissue-needs are not so far apart in their results as they are in their original goals. The end results of activities designed to satisfy feeding and breeding needs are economic enterprises and the family respectively. How to further a material interest which will be productive of consumer goods or of goods exchangeable for food and shelter, how to rear and educate children, are matters of increased knowledge. The need to know has as its aim the acquisition of true universal propositions, but these have by-products which serve the more importunate drives. Man sees in his children a continuance of his own being and some sort of guarantee of ultimate security: the generations will go on from him and pass beyond him.

Man is drawn toward knowledge and security as firmly as the aphid toward the light. The existence of vast libraries and cathedrals offer an abundance of evidence from the standpoint of behavior. For surely there exist many books containing the results of the search for knowledge, and many places of worship devoted to the consecration of security. To assert that the human individual is lodged solidly in the grip of his drives is no more than to say that if he has learned more about the external world and been more active in seeking its assurance than have other animals, this means only that he has come more strongly under its influence.

The arrangements within the organism which are designed for achieving need-reduction are present after need-reduction has been effected or when the elements in the environment requisite for the need are missing. The activity of the animal continues as spontaneous activity or play. All activity not explicable on the basis of tissue-needs or drives is displacement activity (17, p. 362f.). Human cultures can be accounted for either on the basis of the needs or drives or of activity originally designated for drives which has been shunted off into other channels. The tendency of diverse cultures to develop the same set of folkways and customs would tend to corroborate this view (7, p. 126).

It remains to point out after the diversity of human activity its severe limitations. The efforts of the human individual motivated by whatever drives have their restrictions defined by the animal condition.

THE DIFFERENCES BETWEEN HUMAN AND ANIMAL BEHAVIOR

We have seen the enormous range of the similarities between human and animal behavior. It will be equally important to take note of the differences, for although the differences are numerically smaller and less basic, they operate to bring about enormous effects.

Of the six drives we have undertaken to consider basic: thirst, hunger, sex, curiosity, activity, and the avoidance of pain, the first three (the primary drives) are handed on to the human intact; he may surround them with custom and execute them under approved social conditions, but he does not disturb them essentially. Under the sophisticated cultural patterning to be found in the dining room and bedroom, the primitive animal drives to drink, eat and mate continue to exist. But it is the manner in which the individual reaches such goal-satisfactions and need-reductions rather than what he does with them afterwards that marks them as peculiarly human. Many of the more familiar elements of human culture, such as paintings and art galleries, cook books and restaurants, surgery and hospitals, may be regarded from the viewpoint of the human individual as preparatory responses or as permanent possibilities of need-reduction.

The reduction of the animal needs: thirst, hunger and sex, make possible the *immediate* survival of the individual and the species. The reduction of the human needs: to know, to do and to be, are efforts to make possible the *ultimate* survival of the individual and the species. Man because of his relatively large size and low metabolic rate does not have to eat continually, like the shrew for instance, and can devote his free time and energy to the reduction of other needs, such as the needs for knowledge, for construction and for ultimate survival.

The change-over from primary to secondary drives occurs in a number of ways: by extension, for instance, and by transformation. First of all it is necessary to remember that the responses in man to the primary drives are well-formed; that is to say, as naturally occurring they are not unconditioned, like the primary drives in the other animals, but are maintained in established channels of behavior. But by now, presumably, the picture is not predominantly the simple one of a reflex arc but instead the role of internuncial neurons and mediating processes has been sharply increased, and there are ideational as well as overt responses. It is already in his peculiar kind of response to the primary drives that distinguishes the human individual from other animals. The elaboration of the preparatory responses is customary, planned, deliberate and anticipatory.

In the first place, in man a strong affective tone accompanies the consummatory responses (16, p. 330), and in the second place some of the consummatory behavior is transferred to the preparatory phase which usually precedes it. Man drinks like monkeys and cats, but unlike them usually from a glass in the right hand with the arm raised and without the body position noticeably altered. Man brings the food to his mouth, not his mouth to the food, thus necessitating the use of artifacts and of other ingenious preparatory techniques. The extension of the primary drives into the secondary takes place in terms of a secondary interest in the unconditioned stimuli of the primary drives, as, for example, when the ocean which was regarded first as a good feeding ground comes to be a source of knowledge through the study of the chemical and physical aspects of oceanography. The responses to the stimuli of information and permanence are conditioned responses.

All animals are adapted to their environment; indeed those that are not do not survive. That this is not a conscious process makes it no less a crucial one, as Darwinian evolution recognizes. But the distinction between the animal and the human is that the human can make an individual contribution to his own adaptation. In the lower organisms preparatory responses are going on all the time, as for instance the preparatory feeding movements of salivation or muscular contraction. What is peculiarly human is the extent of the externalization of the preparatory responses. The human individual contributes in this way to his own process of conditioning and he does so by making suitable alterations in the material environment.

Indeed, as we shall discuss more fully later, adaptive behavior in the human may be defined as continuously revised self-conditioning. At the psychological level the self-regulating system includes besides the organism itself highly complicated artifacts: combinations of tools and inter-personal sign-relations. When consciousness is given over entirely to the reduction of the primary needs, it has not justified its existence as human, unless it happens also that the future demands of those needs are being anticipated. For the skills insure that such need-reductions shall be performed automatically. The serious business of consciousness is not merely the secondary needs, either, but the anticipation of future need reductions also.

An important difference between human and animal behavior lies in the methods of need-reduction. The use of artifacts by sub-human animals is limited to a few species and there only to certain types of artifacts, mainly tools, which seem not to change. Some animals, as we have already noted, employ artifacts of both varieties for the reduction of the primary needs, the bird nest and the beaver dam, for instance. But the human individual employs artifacts to accomplish need-reduction in the case of all six of his needs, glasses for drinking, knives and forks for eating, beds for sex, books for knowledge, buildings for achievement, and churches for security. There are no records of human individuals without artifacts. The earliest men, now estimated to be more than a million and a quarter years old, were tool-users, and the most primitive tribes alive today, such as those of central Australia (2), or the interior of Brazil (18), are tool-users even though their tools are few and primitive in the extreme. They certainly do also have languages. Human behavior in all of its manifestations is shot through with artifacts. Where the use of tools is not present, speech and writing is, and it is a rare occasion in which one or the other is not used and usually both. In addition, there are preparatory responses for all six of his needs. Customs and institutions prescribe in many cases the routine of the preparatory response.

Man is distinguished from the other animals by the high development of the use of signs. This exists, if it exists at all among other organisms, in rudimentary form, such as the dance of the bees to indicate the direction in which honey is to be found. There are quite possibly monkey languages which we do not understand, and some others. But certainly no sub-human has developed the sign language to the extent that the human has. In addition, he combines both kinds of artifacts: he has tools as well as sounds to stand for signs, for instance written words to represent signs.

In the stereotyped behavior of the higher animals (other than man) there is no feedback from artifacts although there are artifacts. Artifactual behavior is and remains an instinctive affair emanating from the animal and uninfluenced by the effects of his actions on possible products. His behavior does not alter because there are artifacts as a result of it, but artifacts result from his behavior which produces them as it were automatically.

Man no less than the other organisms is stimulus-bound. However, in his case the stimuli are those he has devised for himself, the tools and the signs of his culture. Unlike the other animals, many of his responses are those he has anticipated and planned to produce in himself. As he alters materials through the making of artifacts, so the artifacts in their turn alter him; and the effects in both directions add up to a round of interactions, until the part of his environment he has constructed molds him in ways best suited to deal with their unexpected properties. Some other animals do produce artifacts, but man alone becomes to some extent the creature of those he himself has made. In all animals the consequences of behavior feeding back into the organism increase the probability that they will occur again (habit), but in the case of the human individual there is in addition a feedback from artifacts which insures that future behavior will be appreciably altered.

The drives which in the human most urgently call for examination are the secondary drives. In his case these become greatly extended and developed. The behavior *sui generis* of man in the world is dictated by his desire to know about the world, to change it, and to remain in it. It is here that the generalized drive of aggression takes generic form, but it is expressed also in two others. Curiosity, or the drive for information, is elevated into the search for complete knowledge; and the generalized drive of aggression takes the specific form of the need to do, the need for activity or achievement; and the avoidance of pain, or the drive for security, is transformed into the search for ultimate survival. Thus the additions in the case of human behavior specify for the material object that it shall stimulate a drive when it can be the source of knowledge, when it can be overcome or transformed, and when it can be the source of the continuance of existence.

The primary needs when excessive, that is, when not met with need-reduction, are in the sub-human animals disintegrative (6, pp. 191-92). There is no successful displacement. Hunger must be met with food and thirst with water, and there are no effective substitutes. But the secondary needs in the human individual lend themselves more readily to displacement. The chief characteristic of human behavior is its tendency to prolongation once aroused. Man is capable of sustained action, due no doubt to what one investigator has called his "high capacity to be conditioned" (4, p. 897). A response tends to exceed both in strength and duration anything that could be said to have been aroused by the stimuli. In human behavior stimuli trigger responses but never equal them in size or force. Thus when the need that was triggered by the stimulus has been reduced, displacement provides the necessary safety-valve. The need to know can be displaced to authority: parents, a church or a state. The need to do can be displaced to men of action: professional soldiers, athletes, actors. And the need to be can be displaced onto a ritual cycle.

The last three drives, which are also those for understanding, for achievement and for security—knowing, doing and being—like the primary drives, are tissue-needs. Thirst, hunger and sex are biologically more primitive, but knowing, achieving and being are characteristically more human. The secondary drives of knowing, doing and being are raised to such a position of importance only in the human individual, but must be studied there as special cases of the interaction between the behavior of animals and a changing environment. The animal aim to dominate the environment assumes in the human individual more subtle and penetrating forms. He may conduct laboratory experiments, paint a mural or look for super-natural guidance. But to seek aggressively through science to discover the laws of nature, to isolate the qualities of nature by means of art, or to take steps calculated to insure survival beyond nature by means of religion, is to be no less a mechanism reacting to the forces by which it is surrounded.

The mystery of human behavior is deepened if we do not take into consideration what the behavior is about. Presumably, it is about survival of both the short- and long-range varieties. Aggression may be characteristic of the generalized drive, which is to survive. It is motivated by a general arousal and undertakes to satisfy hungers: the hunger for water, for food, for a mate, for knowledge, for achievement, and for security.

Yet none of these, from the most primitive which the human individual shares with the sub-human animal to the most sophisticated which he possesses alone, can be understood by means of a study of the organism in isolation. Survival where, when, in what? All behavior occurs in terms of an interaction with the environment; and each need upward involves the human individual with a larger segment of the environment. Thirst requires only a little water, but ultimate survival requires the whole universe.

Such behavior is susceptible of individual differences, for no one individual will endeavor to reduce his needs in exactly the same way as another. But general motivation is species-predictable. Man is the animal in whom the reduction of needs involving immediate survival sets off other needs involving ultimate survival.

THE HUMAN NEED TO KNOW

Although all animals possess all six of the basic tissue-needs or drives, it is in varying degrees. In the human individual the drives which mark them off from all other animals are the secondary drives, which are for knowledge, doing and security, for it is in the tremendous and elaborate development of the anticipation of these drives that man has excelled. It will be valuable, then, if we discuss them, and we shall do so briefly here, one at a time, and then more elaborately in separate chapters.

The need to know is a more familiar one, perhaps, than the need to be. The human need to know has its source in the animal need to approach and explore. We have noted already that Pavlov recorded an "investigatory reflex" (13, p. 12) which is called out when changes in the environment cause both men and other animals to orient the appropriate receptor organ toward the quality in the agent which is the source of the change. This is done by adjusting receptors so that they are more broadly exposed to the unknown in the environment, and also by movements designed to bring the unknown nearer in order if possible to manipulate it.

We had better distinguish at the outset between learning as it concerns the need to know and learning as it concerns the other needs. Much thought and experiment have gone into the understanding of learning theories (9). These have meant usually theories of how the animal finds his way to feeding and breeding opportunities. But there is learning in the case of knowledge for its own sake, also; and therefore we shall have to include under the term the acquisition of abstract knowledge the activity peculiar to the attempts to reduce the need to know. According to some animal psychologists, there is the tissue-need or drive labelled curiosity, manifested by approach and exploration. But in the animals other than man curiosity is a preparatory reflex; what is approached and explored is expected to be something capable of satisfying the other drives, goal-objects calling out eating, drinking or mating behavior. In man the need to know is in addition a drive to satisfy curiosity concerning the nature of things, the drive for knowledge for its own sake.

In the terminological usage adopted here 'reflex' is reserved for sub-human animal reactions, and 'response' for the equivalent human reactions. A response is a reflex in the human individual. Even the importunate drives are not the same for him as for the sub-human animals. In the human individual they are marked for instance by the fact that the preparatory response is more complex and elaborate, and has to some extent taken over the functions of the consummatory response.

The motivation in the case of knowing, then, is the reduction of a cortical tissue-need. The human need to know is the need for abstract knowledge, generalized or universal knowledge not directly connected with any possible practical effects. And it is peculiarly human; no other animal pursues such knowledge for its own sake. "All men by nature desire to know'" said Aristotle (1), and he might well have added, only men. That knowledge may, and often does, have such effects is incidental to the purposes of this study since it plays no part either in the functioning of the need or in its reduction.

That curiosity is a drive native to the human individual will be recognized by anyone who has had extensive dealings with children. As soon as the child has gained sufficient control of language, in short, when he is four years old, his questioning goes on incessantly (3, p. 49). Childish questioning begins at two years of age, but at that time is practical in intent, usually concerned with something the child wants or expects. A little later, Piaget has pointed out, the questions are concerned with "pure" knowledge, that is, knowledge not directly connected with any practical motive (14, p. 173). By the age of six, the questions are better organized and can be classified. The principal types of questions according to Piaget are those seeking causal explanation, motivation and justification (14, ch. V, I). It is clear by now that the questions are aimed at understanding. Although the need to know, defined as the drive for the acquisition of pure knowledge, gets shunted off or covered over in later years, it is always there, incorporated in the resources of the central nervous system. In the adult often buried but tending to assert itself none the less, the need to know can be stimulated to movement toward the acquisition of those recurrent things, the abstract relations and true general propositions.

As necessary as the human component in knowing is the artifactual component. Knowing, except at the most elementary levels where perception and recognition suffice, requires the use of artifacts. The simplest level of these is that of a colloquial language containing a minimum of vocabulary and syntax. Later developments include writing and provision for storage. In the beginning, semiotic artifacts suffice, but these are later supplemented by the addition of tools, such as writing materials, books and libraries, in addition to all the elaborate paraphenalia of communication recently added: telegraph systems, radio, television, and now (1963) communication satellites. A language or writing material can be construed as a sort of stand-by of artifacts, to be called on when the occasion for knowing arises. Thus knowing, like the other drives, requires in the human the supplementary drive of doing; for artifacts, whether tools or signs, must be constructed.

THE HUMAN NEED TO DO

The human need to do is the need to make changes in the environment. It includes everything from spontaneous activity to the species of activity involved in the carefully planned exploration of nearby outer space. The need to do supplements all other needs and is included in them as a necessary component. To know or to be, for example, are expressed in terms of some appropriate activity. The need to do is the need specifically expressing the generalized drive of aggression.

Ego-expansion is accomplished by the need-reduction of the need to do. This is another effect of the element of aggression ingredient also in the drive for knowledge and for survival. Constructions result from the need to do; to make something that may survive is like knowing something that may survive or identifying with something that may survive: it reduces the drive. They are manifestations of one definite aspect of human nature, man as *Homo faber*.

There are many varieties of the need to do. In human society it is often the need that seems to motivate the human individual once his primary needs have been attended to. Let us mention a few at random in order to make the topic more familiar. The need for activity, for achievement, often takes the form of the need for social approval, political power and capital accumulation.

The need for social approval is in a sense a familiar form of aggression. It requires from others an attitude in which the approval carries with it some seal of endorsement, of superiority. It is as though one individual had got others to say, "You have compelled us to admit that you are superior." For in social approval it is hardly merely equality or belonging that is being sought. Thus in seeking social approval, the individual is through his actions or his achievements in a sense compelling others to acknowledge his superiority, and this is a variety of aggression.

The need for political power is a more obvious form of aggressive activity. The political leader dominates the society in which he moves. It is in effect power over other human individuals and their goods, the most effective form of aggressive activity of short temporal range, so far as society is concerned. Indeed power over individuals and their goods is political in essence whatever institution it may represent. At the time when Gandhi was assassinated, his material possessions were very few and his identification was with the religious life. Yet he moved in the domain of political power and was *de facto* the political leader of an independent India.

Of somewhat lesser range yet still formidably effective is the need for capital accumulation. The possession of material means has been in many societies the dominant motive behind the self-conscious activities of the individual. In all societies, perhaps, except primitive societies, and among the advanced variety, in ancient Sparta and modern Soviet Russia and China, the man of wealth can to the extent of his wealth control the individuals and the goods of his society.

The need to do, like the other secondary needs, can be traced to developments from the primary needs. Thirst, hunger and sex cannot be satisfied without activities involving changes in some segment of the environment, changes such as the reduction of the volume of streams, the death of other organisms, the inception of pregnancy in females of the same species. Social approval or political power, for instance, can be traced to primary needs; the first to insure that men will cooperate voluntarily in need-reduction, the second to compel them to do so. Further, the will-to-power is the need for survival turned into one of the primary need channels. Need-reduction in all such cases necessarily involves aggression and activity. In the human individual it also may involve the construction of artifacts.

The need to do in the human individual can be traced to effective components of the secondary drives. Thus, the efforts to find and so to speak possess permanence as persistence takes the form of the control of the behavior of many men or the possession of many women or the control of many artifacts. Approach-and-exploration is a form of doing, a way of taking possession through knowledge of an unknown territory. What is explored is no longer unknown and so no longer feared. Thus activity as such increases knowledge and serves survival.

The need to do is the need generic to artifacts. Only this time not their use merely but their construction. The human individual is a builder, and no different in this regard whether he builds a skyscraper, a symphony, a rocket for the probing of outer space, or something considerably less ambitious, such as a stamp collection or a flower arrangement. Artifacts, whether tools or signs, have to be *made* whatever other need they may subsequently serve.

Of course the need to do, conceived as the specific form of

the generalized need for aggression, however much it may be responsible for construction, is not confined to it. Aggression as such is as often expressed by destruction. The blind impulse to destroy, which sometimes overtakes individuals and even whole societies, contributes equally to the need-reduction of the need to do.

Men destroy as much as they produce, and they have an aggressive need which is operative equally in both, even though logically and factually the one seems the opposite of the other. But that men have conflicting motives which come into play upon different occasions is certainly verifiable. It has puzzled students of human behavior for many millennia.

A further distinction in this regard may be helpful. Aggression is constructive when it is serving other drives; it is destructive when operating alone. Human individuals certainly have the need to do something. Muscles otherwise deteriorate, and whatever deteriorates in the organism hurts the whole organism to that extent. However, when aggression runs wild it interferes with the need-reduction of the other drives. When it is harnessed to their service, it can express itself constructively. For it holds true that the need to dominate the environment is never indifferent to the other needs. The need to do is never neutral; it works either to further the need-reductions of the other needs or to block such need-reductions.

THE HUMAN NEED TO BE

Next we shall have to consider briefly the need to be.

The secondary drives themselves are related, and the changeover from knowing to being occurs naturally. The need to know and the need to be both involve survival. The need to know in terms of pure knowledge is an extrapolation of the need to know about eating and mating opportunities, and the need to be is an extrapolation of the need to know. The unknown is a fear or threat to the continuance of being. The dark is unknown and may contain monstrous appearances. Learning is fear-reduction. The familiar is no longer to be feared. Thus knowing serves being. It is necessary to know about permanence through inquiry into it before it is possible to move toward an association or identification with it. The need to be is not only a further development of the need to know but in a way a culmination of all the other needs. For it is a need of the entire man.

If knowing serves being, so also does doing. The escape reaction in animals is a violent activity. In the positive form, which the attempts at need-reduction take in the human individual for the need to be, there is much activity also. The individual makes preparatory responses in terms of his need. He builds institutions which are designed to bring him closer to it, and he devotes a considerable part of his active life fulfilling the requirements which he has in this way imposed on himself. Association or identification with a goal-object means in the case of the need to be the outlay of enormous efforts, whether feasting or fasting, pilgrimages to holy places or wars fought in defense of a faith.

Reducing the need to be, then, can be seen to employ an enormous collection of artifacts, everything from a special language, such as the Maya priesthood reserved to itself, to large cathedrals, holy relics and many others. Religion like any other institution requires the construction of large artifacts and the expenditure of huge sums. Special virtues are attributed to certain artifacts in most religions. There are special words which cannot be said, as for instance in some religion the name of God which cannot be used except by specially qualified individuals and then only on certain special occasions. There are sanctified structures which cannot be visited except by priests and then only on holy days.

It is less likely that psychologists have recognized also in the need to be an animal drive. For in animals other than man, the need for survival, like that of curiosity, is even more rudimentary. All animals have the urge to preserve themselves, as can be observed negatively in their behavior by the fear, rage, escape and avoidance responses; these are efforts at survival but in the animal other than man there is no positive response, no goal-object for the drive. Such a need in man is as much a drive as any. The response which in all animals is negative, as for instance the avoidance of tissue injury (pain) in man alone is also positive, an approach response, and takes the form of a drive for security, the need for devotion to permanent objects. The recurrent abstract objects of knowledge are exchanged for the persistent concrete or material objects of security: attachment to or identification with those things which seem less likely to perish. In man, the need to be is a positive drive, a need for ultimate survival, manifested by the behavior of association and identification, the movement toward objects exhibiting evidence of permanence.

The need to continue to be, the need for ultimate survival, is not in these terms as familiar as the need to know, yet the evidence for it is convincing enough. Man is the animal with foresight. He knows something of what he does not know, and he foresees that he will die. Both knowledge and continuity of activity, therefore, are necessary for him if he is to survive. Not having the necessary guarantee of survival means that a state of need exists. Man is the only animal that knows about death. There is in him a deep and abiding instinct for self-preservation; and what is this but the need to be, the drive to continue an existence already begun? Almost every religion is a result of the operation of the need for ultimate survival; societies without religions are rare. Behavior called out by the need to be takes the form of an association or identification with permanent things: with mountains, the sky, the sun, and finally perhaps with the universe considered as a whole. These things lack the transitoriness of animal life, and therefore possess something desirable to man, namely, persistence. Reaching out for such an association or identification is exhibiting the tissue-need or drive to be.

The mechanism of the need for survival is somewhat different from that of the others. The central nervous system as a whole is involved in each need, though usually through one organ. But the need for survival has no special organ. It is a need of the whole animal, as for instance in the escape reflex, which is most certainly evidence for an effort to continue to be. The fear which leads to escape involves all sorts of functions, cortical, hormonal, circulatory and digestive, to name but a few. Both autonomic and peripheral systems are activated. The intergrative action of the nervous system puts it finally at the service of the most generalized drives.

It will be our task next to study the secondary drives one at a time and in detail, first the drive to know, the drive to do, and then the drive to be. In each case, we shall employ as our model the reverberating circuit of the reconstructed behavior theory set forth in Chapter II, with extensions appropriate to the additional facts uncovered in the study of the particular secondary drive. We shall discuss the activity of the human individual and his attempts at need-reduction, but only up to socialization.

Before we can do this, however, it will be necessary first to devote a chapter to the peculiar human version of the behavior prompted by the primary needs.

Chapter 5

THE PRIMARY NEEDS

WE HAVE NOW to consider the primary needs in the human individual. These do not differ physiologically from the same needs in the sub-human animals. They are joined by others which, however, do. Immediate survival follows the first of the primary needs and precedes the last and the secondary needs. For immediate survival, clothing and shelter are necessary. Also the means to procure water, food and women. For the less physically able, medical services should be added. These come in the order of necessity after thirst and hunger, and before sex, and well before the needs to know, to do and to be.

Feelings of thirst, hunger and sex lead to preparatory and consummatory responses and rewards with their visceral functions which are followed in turn by pressures in bladder and rectum and irritations of genitalia. Between these two sets, one of which initiates a process and the other of which terminates it, there lies a long and intricate series of complex functions operating autonomically.

Our study will be devoted chiefly to human behavior with respect to the secondary needs, but the primary needs produce manifestations sharply divergent from the other animals and thus sufficiently peculiar to the human individual to be worthy of attention first.

TROPISMS

The original material object in the environment which excites the organism is the same for the human as for other animals. It is water, in a condition to be drunk; food, in a condition to be eaten (that is, other animals or plants either living or freshly killed); or a female in estrus. The tropism would show no sharp cleavage either, for with man as with the other animals there would be an orienting movement in the direction of the object (attention arrested) and then a movement toward it.

It is not the whole object which calls out such a dynamic response but only some part of it. The object may furnish the stimulus through its very existence and presence, but there is always a cue. The water looks inviting because clear, the food smells good or the girl beckons. The cue is a part which acts as an agent for the whole. It acts for the goal-object and draws the human individual toward it. But the entire object, and not merely some part, is altered in the ensuing process.

RELEASER

In the human individual there is a corresponding mechanism designed to receive such stimulation on which it acts as a releaser. The throat is dry, the stomach empty or the testes full. Again it is not the whole organism which makes the initial response but only some part. The human individual is prompted to act through the effect of the cue on the releaser. The arresting of attention is a function to some extent of deprivation in the human individual. A man who has just had a lot of water to drink will not be moved by the sight of it. A man who has just eaten can pass a restaurant with impunity. And one who has just had sexual intercourse will not be greatly stirred by the sight of one more nude woman. Deprivation and satiation are prime regulators of releasing mechanisms.

THE PREPARATORY RESPONSE

It is at this point that the distinction between the behavior of man and of the other animals diverges so sharply that its effects amount to those of another species. For it is just in the character of the preparatory response that the human peculiarities begin to show. The preparatory responses of the other animals are direct, immediate and fast. Primarily it is a question of approach. The water must be reached, the animal to be eaten must first be killed, the plant uprooted, or the mate mounted. The preparatory reflex is followed quickly by the consummatory reflex: the water is drunk, the food eaten or ejaculation achieved, followed by the interim reward of the pleasurable sensations of drinking, eating or copulating, and the final reward in all three cases of at least a temporary need-reduction.

But in the case of the human individual the treatment of the primary drives involves more elaborate behavior. There is what may be called here a generalized preparatory drive which is non-specific with respect to the separate needs. The human individual anticipates that he lives in a society where for the reduction of his needs, primary and secondary, he will require the cooperation of his fellows. The division of labor has made this particularly necessary. He will need the economic means, therefore, to insure that he can obtain aid in all his efforts at need-reduction. Hence the importance of work and before that of training for work. The economic function as a means is essential to making ready for the reduction of the primary needs as well as to immediate survival. It is important to be able to purchase in addition to water, food and a mate, clothing, shelter and the medical services. Thus the fundamental material means in a society, such as economic exchange, transportation and communication belong immediately before—as a condition for—the reduction of the needs. They therefore must be considered the preparatory responses *par excellence* in the performance called out by the primary needs.

Thus the distinguishing feature of the preparatory response to the primary needs in the human individual is his indirectness of approach. Other activities, usually of a ritual nature, interpose themselves between the tropistic effect of the object and the consummatory response of the individual. A man will work at something unrelated to hunger in order to obtain the money to buy food, and so for the other needs.

In the first place, human behavior with respect to the primary drives involves anticipation. The human individual aware of his thirst goes in search of water. But he has known from past experience that he will be thirsty from time to time and so he provides water for his own future thirst. And similarly with the other primary needs, food can be stored and women married.

There is a certain amount of generalization involved in the anticipation of primary needs and the consequent provision for future need-reductions. It is based on a comparison of present needs with past ones, and an induction to the generalization that future needs and need-reductions are apt to resemble those of the past and present. Plans for anticipation and provision are possibilities considered as probabilities: the meeting of absent conditions here and now.

To anticipate means to be aware of the existence of the problem abstractly. A need must be provided for in advance against the contingency of its arousal. There must be an intention to prepare for it. Intention is not a new thing in the world, of course, not, that is, if we admit the phenomenon of growth into form as this takes place in every organic species. But deliberate intention is newly introduced at this stage, and consists in the existence of a developed consciousness. Deliberate intention begins with the awareness of aims, and ends with their pursuit.

In the second place, preparatory responses involve the use of artifacts—of tools and signs specifically designed to serve the reduction of the primary needs.

The list of tools in the case of any one of the primary drives would be enormous. It would have to include everything from drinking glasses to public water purification plants and city plumbing systems. In the case of food it would have to include everything from dining rooms and kitchens to farms and farm equipment, slaughterhouses, quick freezing plants, groceries and markets. In the case of sex it would have to include everything from dance halls and living rooms to bedrooms, including furniture, clothing, cosmetics and jewelry.

There would have to be an even longer list of signs for each primary need. There is in fact almost an entire technical language used in connection with the operation of an urban water system; food production and distribution and consumption has produced another vocabulary; and everyone is familiar with the elaborate literature of love.

Language is a way of dealing with tools. Objects are named and new objects require new names, and there often are new tools. Names are in fact being coined every day. Yesterday, we acquired some of the terms of the new physics: electrons and mesons and quantum mechanics. Today we are acquiring some of the terms of the new technology: masers and photosynthesis and cryogenics. The more elaborate the artifacts the more complex the language. Water purification plants and their physical chemistry, food production and its biochemistry, the sex hormones and their chemical control of fertility, are no exceptions.

In the third place, preparatory responses for the primary needs are more than anticipatory and involve more than tools and signs. They are ritualistic. Not only are there established things to be done in preparation for the consummatory responses but there are established ways of doing them. In modern western civilization it is considered unthinkable to drink from one's cupped hands in polite society. Not only must there be a glass but there are well-defined lines of behavior in connection with it. It must be held in one hand rather than in two and the mouth cannot be lowered to it but instead it must be raised to the mouth. There are special occasions for sipping and others for draining the entire contents at a gulp. There are special occasions for drinking wine or whiskey and a special ritual for each of these. The rules and variations are practically endless and the ritual necessary to learn for anyone wishing to be considered a member in good standing in the society.

The search for water has no special ritual but the search for food and mate have. That there are elaborate hunting rituals and even more elaborate courting practices is well known. The tradition of enjoyment of the chase combined with the notion that the fruits are for the vulgar belongs to this stage of the primary needs.

Thus we come to a fourth consideration. The manner of reduction of the primary needs, that is to say, the tools and signs to be employed and the ritual practiced, call for social approval. In most instances the human individual will see to it that what he does in all three directions is similar to what is done by others in his society. Conformity in all but a few cases is essential to enjoyment.

The primary needs are common to all human individuals as indeed they are to all animals of whatever species. But the tools, signs and ritualistic behavior peculiar to need-reduction varies for the human individual from society to society. Every human culture has its own set and their use must be learned by the human individual if he is to be a member.

THE CONSUMMATORY RESPONSE

In the consummatory response, the chief feature is the use of the artifacts and signs by means of the ritual behavior which had been designed for the preparatory response. Now for the first time the three elements of the preparatory response are fitted together and function simultaneously. A man fills his glass with water and drinks it, observing at the same time how thirsty he was; or he sits down at a table and converses with his companions while consuming food; or he makes love to a woman in her boudoir while assuring her how very much he loves her. The man dying of thirst who reaches for a water hole in the desert, the man found starving who is first given food, and the rapist are instances in which the human individual makes straight for his goal object. But except in such aberrant cases the consummatory response of the human individual is never simple. The consummatory response to the primary needs may be merely a vehicle and not a need-reduction at all except in a kind of ancillary fashion. The primary needs may in fact carry all sorts of other services, for a number of other needs may be involved. Prestige may depend upon where one dines, what wines one drinks, who one's mistress is. Social approval or self-love may be equally represented in these ways.

It is at this stage that it is possible to recognize in the artifact which has been prepared to reduce primary needs a compound conditioned stimulus (the CCS), and a conditioning to the CCS in the needs themselves. A flavored water, a fish cooked in a sauce containing condiments and spices, an accomplished courtesan—these are the CCS appropriate for the consummatory response which will effectively reduce the primary needs in the human individual.

REWARD

As soon as the goal-object has been reached: the water drunk, the food eaten, the copulation completed, behavior passes over to the physiological and becomes identical with the behavior of the sub-human mammals. The goal-object in each case will be transformed as a result, and the human individual affected. Some of the water and much of the food will be assimilated and the mate perhaps impregnated. The individual will be nourished and then there will be psychological effects of all sorts: a restoration of the sense of well being from the nourishment, and from the mating a variety of possible effects: for instance an increase or decrease of desire or of love for the mate, or an increase or decrease of ego reinforcement.

The enjoyment the individual derives from his primary needs comes as much from the artifacts by which he reduces them as from the physiological sensations themselves. Thus the wine drinker will enjoy tremendously the use of an old goblet, and the diner old silver and table china. The entire force of the reward may even be entirely shifted to the artifacts which were formerly employed in the service of primary need-reductions but are so no longer. Old chairs and other antique pieces of furniture too frail to use become cherished for their own sake; old houses are turned into museums; old ruins preserved for their history or beauty; even old motor cars are valued although no longer utilized in the service of transportation.

MUTUAL NEED-DETERMINATIONS

Specialists in particular aspects of human behavior are often led to see some one need as more basic than the others and frequently even as determinative of the others. Thus Freud regarded sex in this manner and Marx economics. The primary needs lend themselves more readily to this kind of treatment than the secondary. Freud thought the source of all human energy was the sex drive, while Marx gave primary reality to the exchange of goods, with the hungry man furnishing the broad base of society. A favorite in history has been the need for ultimate survival, the need for religion. But no one as yet has specified water, knowledge or activity as basic. It is the thesis of this contribution to the theory of human behavior that the drive of aggression, the need to dominate the environment occupies this place, with the other needs ranged in proportion after it as stronger or weaker and in any case more specific instances of it. The drive of aggression is spelled out as the needs for water, food, clothing, shelter, medical services, a mate, knowledge, activity and ultimate security, respectively.

Each need of course is quite capable of preempting the position of the others, and as we shall see in a later chapter a need out of place always results in aberrant behavior. The distinction is not an absolute one, but it is based on the difference between the importunate and the important. One does not seek the most general knowledge in order to be free to wear warm clothing, but one does wear warm clothing in order to (be free to) seek the most general knowledge. The importunate is insistent and preempts attention, but it is the means-*by*-which of human existence, not the end-*for*-which. The important is the end-*for*-which, and it is given in the secondary needs. We have noted in an earlier chapter (Ch. II) that in the order of importunateness the primary needs take precedence over the secondary (and in fact that is why they are here called 'primary'), but in the order of importance the secondary needs take precedence over the primary.

Thus the needs of man exist in a hierarchy of graded support, those on the lower level making possible those at the higher, all building *on* what one might call the smallest sip of water, yet building toward greatness of achievement and ultimate survival. The movement of evolution seems inclined toward an increase in the complexity of matter. The human individual is the most complex of single material entities and his society more complex still. With its individuals and their tools and signs, we see the direction that progress is slowly taking. The human needs serve this complex and they serve it best when functioning in series and in their proper place, like a smoothly running internal combustion engine which can drive a vehicle only when its pistons observe the firing order.

The primary needs have been studied more intensively than the others. We shall move more decisively, therefore, and in greater detail when we come to discuss the secondary needs.

REINFORCEMENT

In a settled society there is achieved a sort of equilibrium between the human individual and the artifacts necessary for the reduction of his primary needs. The more the individual settles for certain ways of reducing his primary needs the more he becomes committed to them and reluctant to change any of the details. Every consummatory response deepens the committment. Although the individual is unaware of the extent of his involvement it remains strong. The continual round of interactions between the individual and the artifacts responsible for the reduction of his primary needs reinforces his reliance upon them and his expectation that they will continue to be available. He becomes dependent upon a set of elements which belong irrefrangibly to the external world yet remain available for utilization by him, needing him so to speak for their fulfillment. The greater the delay between tropism and consummatory response the greater the degree of involvement. Water stored in tanks, food kept in deep freezes, women passively waiting, secure his allegiance and emotional identification with their potential need-reducing properties. Thus, habits rapidly become established and themselves reinforced.

REVERBERATING CIRCUIT

What we have been describing is the routine activity of a reverberating circuit. Artifact stimulates man, man derives need-reduction from artifact but thereby changes it, the artifact (now to some extent a fresh artifact because changed) stimulates the man again, and again he derives a need-reduction from it but this time slightly more effectively as a result of the change, and so on in a continuing round of interaction. This process of reinforcement by establishment of ritual cycle is more evident in the case of goal-objects which are not destroyed in the process of need-reduction, as for instance in mating. By an act of mating the female is altered to some extent, for instance emotionally or through pregnancy. There is no invariant except the existence of an ecological process itself. Otherwise, change is the rule and especially rate of change. Given the enormous number of variables, the rate of change would be difficult (though not impossible) to calculate.

In any cycle of need-reductions the repetition is self-destructive. Monotony is a kind of anti-productive element inevitably bringing about a decrease in the frequency and intensity of consummatory responses. The stimulus has a feebler cue effect and the releaser operates less efficiently. The preparatory response is mechanical and the consummatory response smaller and weaker. Living always in the same house, wearing always the same clothing and eating always the same food offers the advantage of reinforcement to the sense of security but also dulls the primary senses. And we have already noted that in the order of importunateness the primary senses take precedence over the secondary. Thus periodicity of unrelieved need-reductions loosens the connections between the human individual and the external world, and the drives tend to reassert themselves. Hungers of all sorts are stimulated afresh only through the introduction of elements of novelty. Thus the reverberating circuit of needs and need-reductions tends to destroy itself and to leave the old drives hanging while the individual goes in search of new goal-objects capable of offering more powerful need-reductions. A man who is faced always with the same goal-objects for the reduction of his primary needs goes at last in search of new goal-objects which if they are less effective than the earlier are at least different.

Chapter 6

THE NEED TO KNOW

IT WILL BE our task to study next the first of the three secondary drives, the need to know. The need to know is the need for certain knowledge. By certain knowledge is meant knowledge of the absolute truth. The need to know is no less a need because the absolute truth is hard to come by or because alleged versions of it often prove limited or false. The generalized drive of aggression, defined as the drive to dominate the environment, takes a specific form in knowledge-getting. We have noted that a need is a lack on the part of an animal of some component a material object can supply which is necessary to survival. Knowledge-getting is a macroscopic event involving the activity of animals in the natural world. In its earlier, primitive stages, the animal does not need to know that he needs to know nor even that he knows, and this applies also to the simplest of human knowings. But it happens that the effort to gain information, like the effort to survive as an individual, leads to overt behavior which can be observed by an independent investigator.

The need to know has this in common with the more primitive needs, that it hooks up the organism with a material object. It has its counterpart and perhaps origin in the investigatory reflex of the sub-human animal. We have already referred to the work of Pavlov and his pupils on this reflex as it occurs in dogs, and the same type of inquiry is still in progress. According to Berlyne (1) rats exhibit curiosity by means of approach-and-exploration.

There are important differences between the primary drives and the need to know. Where in the primary drives the material object was the whole object: food to be eaten or another animal to be mated, this time it is a part of a material object. Where in the primary drives the goal-object was altered in the process, this time it remains unchanged. For the goal-object of the need to know is not always the property of some one object only but often of many and even of all. The goal-objects of the need to know are the similarities and differences of material objects, and these remain unaltered, they do not suffer change in the process of being known.

THE TROPISM OF KNOWING

In the human individual, the need to know relies upon more primitive conditions, and its explanation must begin with them. The aimless and spontaneous behavior observed in the animal may be due not to uncontrolled and irregular motor activity but rather to the motivation of searching manifested in approach-and-exploration: after choosing a goal, the limiting of stimuli to just those influences which would further the efforts toward that goal, a painful process of grasping piecemeal the "insignificance of all irrelevant stimuli" (14, p. 320). As is the case with all needs, there is first a material object. When an animal is confronted with a material object which excites a need, he moves toward it, and when the human individual is confronted with a material object which excites his need to know, he behaves in a similar fashion. The strength of his response will be proportional to the duration and intensity of need-deprivation. If he has developed without access to information, then for the time being at least he can be said to be knowledge-deprived. The effect of such a confrontation is an orienting response, the recognition of a tropism.

The second term in the psychological circuit of knowing, then, is tropism. The tropistic object in the case of the need to know is the 'naturally occurring relation,' defined as the similarity or difference of material objects. An example of naturally occurring relations would be the similarity of the shapes of these two trees, the difference in color of those two rocks. Naturally occurring relations are as much a part of the world as the material objects in which they inhere. The human individual who recognizes them is no more responsible for their existence than he is for his own recognition of it. Perception depends upon stimulation, and stimulation issues from the environment. Thus perception is a function of the environment (8). It is from a comparison of the similarity of members of classes that the recognition of classes arises just as it is from a comparison of the difference between members of classes that the recognition of individuals arises. The naturally occurring relation can be separated out from the material objects in which it is found and preserved in knowledge, often without disturbing them. Also, it can be combined into propositions, by means of which it is possible to represent absent objects. Its attraction lies in its permanence, its ability to recur unchanged indefinitely in other material objects in the future as it does in the present and evidently did in the past. As we shall see in the next chapter, it seems in this way to have a power to continue to be which is exceeded by little else that we are able to discriminate in the environment.

The choice of goals may be influenced by previous occasions of success or failure, or by the existence of a threshold which determines the degree of inertia which must be overcome before behavior can be aroused. But at the present stage in the evolutionary development of the cortex there are instinctive patterns of behavior which determine that relations shall function as tropisms. The figure-ground organization in perception, so favored by the *gestalt* psychologists in their investigations, is the first stage in the process of abstraction from material objects to classes and propositions.

For man the similarity of material objects constitutes a tropistic feature. Such phenomena exist continually and are available to all perspectives. But it would be idle to expect any animal to make a specific response unless that animal were intrinsically equipped to do so. Tropisms ordinarily issue from objects present to sensation, but here they operate as conditioned stimuli and play an intermediate role, the role of language. Signs are material objects employed to refer to other material objects, and this may mean all material objects of a certain specified class, those absent as well as those present. Behavior elicited by the need to know is very much conditioned by artifacts. The artifacts peculiar to this need are signs. Signs are artifacts, semiotic objects, of permanence, and exhibit sign-recurrence. Sign-behavior is the kind of behavior peculiarly designed to deal with absent objects.

A tropism in the case of knowledge will be called a gnoseotropism, and the behavior it elicits gnoseotropistic behavior. There is more to a tropism than merely an orienting response when there is more to the tropistic object and more to the animal. Gnoseotropism means orientation in depth by the human individual to a material object which may be complex indeed and requires considerable penetration of perception and even understanding (22, p. 435).

In order to consider relations in terms of tropisms, in the active sense, that is to say, as seen from the material object, we shall have to note how relations exert a compulsion on the knower. For this we shall have to turn to the work of a man who should receive the credit for recognizing the compulsion involved in abstract knowing, Charles S. Peirce.

In his theory of signs, he called attention to the forceful element which is involved in the act of communication (7, pp. 133, 252-53). The sign relationship is an interaction of three events, in which one idea affects another (2, 6.139). Ideas have an insistency about them. Indeed Peirce's very definition of a sign conveys this forceful element. A sign is "anything which determines something else (its *interpretant*) to refer to an object to which itself refers (its *object*) in the same way" (2, 2.303). What a sign stands for is its object, and it stands for that object to somebody in whom it arouses a more developed sign or interpretant. The sign stands for the "common characters" of the object, and in this respect is called the *ground* (2, 2.418). In "common characters" it is possible to recognize what we have called relations: the grounds of signs are relations. Thus the tropism we are looking for in the case of knowledge is implicit in the theory of signs, at least as Peirce analyzed it.

One inference that stands out clearly in Peirce's contention that signs are forceful is the stability of the relations which the signs represent. All signs are names, and the signs of relations are the names of recurring but indestructible things. The stability of relations is of a peculiar sort. Relations do not persist, but they do recur. Circles can be destroyed, but there will be circles again. Knowledge-as-such is acquaintance with permanence-as-recurrence. (We will study human behavior in relation to permanence-as-persistence in a later chapter.)

What Peirce did that is so pertinent to our purpose was to point out the tropistic character of signs for human individuals, as in the observation of diagrams. A sign exerts a compulsion on those capable of reading it. No one can refuse to recognize in a pointing hand the indication of a direction, though he may fail to carry out the appropriate behavior. Language exercises a definite force upon those who can read or hear examples of it. A choice in such cases does not exist; it is not possible to choose not to comprehend an idea any more than it is possible to choose not to notice noxious odors. From the simplest sign to those complex combinations of signs called language, the human individual is compelled to attend to it by his understanding of it.

Knowledge, then, is the element of compulsion in all tropisms above threshold as the stimulus to sign-behavior. At this point it is necessary to recall that the secondary drives of the human individual are less pressing than the primary. The more importunate drives, corresponding as they do to the more strongly conditioned stimuli, will dominate: eating over mating, mating over knowing. Exposure to stimuli furnishes the opportunity for selecting the more strongly conditioned stimuli. But when an animal has been fed and mated, it is available for another set of stimuli; and, then, given the cortical equipment to apprehend impinging relations, knowing occurs. In the processes of the psychological circuit, the acquistion of abstract knowledge starts from the perception of relations, of forms and qualities —in the case of visual perception, for instance, of colored shapes.

Approach-and-exploration behavior is familiar enough. A chimpanzee or a kitten will move toward any small object to examine it. The object may after all be good to eat but if not is usually discarded. In the same way the human individual approaches knowledge; it may be useful, but if not, in his case, it is not discarded. For he has learned that what is not useful directly may be useful indirectly and so worth saving. This was a giant step. Knowledge which can lead directly to reductions of the primary needs is called concrete knowledge. That raw cassava root contains a poisonous sap but dried and cooked is good to eat, is an example of concrete knowledge. Knowledge which does not necessarily lead directly to reductions of the primary needs is called abstract knowledge. That the square of the hypotenuse of a triangle is equal to the sum of the squares on the other two sides, is an example of abstract knowledge. Abstract knowledge can of course lead to need-reductions of the primary needs indirectly. But it can lead to reduction of the secondary needs directly, and this is obvious when we remember that the first of the secondary needs is the need to know.

In place of animal approach-and-exploration, there is, first, learning, and then manipulation and alteration. Learning is here defined as those changes made by the environment in the animal which make it possible for the animal to change the environment. In the need to know, the conditioned response becomes a kind of elementary learning. It begins with what Pavlov called "generalization of stimuli" and rests on the fact that natural stimuli are flexible and have a certain limited group range (19, p. 113). Hull observed that in the higher organisms learning often occurs with no need-reduction (11, p. 387). The process begins with insightful learning and operates against a background of more primitive scanning, such as saccadic eye movements. But this is not the whole story, for there is one more human dimension. Exploration reveals that there are some phenomena which cannot be manipulated and altered in the ordinary way. As we have already noted, naturally occurring relations often are treated in absent form by means of sign-learning (7, pp. 133, 252-53). Similarities have to be detached from their material objects and examined at leisure, the similarities of shapes or of numbers, for instance. Approach-and-exploration in such cases has to take the form of the ingestion of a representation, the reception of a concept in the mind.

There is learning in the energy which excites the receptors. The alterations of the organism consists in the activity of the central nervous system, in particular the reticular formation of the brain stem, and the cortex. Learning may be, as Guthrie has pointed out, intentional or not (9, pp. 203-11). For the adult, learning takes place through the feeling or through muscular exertion, but it is the reason which knows. To make contact with the world as it is in itself requires all of the faculties working together. The understanding of the whole of his environment—the attainment of complete knowledge—would have to be an effort of the entire man.

Learning as the term is extended here of course means acquiring pathways not to water, food or a mate but to the knowledge of relations. Knowledge for its own sake—whatever may subsequently be its incidental practical consequences—is a goal for the human individual. Innate capacities determine learning, and learning determines later learning. Curiosity, the expression of the need to know, is satisfied only by novelty. The intact animal learns to ignore a monotonous stimulus; because imprinting is cortical, the same object can serve as a stimulus repeatedly only to the decorticate animal. The limitations of the simple stimulus-reflex cycle become more apparent the more complex the animal. The decorticate animal is the least alert, the intact animal is almost never free from the disturbances in the immediate environment. And when we come to the human individual in whom the level of arousal made possible by the activity of the non-specific projection system is high, such an abstraction as the stimulus-response cycle almost never applies without qualification. Old knowledge is often ignored: to be stimulating, it must be new knowledge (13, p. 55). If there is a need and there is already knowledge, then clearly what is known did not reduce the need, and new knowledge is needed. Movements intended to aid need reduction include experiments to determine properties, the comparison of material objects, the relating of abstractions, and calculations with graphs.

Knowing is not necessarily fully conscious, but there is a hierarchy of degrees of consciousness required for knowing. By "consciousness" is meant here the awareness of perception, made possible by ascending arousal impulses from the brain stem reticular formation (16, p. 49; and 4, p. 378), particularly in such starting states as wakefulness, attention or arousal (16). This will mean also of course the awareness of the content of perception; and it is the awareness of this content which is necessary for knowing. One knows that one has learned this or that one believes that. The perception of naturally occurring relations means that by looking deeper into the familiar material objects in his environment the human individual discovers exciting novelty in the midst of the most monotonous familiarity.

The equivalence of stimuli is itself a stimulus, and gives rise to the increasingly abstract character of the learned material. The progression of learning, so far as abstract knowledge is concerned, follows the scale from the knowledge of particulars to particular knowledge: from the observations of material objects to the selection of empirical relations to the construction of empirical generalizations to universal propositions.

Impressions are received through every avenue of sense as well as through the movement of muscles. At the end, these impressions become knowledge by means of interpretation; but there are direct capacities of the knower as well, such as those engaged in the perception of relations, where interpretation so to speak rides the ascending neuronal pathways. For surely a very thin line if any exists between the selection of what is to be perceived and the interpretation of the received impressions. There are no creative powers proper to the human individual. What is referred to as 'creation' usually proves to be discovering, selecting or sorting. But knowledge as such is the name for the content carried by the intermediate processes which are characterized by a long delay between stimulus and response.

THE RELEASER

Relations are to be found in the environment between material objects, and in the human individual within cortical connections; but it is the act of recognition functioning as releaser which connects them by eliciting in the individual a curiosity about particular things and relations, manifested in the naming of particulars and the classifying of common objects by means of general terms. The objects exhibiting similarities are stimulus-emitters in this case, and the respondent has capacities which are released in the process. For the human individual, to think is no less an instinct than to eat or to breed. Thought is simply the extended product of the discrimination between beneficial and noxious stimuli in the environment. But there must be a cortical correlate of the type of naturally occurring relations, else neither would such relations excite the mind of the knower nor would he respond to them as to stimuli. It is seldom the case that an act of recognition does not connect something known with something else apprehended. Remembering has to be triggered by recall. But discovery consists for the respondent in three and only three mental operations: (a) he can apprehend true ideas, (b) he can recognize new ideas, i.e., hitherto unknown relations between true ideas, and (c) he can invent false ideas. True ideas are those mental concepts having a one-to-one correspondence with situations, actual or possible, in the concrete world. 'Mind' is a much abused term. But if we allow ourselves to mean by 'mind' consciousness plus the unconscious, then we shall be in a position to state an hypothesis regarding its capacities. There is nothing in the mind that was not first in the external world, except certain types of apprehension, discovery and invention, as set forth in (a), (b) and (c) above. If it can be shown for any mental activity that it is an instance of some one of these three types, then the hypothesis may be regarded as at least a partially established theory.

It is well established that there are afferently aroused physiological needs and effector activities which terminate in consummatory responses. Behavior is a product of internal changes which begin with the perception of consummatory stimuli, but the nature of these is a matter of speculation. Deutsch's hypothesis of a chemical change leading to irritation seems a good one, even though for the moment the nature of that chemical change remains unknown (5, pp. 23-34). Searching occurs in terms of curiosity. But what internal change triggers curiosity? Deutsch's theory that the stimulus produced by a need does not evoke a response but terminates it would mean that the acquisition of information shuts off the search for it, that curiosity is interrupted by its satisfaction. Just as eating stops when food enters the stomach, so inquiry stops when knowledge enters the mind. Any further process is exclusively cortical, and takes place by means of closed circuitry: communication between areas of the brain.

The specificity of the need to know is better explained by Deutsch's hypothesis than by the older version of Hull and others whereby needs stimulate receptors; for on this latter version how could it happen that the only object which could satisfy the need is chosen for the purpose? The consummatory response which results in need reduction could very well not consist in the stimulation of receptors but rather in that of the required factor. These are proximal variables; they are attainable in the immediate environment. Both food and a mate can be perceived and sought; impulse signalling can locate them and motor activity can bring them into range. But there exist other variables of a more distal nature, variables not available to sense perception. Knowledge is required to begin with if there is to be a reduction of the need to know.

In the nervous system, most probably in the brain, there takes place an imprinting of the sequence of external events. And these events can include abstract knowledge: the relations between material objects or between events—naturally occurring relations. They must include also new knowledge.

Cooperative behavior is important to the knowing need. Participation in group actions makes it possible to accomplish need-reductions not otherwise possible to the individual. Schools and their functions, libraries and their contents, scientific investigations, geographical explorations, institutionally-sponsored inquiries of all sorts, produce much information necessary to human knowing. However, it is important to remember that such group endeavor is in the service of an individual need. It is an effort to obtain need-reductions not otherwise obtainable with merely individual striving.

THE PREPARATORY RESPONSE

The preparatory response comes under the general heading

of operant learning, which is motor, as compared with sensory or cortical learning (22). Another approach to the same stage in the psychological circuit is that which regards it as learned motivation (10, p. 161). The development of sophisticated behavior from more primitive drives amounts to a qualitative difference which could only have been acquired. Man learns by doing, but for this it is necessary to take anticipatory action. Ideals are plans considered as approximations, plans for a series of actions designed for approaching a goal. Operating by means of thought in terms of the ideal means responding to stimuli from absent objects. The human emphasis is on preparatory responses, for they change, while the consummatory response remains the same. In the case of the primary drives, for instance, it is the responses which are elaborated. Eating is eating, for example, but the preparation of food varies widely among different people and for the same person at different periods of his life. Human behavior has the advantage of not being tied down to specific innate behavior patterns, which exist in man but are much more general. Thus, his capacity for learning is greater, and he has a greater potential range of behavior. The urge to grow food, to prepare it, to perform rites of passage, constitute instinctive patterns of behavior in man; indeed almost the whole of human culture, one might say, is of this character.

From the preparatory response in the human individual it is so easy to slip over into displacement activity. Preparations for consummations which are never effected are of this character. The need to know when it is not concerned with immediate practical knowledge is generically the same as intellectual play: a detached interest in winning to a certain awareness which consists in nothing beyond the knowing itself. What is this if not a description of the search for knowledge for its own sake, surplus motivation leading to displacement activity? That the game of learning without primary need-reduction in view happens to result in the acquisition of knowledge having more than theoretical interest is an indirect effect and has no influence on the game itself considered as a pure displacement activity capable of discharging energy called out in the service of more primitive drives.

Planned experience is the archetype of anticipatory response in man (18). A work of art or the design of a scientific experiment is a preparatory response undertaken in view of operant learning. Concept formation, which may be defined here as the acquisition of a formula for a common response to elements of similarity among dissimilar stimuli, is a species of behavioral decision theory (12) and a continuation of sign-behavior. Plans may be made for extensive feeling, e.g., to attend a concert; for extensive reasoning, e.g., to read a volume of mathematics; or for extensive action, e.g., to travel through Asia. Plans may be simple, as for example to cook a chicken, or they may be complex, as for example preparing for a career.

THE CONSUMMATORY RESPONSE

In the case of the need to know, the consummatory response consists in the assimilation of the object of knowledge by the individual. Need-reduction is accomplished usually through the acceptance of some propositions considered the absolute truth, as for instance a creed guaranteed by a church or a state. Philosophy is the response made when naturally occurring relations stimulate in man the need to know. The information which has been sought and acquired becomes part of him, through memory traces. He has absorbed it in the same way in which an animal absorbs food by eating. There is only the difference that the animal destroys the food by eating it, whereas knowing does not affect knowledge. Universal propositions remain uninfluenced by the knowledge of them. But this is not true of the individual: because of the consummatory response of knowing, the knowledge does affect him. Just how much it does is a question of depth of the impression reached in the response, the more primitive the somatic level the more powerful the effect.

REWARD

Need-reduction in the case of knowing, as in the more primitive instances of feeding and breeding, is the basis of reinforcement in simple conditioning. The more a subject is content with what he knows about the world the easier it is for him to settle in with his knowledge and to look for no extension of it. His life of inquiry is for the moment at least ended—he *knows*. There is an adaptation to expected stimuli and as the neurophysiologists say of other species the repeated stimulus fails to awaken the sleeping animal (13, p. 55).

The pleasure of understanding is the reward germane to learning. Knowing is a kind of having, by getting information inside the skin. Learning takes possession of relations, and no less so because the relations are not thereby diminished. As when no one is in possession of a truth docs not make it any the less true, so when many know a truth that does not, either. But for the knower there is a participation in knowing which comes from understanding. And that understanding is diffused makes it no less a sensation, for it is sustained. Knowledge can be recalled; the feeling which occurs in the case of knowledge is the conviction that lawfulness is a world-condition, a pleasurable feeling because a conviction that reinforces security.

Let us analyze the steps leading to this reinforcement. Any segment of a circuit is a causal series, in the sense of Cournot's (3, pp. 39-42) and Russell's "causal chain" (21, pp. 453-59). It is possible to see in the stages of a reverberating circuit each of which sets off the next an illustration of the logical connectives between classes (as for instance 'and,' 'or,' 'not'), and it is the sense of discovery implicit in the recognition of the existence of causal chains which is responsible for the pleasurable feeling. Discovery in the case of knowledge is sudden insight and insight is the threshold of latent learning. Bits of information assimilated in connection with other causal chains are seen to have cross references and to constitute themselves an additional set of relations. The act of discovery is a sudden movement that cuts diagonally across causal chains. What is discovered of course are additional pieces of theoretical knowledge.

There is more security to 'all' than to 'some.' But truth of any size is a value (17). And the quality which emerges from the theoretical nature of abstract knowledge carries the satisfaction of the need to know because a "possession forever." 'All' includes future instances with those of the past and present. We have said already about the function of knowledge that by means of abstractions there can be a representation of absent objects. Universals are classes whose members are all possible instances as well as all actual ones. Thus, universals are abstract representations of recurrent material objects, and in this way possess some permanence, or at least more persistence than the instances themselves. When a class is abstract and its members concrete, then we can say that the class possesses a permanence not possessed by its members. But this is not always the case, for the members as well as the class may be abstract, as for instance in pure mathematics.

REINFORCEMENT

Reward and reinforcement in the case of knowing is the result of pleasure and understanding respectively. Contact with any element possessing permanence provides both the pleasures of understanding and the comforts of security. These are felt as a kind of belonging, a diminution of strain, and a general sense of the fitness of things. For the universals at least are secure as men wish themselves to be. Understanding is pleasurable, but discovery even more so. These are the reinforcements which act in the case of knowing. The utilization by animals of information with which they have been previously confronted depends upon some other mechanism not as yet isolated. The hypothesis is here adopted concerning the operation of a principle of parity: that any pieces of knowledge can become relevant pieces when acted on by the perception of their similarity. Motivation is disclosed by the behavior of understanding, and the understanding of anything finally requires the rearrangement of its elements in a system.

When an artifact, more specifically a tool, triggers responses which result in further alterations, we say that a psychological circuit has been fired. And when the artifact is a sign which triggers responses resulting in further sign-behavior, we say a cultural circuit (6). That such semiotic objects can initiate responses in the same way that material objects can, we have already noted in what Peirce called the observation of diagrams. It is possible to make discoveries by studying the relationships —for instance, those between equations, which were not noticed before the equations were written and then observed together.

The degrees of knowing mark the amount of emotional acceptance and dislocation the knowing occasions. The intensity and breadth of emotional acceptance is indifferent to the amount of truth and falsity in the knowledge. The feeling of pleasure in the discovery is the same for false and for true ideas. (And the social acceptance, as it happens, is greater for false ideas than for true, a phenomenon which will be examined in another place.)

The acquisition of concepts provides the stimulation for belief. By 'belief' here is meant the feeling that an item of knowledge is true. The neurophysiological concomitant of belief ranges from the faintest memory traces to integrations occurring at the highest level of the central nervous system (6). Belief is a comfortable state (as contrasted with the discomfort of its opposite, doubt). Most beliefs are prejudices which are adopted emotionally and afterwards defended through the use of logical fallacies. There is a tendency to accept as true whatever is asserted, a tendency which can be accounted for quite easily by the fact that every proposition asserts its own truth.

Not all beliefs are conscious, indeed few are. There are beliefs at every integrative level. For physiological belief for instance we have the feeling of hunger, which implies that there is food in the world. Such an implication is included in what is meant at this level by 'belief.'

Emotion is the response of the whole organism to the blocking of behavior. Blocked behavior induces more intense feelings. Belief is natural to man but absolute belief is the response to blocked inquiry. When the need to know cannot be active, the intensity of the emotion is turned into belief, swelling it to abnormal proportions. Then the belief becomes an end in itself and can itself be the cause of secondary types of inquiry. Such issues arise now as for instance why other men are not as strongly set in the same propositions, or how they can best be proselytized.

Believing is both a form of knowing and a stage beyond it. It is possible to know without believing but not to believe without knowing. To know means merely to be aware of the truth of a proposition, but to believe means to be affected by the acceptance of it, and to be willing to act from it. In belief, a certain amount of the security of the individual is attached to the proposition qualitatively. Believing is the kind of knowing which can permeate the whole organism and reach deep levels within it, whereas knowing by itself can be a very superficial affair which floats through the consciousness without having much of an effect of any kind. The concept of unconscious belief is a difficult one to accept though surely not a new one (20). Belief is entirely conscious only at the very highest psychological level. It thus puts an emotional stamp upon knowing; to believe in something that concerns being means to be grasped by it in such a way that a separation would be hard to make and could be accomplished only at the cost of a certain damage.

Every thought, feeling or action on the part of an organism indicates the presence of a belief about some segment of the external world. Beliefs are betrayed by speech and action. It often happens that avowed beliefs are contradicted by overt behavior, and when they are it is the beliefs behind the behavior which should be taken more seriously. When the process is conscious and deliberate, we say that belief triggers the will, and action is the result. But when the process is unconscious, belief may hook up directly with action, and it may even happen that the resultant behavior is against the will; certainly the belief may be so. There are 'ugly' truths which we do not want to believe but which force themselves upon us none the less. The posture of volition which facilitates action is betrayed by such states as intentions, resolutions, impulses.

The step from belief to action, then, involves a decision and the will. Every decision is precipitated by a trial, and in this sense man is an experimental animal. The selection of beliefs relevant to specific actions must be a component of the process. Indeed, thoughts and the results of previous actions may in this way be carried along.

REVERBERATING CIRCUIT

We have already noted that knowledge remains unaffected by being known. Thus in the case of the need to know the material object can only be altered by the response if the propositional content of the knowledge is revised or exchanged for a different propositional content in a subsequent cycle. And this happens when there are a sufficient number of cycles to produce a reverberating circuit, for then a new element has entered into the process of knowing. Knowledge interacts and thus produces novel arrangements calling for corresponding activities. Thought takes place during a protracted period of latency, when there occurs the assimilation of and adaptation to the newly acquired knowledge. The movement of inquiry is formally manifested in such activities as artistic production and scientific investigation for instance.

The cycle of the reverberating circuit is not completed until the alteration of the original material object which had initiated the cycle by its gnoseotropistic effects has been taken into the account. In the case of the need to know, as we have already noted, the 'material' stimulus is the naturally occuring relation between material objects. And, as we noted also, there is no effect on the relation which can be said to have been brought about by its being known. We can speak of a stimulus only when we refer to a single occasion. If an individual is subjected to a class of such occasions, the stimulus referred to becomes one value of a stimulus variable. What, then, could the alteration of the material object in such a circuit mean? Alterations of this character are either constructive or destructive. But naturally occurring relations can be neither constructed nor destroyed.

What can be constructed or destroyed, however, are abstract models. Systems of philosophy are response systems in the sense of Skinner (23, p. 286). Where there has been system-building by using the naturally occurring relations together with the abstract relations, then the representative value of the system can be verified or falsified. The combination of new with old knowledge acquired in the way we have been describing makes such systems possible. The systems themselves are the objects we have been seeking, for while not material in the same sense they have material components which are signs and sign-relationships. And *qua* systems they are identical with other relations which exist between large collections of material objects.

And yet the whole account cannot be given in terms of naturally occurring relations alone. For these are embodied in institutions by means of tools, which, it will be recalled, are material objects employed to move other material objects, and by means of signs, which are material objects which point to other material objects. Many naturally occurring relations themselves related and compounded by means of causal chains are incorporated into institutions by means of tools, and in this way belief is reinforced, so that an external axis is established for the environmental end of the reverberating circuit.

The reverberation time for the complete operation of a circuit may be long. If so, then delayed responses are the cause. Knowledge stored as belief may have to await recall, before objects are altered again. Belief brings about a sharp extinction curve of inquiry. Then, too, responses inhibit their own repetition; some of these inhibitions are dissipated, the unconditioned inhibitions especially. There is a characteristic rhythm to the drive for knowledge. Instinctive patterns of behavior are made available by maturation processes. Maturation reaches a certain definite terminal point of its own, but with stimulation further maturation stages can be developed. The acquisition of abstract knowledge has this effect. Conscious thought implies the ability of the cortex to design, plan and store its own responses. Thus there is besides the instinctive behavior patterns some degree of self-determination. It carries the subject to a new maturation point at which the facility of movement among abstractions—movements in logical space Lewin would have called them (15)—can be attained.

It is necessary, in connection with the need to know, to account for the resumption of the drive of curiosity and the repetition of the cycle. The most powerful incentive is a familiar one: novelty. Novelty is so strong it can revive a need immediately after reduction (22, p. 370). It may be presumed that knowledge as previously acquired is partly false, and that the subsequent application of false knowledge discloses inadequacies. Expectations remain unfulfilled and the unfulfilled expectations (in some cases the drives) lead to a resumption of inquiry. The internal changes, then, are the frustrations of the consummations expected on the basis of the applications of alleged knowledge; the man who thought there was food in the icebox or that a woman was willing.

Thus absent objects furnish the necessary cues: nothing, where something was expected, again sets off the craving for knowledge. The stimulus is the irritation occasioned by a lack: ignorance associated with fright, the fear of the unknown translated into a dread of personal danger.

Chapter 7

THE NEED TO DO

THE SECOND of the three secondary drives is the need to do. We have noted already that a need is a lack on the part of an animal of some component a material object can supply which is necessary to survival. The need was known to Pavlov, though negatively, as the need for freedom, and he recognized what he termed a "freedom reflex" (4, pp. 11-12). The generalized drive of aggression, defined as the drive to dominate the environment, takes the form of activity. Behavior is directed activity, it is *doing*. The entire physiology of the human individual is designed for activity, from the background of simple arousal (3, p. 157), to the proprioceptors and the effects of androgens (2, p. 189) on the production of aggression. The need for some sort of work is well known. Work is a name for doing, when an individual has nothing to do he deteriorates rapidly. The muscles exist only in order to be used, and when there is nothing to push against they do not long remain in a healthy condition. The need to do is the need to achieve. Organs compel the organism to movement. There is need for an activity of the whole organism to construct or destroy a material object, and in any case to transform it.

It is easy to see how the need to do serves the primary needs. An activity is usually required to obtain water, food or a mate, and some kind of construction is usually adjunctive to the continuation of such need-reductions. But the secondary needs are equally involved. Action itself can be a source of knowledge, as when one learns from ordinary experience or from scientific experimentation. As we shall see in the next chapter, action is necessary to survival, since most religions involve ritual observances of some sort.

The fact is that the human individual likes to fight, and as much to obtain what he needs as to destroy what he fears. And he will risk pain if necessary for the sake of aggression in either case; so that it becomes clear that the avoidance of pain, or positively, the need for survival, is not a need that dominates the others under every set of circumstances. Life is struggle, and violence is only a more direct and immediate form of struggle. By ordinary, society condemns such direct methods and provides others which are indirect—in the United States, for instance, the path of due process and the law courts, though not yet operating in the case of international relations. In general, the need to do takes the form in the individual of the construction of something of his own and the destruction of that of another—construct mine, destroy yours. All need-reductions involve activity of some sort, as a means. But in the case of the need to do, the doing itself is the end.

Man behaves in accordance with his experience, which is to say in accordance with the appearances. But if there were no correspondence between the appearances and the material things as they are in themselves, he would pretty soon run afoul of the material things. For his activity consists in movement among material objects and his achievement is their manipulation, the latter more often than not by means of tools. The fact that he does not encounter difficulties of this sort is revealing, and tells us something about the correlation, rough as it may be, between material things as they are in themselves and in their appearances: they are not, as Kant for instance suspected them to be, unknowable. Either they are not there at all or they are to some extent as man thinks them to be as a result of his contact with their appearances.

THE TROPISM OF DOING

Both organism and material object change continually, but the relation between them is asymmetric; in the tropistic phase of interaction the organism is the dependent variable, the material object the independent. The challenge of the object is its presence, its stability which seems to the individual to defy his efforts. For the need to do the existence of obstacles is necessary (5, vol. *i*, p. 280). A famous contemporary mountain climber when asked why he had wanted to climb Mt. Everest answered, "Because it was there." An object or another person, whose very existence or activity seems to constitute a threat or a dare, serves as a stimulus to action. The actor accepts the challenge and is aroused by the defiance which things-as-they-are seem to present to him. This is the manner in which the individual encounters the tropism of the object as it stimulates in him the need to do.

The most fundamental form of this need is exercise, the mere extension of the muscles against something. The strength of the individual's response will be proportional to the duration and intensity of his need-deprivation. The longer he has gone without physical exertion the greater his need. Mere posture is not enough, and more must be antagonized than mere gravity. Thus there must be a force which resists in order for it to be conquered; activity is aggressive and is aimed at victory, alike whether the object is to be increased, as in a construction, or destroyed. In short, the need to do means that something must be done, anything whatever so long as there is animal effort.

The need to do may take many forms. Another primitive form of doing is collecting: hoarding in animals, acquisitiveness in man, the ground squirrel's cache of nuts and the miser's pile of coins for instance. The existence of material objects which it would be good to have for the sake of reducing some need is the starting-point. When the human individual is confronted with a material object which is desirable: real estate, money, women, works of art, he turns his attention toward it, an orienting response, and again there takes place the effect of a tropism. The tropistic object in the case of the need to do is a material object which in some way seems to call for action; it needs to be grasped, used as a raw material in some construction, or even in certain cases destroyed.

The more sophisticated form of doing is achieving; this seems so far as we know more extensive in man. The human individual strives to accomplish something which can be a source of need-reduction for him: making a work of art, discovering a law of nature in science, contributing to the welfare of his fellow-man.

When the human individual is confronted with the raw material which is a sign to him that it offers the means to do something it would have been good to have done, he recognizes in it the prospects of a need-reduction. A tropism in the case of the need to do will be called prattottropism. Prattottropism is the need to do recognizing its goal-object, and prattottropistic behavior is the orienting response to the object to which something needs to be done.

The aim in prattottropism is to achieve something permanent. Knowing deals with naturally occurring relations, which are permanent in the sense that they can continue to recur. And we shall see that the need to be aims at goal-objects which are permanent also but in the sense of persistence. The need to do is occupied customarily with more ephemeral goal-objects. Works of art and laws of science apart, the need to do deals with constructions which are temporary and destructions which are more temporary still. But the element of compulsion in all goal-objects of the need to do inhibits more far-reaching calculations; it makes up in violence what it lacks in permanence. There is an insistence about the demand for doing which issues from the goal-object calling for immediate action at whatever cost.

In such aspects the need to do betrays its nature as one of the more elementary drives; it overrides all others under conditions of deprivation. The movement-producing stimuli from the environment orient the human animal in the direction of the external agent at whatever cost to other needs, at least for the duration of the interval necessary for need-reduction. It is insistent, it is brutal, and it is in a certain sense automatic. Confinement is evidence for the strength of the drive in which external forces are sufficiently powerful to inhibit even the primary drives.

RELEASER

Strictly speaking, any element in the environment which presents the appearance of resistance may act as a releaser for the need to do, for it promises need-reduction in terms of activity. An obstacle to stability probably is what triggers the contractile mechanism. The background of activity in the alert animal is well-established, a constant state of unrest accompanied by spontaneous changes. There takes place an orienting movement to external contact (thigmotaxis); movements preceding external stimulation (1), and even a rudimentary kind of consummatory response, as when for example infants fall asleep on stroking. The need to be active is always present in the healthy animal, but it requires an object which can resist; for only in this way can there be struggle, and struggle is an effective form of activity. Also, there is no achievement without it. Resistance is a challenge, and so it is not merely in the reduction of the primary needs, although of course in them, too, that the need to do finds its releaser. Harmonious elements in the environment are beside the point so far as this need is concerned; they offer no immediate prospect of activity but only of consonancy. Opposition is more effective, for if there is to be activity there must first be something which has to be overcome.

As with all of the secondary needs in the human individual, cooperative behavior is important. Most activities whether constructive or destructive involve greater efforts and larger enterprises than are usually possible to the single individual acting alone. This is true of capital cities which have to be built as it is of wars of destruction which have to be waged; they are cooperative enterprises calling out social behavior. Such group endeavors would not be possible, however, were it not that they fit neatly with the needs of individuals. From the point of view of the human individual, group enterprises constitute opportunities, though it must be admitted that this is not the only point of view: there is the reality of the group also. The individual opportunities in question are the drive outlets and the need-reductions which are the result.

THE PREPARATORY RESPONSE

Like the reductions of the need to know, those of the need to do are planned experiences in man. The preparatory response of the need to do means bringing the individual into relation with the stimulus to activity or achievement, such as the preparations for the expending of energy: designing weapons, making blueprints or writing speeches. Engineering diagrams, descriptions of experiments, accounts of travel conditions, enable the human individual to follow a previous activity or repeat an earlier achievement. The muscles are not usually exerted spontaneously or at random, but such exertions are the result of anticipated activities and expected experiences. Vast enterprises, like military campaigns or cathedrals, are worked out in advance by specialists in war colleges or architects' offices. Even lesser activities are designed, athletic games, for instance, or voyages, either of which may be strenuous. If this is true of the need to do as mere activity, all the more so is it true of the need to do as achievement. The activity over many years may have to be laid out carefully in anticipation of large ambitions. If we remember that almost all enterprises require work, and work is energy expended—activity of some sort—then whether it is the mere exercise of the muscles or the more pretentious fulfillment of some elaborate material scheme the same need is called out.

It is here in connection with the preparatory response that a word must be said about skills. The acquisition of skills belongs to the preparatory response phase of the need to do. A skill is a practical knowledge combined with a mechanical aptitude. Skills are muscular knowings. They are acquired usually only with practice, such as the driving of an automobile, the use of a typewriter or the operation of a computer. The knowledge of and proficiency in a language is a skill, although conventionally the term is reserved chiefly for material tools rather than signs. The possession of a skill is often the preparation for a need response. To know how to use a bow and arrow or a gun is to be able to effect the need-reduction of hunger, to know mechanical engineering is to be able to effect the need-reduction of the need to do by making a construction. Skills, it should be pointed out, are skills chiefly in connection with the specific tools for which through training they furnish the operator. The virtuoso pianist is an extension of the piano, without which his skill would be meaningless, and the expert pilot an adjunct of the airplane.

By means of the preparatory response, it becomes easy to provide a displacement, otherwise men would never have found the means of living together. It is in this sense paradoxical when men cooperate in activity, for mutual destruction would be more conformable with the drives. For although as we have noted the human individual loves to fight, there exists also the activity of displacement. Sports and athletic contests are attempts to turn the love of fighting into harmless channels. The need to do can be reduced directly by means of athletic contests, baseball or tennis for example. But there are also the indirect means of reduction, when greater exertion is demanded. Violent spectator sports, such as prizefights, bullfights and gladiatorial combats, offer a way of participating vicariously in the emotional states of fighting without the risk of personal harm. From his safe coign of vantage in the stands, the spectator can often be heard calling for more blood. Athletic sports and games are ends in themselves; they are not for the sake of winning merely; the loser also benefits. They are first for the doing and only afterwards for the winning or losing. A poor loser is one who is not willing to play the game for its own sake, which is to say, for the outlet of activity it affords.

THE CONSUMMATORY RESPONSE

Consummatory response for the need to do consists usually in struggle. Success in accomplishment is only a requirement of the need to do considered in its second and more advanced phase as the need to achieve. For the need to do as the need for activity, the struggle itself is sufficient for need-reduction. Thus, what is ordinarily called work, as in the making of a living, is the consummatory response to the stimulus presented by some object. Work is energy expended, and whenever there is energy expended there is activity. Working for a living may provide the need-reductions for other needs, the primary as well as the secondary needs, for example. Working to earn the money to buy food or social esteem may also serve to reduce the need for activity or even for achievement.

The primitive phase of consummatory response for the need to do is that which consists in play. Although preparations for activity and, more, for achievement, are the rule, there are important exceptions. There is always an element of sheer spontaneity in the releasing of the need to do. The muscles are there to be flexed and extended, and so activity cannot always await preparations but may have to occur spontaneously. Play, not as in organized games, but as in the sheer love of activity, such as we find in small animals running and jumping or in children's practical jokes, is released in the animal by the existence of a good night's sleep, by the awareness of a sunny day, or often simply by being placed in a space sufficiently large for wide movement. Play is an end in itself; it brings its own satisfactions in muscles exercised and bodies active. In play, there may be no material object transformed except the organism itself. Ground covered is not ground transformed and in play of the spontaneous variety no ball need be thrown. But it may, and the transformation of the goal-object in the instance of play is done at random and without a view to the end-results.

The advanced phase of the consummatory response is an achievement, something constructed or destroyed. Physical constructions are the responses made when nearby objects stimulate in man the need to do. These may result in science because stimulated by the properties of naturally occurring relations, or they may result in art because stimulated by the properties of qualities. In need-reduction, destruction is just as effective as construction, and perhaps even more. By achievement as construction, a material object in the external world has been transformed into something functional, something itself capable of accomplishments. But destruction is in its way no less of an achievement. It is something final, a raw, overt aggression.

Part of the need to do is the need to say. The need for self-expression is the need *qua* need in its aspect of verbal behavior. An utterance is an activity, and the achievement in this case consists in altering the behavior of another person, often in such a manner as to bring about through his actions the alteration of material objects. Speech is from the point of view of response a muscular activity, specifically the activity employing vocal cords, epiglottis, soft palate, tongue, lips and jaw, to influence a listener. Writing is that form of verbal behavior aimed at affecting absent persons: those elsewhere or perhaps unborn.

The habitual modification of sounds or the inscription of conventional signs is an activity called communication, intended to change behavior by means of the transfer of information. The stimuli in the case of verbal behavior are a series of particular signs which may convey particular or general meaning, but the response evoked in this way is always particular.

When there is a speaker and a listener there is also the reference of their language, and this reference may be a material object. And even when the speaker is talking about himself it is usually in the context of some actual physical event, some involvement of himself with material objects. The use of language has to be studied by physics, physiology and anthropology. Physics is called in to describe the sound waves or the writing materials necessary to communication; physiology to account for their sensory reception; and anthropology to describe the contents carried by the materials from the organism where it is encoded and communicated to that other organism by which it is decoded.

One form of the consummatory response of the need to do consists in the educational process. Here admittedly there is a large element of preparation, but the response is sophisticated in that it employs both the movement and the speech aspects of the need. Leadership consists in doing as well as saying what will influence the behavior of others. The behavior of the teacher is intended to be copied by others, and imitative behavior is the kind of behavior which is called out in learning.

Thus from the violent kind of behavior which occurs in wars of extinction to the mild and gentle behavior which takes place in education, we see the range of consummatory responses of the need to do, the need for activity and achievement. The range is certainly a wide one, and indeed it has to be, since it represents the greater part of the life of the human individual. Most individuals are active for the greater part of their lives, and if the activity involved in the reduction of the primary needs occupies the foreground, it plays a role in satisfying the need to do also, for this is a need which though separable is very much involved with the others. There are no completely separable needs and yet none which cannot be distinguished. Human behavior is plastic and it shifts rapidly from one response to another, often carrying out a number at one time but rarely confined to any for long.

REWARD

The reward of the need to be is divided into the usual two parts: activity and achievement. The reward of activity is the feeling of relaxation after exercise, of muscle tonus, the sense of pleasure from the receptors located in muscles, tendons and joints as these alter their position with respect to the body as a whole. Somatically, it is good to have been active, and even necessary if the body is to be kept in condition. Actual contact is transmitted from the skin inward, a pleasurable sensation. Action is in a certain sense its own reward. To be active is to experience a satisfaction at existing, to become aware that one is very much alive. Life is motion, it is activity, the pleasure of relaxation from the tension which the preparation for activity had engendered.

The reward of achievement is the "sense of accomplishment," the feeling of attainment upon the recognition of a construction completed. In this case an external material object has been transformed. A destruction completed, such as victory in battle, could produce the same sense of accomplishment. In both instances it is clear that the need to do is a species of the generalized drive of aggression, the drive to dominate the environment. Some material object has been covered by movement, altered by activity, or some person has been influenced by speech. A man running, a house erected or torn down, or a listener precipitated into action, are examples. In this latter connection there is no difference between an imperative sentence, a declarative statement, and a question. In the effect produced, there is no difference between "Go home!" and "Your house is on fire," and "Did you know that a thief has just invaded your home?"

A thing done is a source of satisfaction whatever its effects. To the extent to which a material object is changed, it is owned; the actor so to speak possesses a little bit of its shape or direction. There is aggrandizement of the ego through a degree of spreading ego-involvement. Doing is more intimate than knowing because the individual has interfered with the object physically and changed it in some way that is his own. Thus he is involved with it in a contact from which its new form can never be dissociated. And to that extent it belongs with him—it is him.

It often happens that there is no reward to a drive because the response is blocked. The reverberating circuit which produces the smooth operation of interaction between organism and material object never becomes established, and so there is no outlet for the responses to accumulate in the organism. Emotion is the response of the whole organism to the blocking of behavior. The emotions, which accompany pleasurable parasympathetic discharges and painful sympathetic discharges, no longer operate merely to restore homeostasis as with the subhuman animals but play in the human individual an important part in the need-reductions of the secondary needs. Each need has its own characteristic emotion. We have already noted in the last chapter how the blocking of the need to know results in absolute belief which then serves as itself a further cause for a different kind of inquiry. The emotion peculiar to the need to do is rage, it occurs when activity or achievement is inhibited. Rage results from confinement, since as Pavlov noted, activity requires freedom. Feelings of some sort always accompany responses. Blocked behavior induces more intense feelings, just as dams raise water above normal levels. When a feeling is elevated by blocked behavior to the point where its intensity becomes itself a motive force, then it is what we recognize as emotion. Subsequent behavior can then be caused by the emotions, usually more violent behavior, and of a particularly violent sort when the inhibited need has to do with overt action in the first place. The emotion of rage resulting from the blocked behavior of the need to do is likely to be more destructive than constructive and more random than planned.

The emotion of rage does not persist. Either it is responsible for the destruction of the object if translated into action, or—often—of the subject if it is not. But the emotion of love has a somewhat different outcome. The possession of the loved object often tends to reinforce the emotion, because need-reduction becomes identified with that particular object. This cannot be so of objects that are destroyed in the process, such as for instance food. But it is true of women and works of art for these are not destroyed and indeed become more intensely need-reductions with repetition of the experience. However, there are changes in the type of emotion. It should be remembered that poets rarely write sonnets to their wives or mistresses but more usually on the occasion of an unrequited love.

REINFORCEMENT

The reinforcement of the need to do is called habit. The more often a thing is done, the easier it becomes to do and the more the actor is inclined to do it. Reinforcement is measured in habit strength, the tendency to react to a stimulus to which the individual has reacted before. Habit is the learning process as it takes place in the striped muscles which determine posture and movement. (The unstriped muscles acquire their habits phylogenetically.)

It should not be necessary to labor the point that the need to do could never be reduced were it not for the opportunities of need-reduction that the external world provides. The exercise of the muscles depends upon material objects which resist to some degree, and achievement depends upon the fact that such resistance is not total. Material objects can be altered and (a special case of a particularly complex material object) by means of speech and writing men can be moved. The freedom of opportunity which the similarities and differences, the potentialities, of material objects and persons provide, is also the freedom of action so essential to the needs of the human individual.

Within the interstices provided by the opposition between freedom and necessity, a kind of possession characterizes doing. Doing is the kind of having that grappling is. When a man digs a hole, he has to that extent the control of it. When he addresses a crowd, he has to that extent the members of it. Whatever an individual does must deal with him. Whatever he changes, is to that extent a new thing and must stimulate him in a new way. The continuity of interaction constitutes a reverberating circuit, with the goal-object of his intended achievement and himself at the poles.

Complete freedom of action is of course never possible. The actions of the human individual are hedged about with all sorts of restrictions. There are the limitations set by the feebleness of his own powers and the strength of those imposed on his efforts by his environment. More things affect him than he can affect, the sun, for instance, which reaches him by its light but which he cannot reach. In addition, there are the laws of existence which apply at every integrative level: the physical laws at the physical, the chemical laws at the chemical, and so on, laws which prescribe what cannot be done as well as what can.

REVERBERATING CIRCUIT

The tendency of a habit to reinforce itself by means of a regular pattern establishes a re-entrant circuit, a continual round of activity, which works toward the completeness of the world through a sense of the fitness of things. The reinforcement of doing comes from the feeling that by means of a cumulative effort something of the world is being put back in order. For when there is continuity of doing, the average effect is no mere activity but a transaction, and the total response an undertaking completed, an operation successfully executed. As the actor becomes more involved with the world, so the world or at least that part of it which his actions affect is (intended to be) made over into something closer to what it ought to be. The deep and all-round conviction that this is the result is the final stage in the reinforcement of the need.

There is always more of the immediate environment than there is of the human individual. No one can foresee all of the consequences of his activity, and anything done may be the occasion for the production of a compound conditioned stimulus to further activity. And so it happens that when he exerts himself to influence it, there are serious repercussions upon him. No matter how powerful he may be or how strenuous his efforts, he is destined to be engulfed and overwhelmed. The doer is eventually always overdone. The cause of his overdoing is the material object his activity has altered. The altered material object now constitutes a different stimulus, which has been called the compound conditioned stimulus, and upon each subsequent occasion the resultant construction, or destruction, is a new tropistic object, and it stimulates in the human individual a new response. Buildings stimulate in other ways than piles of bricks, and a conquered population elicits behavior far different than it did when at war. The adaptation of the human individual to the changed conditions of the environment is no less urgent because he may have played a crucial role in bringing them about.

Chapter 8

THE NEED TO BE

WE COME NOW to the third of the secondary drives as these exist in the human individual, the need to be. The need to (continue to) be is the need for ultimate security. The motivation is that referred to earlier, the need for self-preservation recognized by Pavlov as a genuine reflex involving life or death (8, p. 31). 'Security' is here defined as attachment to permanence of being, and 'ultimate security' as attachment to permanence of being after life. If a need is a lack on the part of an animal of some component a material object can supply which is necessary to survival, as we keep reminding ourselves, then the need for ultimate survival can never be entirely reduced.

Immediate security is a matter of the primary drives. Ultimate security relies upon the last of the secondary drives. Many will recognize here the last specification of the generalized drive, the psychological counterpart of the brain stem arousal reactions. The organism acts as a whole because the central nervous system is basically sensori-motor, intermediate cortical processes however complex serving eventually only as connections (1, p. 254). By means of the ascending and descending control of cortical and sensory reception centers respectively, it is possible that the generalized drive is drained off into more importunate tissue-need channels (the primary drives) before reaching the more important channels (the secondary drives), and even shading off into the tertiary channels as noted by Hebb (5, p. 459).

Thus the more pervasive drive can be traced to a more primitive one. The need to be hearkens back to the animal drives to skirt danger and run away from pain. All animals exhibit the negative reactions of fear, rage, avoidance and escape. Fear is the most powerful human feeling, because it anticipates the annihilation of the entire man. The whole animal is involved in the outcome of the escape response, successful or not. Death involves both pain and non-being, but the first is temporary and the second permanent. Fear results from a confusion of the first with the second. Anxiety is the result of the blocked aversive response of the human individual security-deprived. The higher organisms are liberally supplied with nociceptors (6, p. 34); they sense a threat in transience, and hence seek its avoidance. Freedom from danger of all sorts is the negative version of the continuance of existence. The animal ceases to exist as an animal when it dies. Life is a balance between the activities of approach and avoidance. In terms of avoidance, security means freedom from death.

Every animal makes the effort to be allowed to continue to be. The lower animals express this negatively, in the avoidance response, what Pavlov (8) calls the "defense reflex," while man expresses it both negatively and positively: negatively, in the same avoidance response made by the lower animals but manifested in his case as anxiety; positively, in the active pursuit of permanence through association or identification with persistent things. The need to be in the human individual may be considered also an aversion or avoidance response to the prospect of certain death. Both the need to do and the need to know are necessary to security. The need to know is involved because man is the only animal that knows about death, and the need to do because he must be active in escape or avoidance (11, pp. 171, 178). Ultimately, then, security is the state lacking to the need to be.

By 'being' here is means 'being-in-itself,' or what there is. Being active means being-for-itself, the continuity of the present and future of being with the past as exhibited by the continuity of activity; recognizing as being only what can be discriminated. One who pursues his own being does so in terms of being-for-other. Attachment to permanent or persistent objects constitutes the technology of being, for it represents devices worked out in the effort to continue to be. A concern for being is resolved as an effort to preserve being; and this generally means turning toward those material objects exhibiting a greater power to continue being, such as the artifacts of a religion, its icons and talismans.

A similarity to the interest of existentialism will be evident here. But there is an important and crucial difference. The existentialists—Sartre, for instance (9, p. 73ff.)—are concerned with the relation of consciousness to being. Here, however, it will not be a question of relating consciousness to being, which is a subjective approach, but, instead, of relating being to behavior, with consciousness recognized as a form of behavior. The standpoint of the present work is the continuity of structure with function, and the aim of the present work the understanding of the human individual as disclosed by his objective behavior. The elements of existentialism appearing here have to reckon with the elements of behaviorism, Sartre so to speak making his peace with Pavlov.

It should be clear, then, that the need to be means the need to continue to be, the need for ultimate security, which, it is hoped, can be attained either in this world or the next: in this world as "eternal fame among mortal men" or in the next as immortality. A man too timid to take any action might be thinking of simple security or present freedom from danger. But the aim in both cases, that of the hero and that of the coward, is equally at security.

THE TROPISM OF BEING

Like the primary needs and the needs to know and do, the need to be begins with a material object and its properties. Once again in the tropistic phase of interaction the material object is the independent variable and the organism the dependent variable. This time, the object is any material object which exhibits persistence beyond the life of living animals. This would be true, for instance, of a society, a mountain, the sea, the solar system, or the universe. In each case, power has been attributed to the object; the Greek gods lived on Mt. Olympus, there was also the sea-god, Triton, the Egyptian sun-god, the sky god and moon god, and the universal God of the Hebrews. Even remote ancestors would have to be included. Such a catalogue classifies the goal-objects of the need to be, the far-away gods. Behavior in view of being is usually behavior with no stimulus present but only an observable frequency. It is what Skinner calls "operant behavior" (12, pp. 19-21). It is important to note that in the case of each large, powerful and remote god-object, there is a nearby symbol to represent it to the human individual. A symbol, it will be recalled, is a quality attached to a sign, a material object employed to refer to the quality in another material object. Religious artifacts are too well known to require illustrations: crosses, icons, bodhisattvas. We shall see presently that abstract structures also can be endowed with the needed quality. Abstractions as knowledge acquired through the need to know possess the same property of permanence, only in terms of recurrence rather than persistence. Thus religious systems, which are combinations of both, enjoy the reputation for permanence. Religion had its origin in the awareness that there were material objects which persisted longer than human individuals. This is a simple case of the lure of thigmotaxis, for there is need of contact with these objects.

The material object of the need to be invites comparison with that of the need to know. The object of the need to know is abstract and the attraction intellectual; the object of the need to be is qualitative and the attraction emotional. Whether it be a mountain or a theology, it is the qualitative side which is involved with the human individual, and his reaction is through feeling, not thinking. Thus even when a system of ideas gained through the need to know becomes a source of movement for the need to be, it is the feelings which the ideas engender rather than the thoughts which they impart that is relevant here. The excitations of the two needs are complementary rather than conflicting.

When the human individual moves into the energy field of an object which is tropistic for the need to be, he behaves by moving toward the object. The confrontation of the human individual by the material object excites the individual to an orienting response.

The adjustment of the central nervous system is eventually

made by a compromise between competing excitations. The scanning of exploration is a search for threshold constants contained as invariants in the enormous recurrences represented by abstractions. In addition, far-away objects excite distance-receptors (10, pp. 348-52). Human behavior can be characterized as an attempt of the central nervous system to respond to distance-receptors.

Neurophysiologically, the individual reaction is in fact an orienting response. Given two competing excitations, the decision is reached by means of a tropism. A tropism as the term is used here means a movement-producing stimulus: the response of reorientation made by an organism to the stimulus from a particular object in the environment. It is the altered posture called for by an irresistible pull—in this case from a higher integrative level. It is a thesis of this study that human motivation finally can be explained on the basis of sositropistic behavior, where by 'sositropism' is meant a compulsory movement toward opportunities of security in a domain containing both safety and danger (2, pp. 45-127). By 'sositropistic behavior' is meant responding to the qualities of material objects which appear permanent (*i.e.*, persistent). It involves the shifting of an entire organism to a particular dependence as a response to some item supposedly permanent. Every tropistic object is surrounded by a field in which its energy operates. As with heliotropic plants and animals, the sositropistic objects are those which attract insecure individuals by their possession of security.

The tropistic object in the need to be is any object exhibiting the appearance of permanence beyond the life of the human individual. A tropistic object stimulates him to move toward it by arousing his curiosity. But weak persistence or semi-permanence is not sufficient to overcome the threshold of inertia; there must be a feeling of eternality whatever the facts. The human individual will act then in such a manner as to form an emotional attachment to it, either by association or identification, by dedicating himself to it or working for it. He will try to move toward being (toward security or salvation) by feeling an association (weak) or an identification (strong) with the secure object (the permanent, persistent or recurrent object).

Since there is a rank order to needs, we should expect to find the same among tropisms; only among the important tropisms it appears as a compounding. The need sets a direction according to the lessening of pressures, which allows first the need for knowing and second the need for being, to dominate at least temporarily. A security system is any system of beliefs about security, such as a philosophy or a religion. An absolute security system is a security system whose truth has been placed beyond possible doubt, accepted without reservation, and attributed to perfection. It is customary to have for the need to be the transfer from the need to know of a security system but, unlike the need to know, having attributed to it the additional property of absoluteness; a system in which hope may be centered and to which faith may be surrendered. For the estimation of any sositropism, the given security system must be known. The acceptance of such an absolute system may be deliberate, as in the case of a religious conversion, or not, as in the case of one who grows up in a religion. One who believes in a transcendental religion will differ in his orientations from one who does not.

RELEASER

The cues in the stimulation of sositropistic objects are any signs of persistence; these usually are indications that an object is remote or that it is large and immensely strong. It lies within the phylogenetic inheritance of man that objects which are far away and gigantic also seem powerful: the gods on the mountain top or those in the sky.

What is true of the thirsty animal attracted by the sight of water is equally true of the man who responds to a far-away object with emotion. It will be recalled that the concept of 'releaser' applies to any object (or the property of any object) to which an animal reacts. In this chapter it will mean the property of an object to which a human individual reacts in terms of his personal security. The prospect of a permanent object releases in man the craving for transcendentals (7, Ch. III). Since absent objects include those which are far away, and abstract structures represent absent objects, abstract structures represent far-away objects. Thus abstract structures can also release in the human individual the craving for transcendentals.

In the case of the need to be the question of just how much of a stimulus is required to produce impulses above threshold value is a difficult one. How much need for survival must there be before the prospect of a distant object suggesting permanence can evoke responses? The answer probably involves the factor of deprivation: how strong has the threat to existence been? Those with a tenuous hold on existence feel it more insistently, the sick and the old, for instance. But susceptibility however strong still requires a trigger to set it off.

The releaser in the case of the need to be is the appearance of permanence-as-persistence. We have seen that knowledge-as-such is permanence-as-recurrence; but recurrence means intermittent absence as well as sure return, and the absence not only does not afford the requisite security but actually marks an interruption in it. That is why knowledge-as-such is not usually a goal-object for the need to be, and can participate in it (as in fact it always does) only in a secondary way, by attaching itself to some object which can exhibit the appearance of permanence-as-persistence. The single but significantly large exception is Hinduism. The doctrine of the eternal return is an instance of permanence-as-recurrence occupying a central position in a world religion. The craving for transcendentals cannot be satisfied by anything to be found in nature and so may be sought in the posited cause of nature which (it is assumed) lies beyond nature: the super-natural. All other drives are proximate and their goal-objects contained within nature, but there are no ascertainable limits to the goal-objects of the need to be. Hence the prevalence of the identification with the posited cause of all material objects: the reason for the cosmic universe. The drive for ultimate security may be felt in its extreme form as a yearning for infinity, a mystic religious experience.

A structure of tensions is always necessary for activity. The individual must somehow be braced in the direction of motor responses. The need for being is a posture of the entire man, to whom transcendental cravings are natural. The difficulty here, of course, is the abundance of unknown variables; the complexity of nature (in this case, of human nature) always exceeding the efficiency of our mathematics. Here is a situation, however, involving quantitative modification under controlled conditions. A compounding of such decisions could account for much of human behavior. Statistical studies of the probabilities involved in the matter of choice might reveal a trend resulting from the adoption of some need satisfaction as a goal. Where an organism is allowed by the environment an uninterrupted continuance of its existence, there is a reduction of the need for being. The satisfaction of such a need, then, is negative.

Cooperative behavior, as we have seen, is characteristic of need-reduction in the human individual. Participation in group action not possible to the individual alone is certainly true of most efforts at need-reduction in the case of the need for survival. Life is short, and survival is attached first and most primitively to progeny. The survival of the species, while not guaranteed, is a good risk for the individual. The species may endure. The horseshoe crab is over four hundred million years old and has remained throughout that enormous span of time unevolved, even though many other species, such as the dinosaur or, in our own time, the dodo, has become extinct, and man himself is largely changed from his remote ancestors. To devote oneself to one's progeny seems a chance worth taking. The species is no short-range self, like the self itself, nor a nearby god, like the black stone at Mecca. It has the merit of including elements of the self yet extending into the future as far as it has already come from the past.

THE PREPARATORY RESPONSE

Such considerations and activities make up the preparatory response in the case of the need to be and range all the way from mere expectation, through plans for search or adoption, to discovery of a security system.

Theologies are qualitative response systems which promise survival. Irrespective of their truth or falsity (and since they conflict no more than one of them can be true), the overwhelming statistics as to the prevalence indicates that they are necessary for some need-reduction in the human individual. The need is of course the need for survival, for ultimate security, for the escape from the pain of death.

The human individual knows that he must die, but has thoughts larger than his fate. The human individual living as he does in the mesocosm can *know* about the microcosm, the world of the very small a world of electrons, atoms and cells, but he can *go* only to the macrocosm, the world of the very large: at present by means of artificial satellites and rockets to the moon. Attempts to reduce the need to be consist in trips to the macrocosm. The older attempts were efforts to get in contact with the supernatural by means of mystic states, prayer, meditation, ecstacy, "union with God." Such efforts are continuing, as for instance in the use of lysergic acid. But go or not, the individual is committed to a dedication in a desperate play for survival. He embraces in his imagination a universe more immense than the one with which he comes into contact, and so he must invent for his consolation a symbolic contact which he is able to establish with the universe as a whole. Sign-artifacts are more recurrent than persistent. But symbols, defined as the attachment of a quality to a sign, usually involve material embodiment for such an attachment and so are more persistent than recurrent. Thus the need for survival by means of attachment to objects of salvation shifts the preparatory response to symbolic artifacts and to beliefs connected with them. Religion is the formalization of a socially accepted method for getting in touch with absent being. With material symbols the skin once again plays a role in need-reduction: there is touch, as when participating in the Christian sacraments. Institutions are encrusted around them in order to preserve the promise they represent. Those beliefs are cherished which contain a promise. Hence the 'world' religions, such as Buddhism with its promise of a paradise of non-being for the painful (*nirvana*), Christianity with its paradise of the good (heaven), Islam with its paradise of plenty, Judaism with its future of paradise on earth (the *olam habima*).

The need to be is a search for duration, and the acceptance of a security system is the discovery of duration. The preparatory response rests on faith in the efficacy of an absolute security system. The construction of a church is an example of the preparatory response of the need to be. The artifacts of an absolute security system which are to be employed in the consummatory response are segments of anticipatory behavior, actions carried out in preparation for a full response and in view of the coming need-reduction. It is at this point in the reaction formation that the preparatory response can give way to displacement behavior. In place of the need for survival, the religious life can be handed over to architects concerned with church construction, to composers concerned with the construction of hymns, oratorios, motets and plain chants, as substituted goal-objects. Such activities, it is true, are explicable by drive, since they serve institutions in which individuals cooperate in the efforts at need-reduction for survival. But they can also and so easily displace the drive onto aesthetic objects as ends in themselves.

THE CONSUMMATORY RESPONSE

The consummatory response is the exercise of ritual observance. If such observance marks a faith in duration, then what the individual does about what he feels is the surrogate for the continuance of his existence. The commonest example of a transfer process from the individual to his chosen goal-object exhibiting the much-admired permanence-as-persistence is what the anthropologists have called "imitative magic" or "contagious magic." According to J. G. Frazer both kinds of magic are predicated on the idea that results may be obtained on the supposition that an effect resembles its cause, or on the other supposition that things which have been in contact but are so no longer may still exert action at a distance (4, vol. I, p. 52). "Contagious magic" is the primitive form of what we have been describing in various places in this book as a need for contact, a comfort that begins at the skin, which is the organ of security.

The consummatory response of the need to be, or more properly, of the need to continue to be, is the perfect archetype of operant behavior. It takes place with no stimulus present and observable but being cyclical it does exhibit frequency of occurrence. It is a motion carried on in the absence of a goal-object which, it is supposed, was once present. The search for security occurs in bursts; it is both self-stimulating (doubt) and self-terminating (belief).

Thanks to its role in need-reduction all belief is comforting. Faith is merely the feeling of belief unsupported by reason. Beliefs about the super-natural, and, more importantly, about the individual's contact with large and distant objects possessing permanence, are as culturally-conditioned as types of food production. The Australian aborigenes, for example, talk about links with "the eternal dream-time" which set them free from the limitations of space and time by means of the activities of totemic lodges and cult societies, with their ritual reenactment of myths (3, pp. 187-221).

With repetition belief becomes stronger. Every additional act of observance called for by an absolute security system deepens the acceptance of that system. Ritual reinforces belief. The consequent need-reduction consists in the sense of safety arising from the identification with an object believed permanent. The consummatory response of belonging, with its exercise of ritual observance, is a need-terminating response. But there has been a sharp reversal of roles: the subject is now devoted to the object. For the assimilation, which took place with all primary drives, and even with the secondary drive of knowledge, the assimilation of food, for example, and knowledge, there is now substituted a dedication: the subject now finds his salvation by losing himself in the object, becoming immersed in it. Goal-orientation means a transfer of habits to objects, as for example a ritual, *e.g.*, a habit which has been assigned to a material object or a set of material objects.

The consummatory response of the need to be consists in the attempt of the individual to become assimilated to the object: the persistent, far-away object of which the individual would like to become a part. It is clear that the degree of ego-involvement is greater in the instance of this need. But ego-involvement here is the equivalent of attainment. To get within the effective field of a persistent object is somehow to occupy its perspective, at least in part, and so to see from it as though, in Spinoza's phrase, under the species of eternity. Success means to reach a goal, to try for identification with a permanent object and to achieve it. This can be done in one way but not in another. It can be done in terms of sign-relationships but not in terms of overt behavior. The body perishes, it does not persist, nor, so far as we know from any empirical evidence, recur. But the substitution of sign identity with actual identification substitutes for goal attainment a symbolic attainment, and this is success in terms of the drive to be.

It is possible to see in the flourishing days of a religion on the part of individuals who subscribe to it something of the consummatory response of the need to be. Religion is an effort to be included in some domain larger and more permanent than mere existence. The goal of religion in life is to plan the survival of death.

REWARD

Much has been written on the rewards of faith. Here it means a need-reduction of the need to be, consisting in a *feeling* of security. The individual experiences a serenity in the conviction that salvation has at last been assured. His reward is the assurance that he is no longer responsible for his own safety. Ultimate security is promised in return for the combination of faith with ritual observance.

Reward in the case of being consists in the safety and semi-permanence offered by a religion, where religion is understood to be the institution of a church incorporating the attachment of knowledge-as-such to a material object—or posited cause of a material object—exhibiting the appearance of permanence-as-persistence. Men erect their highest buildings in honor of their deepest beliefs. Security systems end the painful state of doubt; they meet the needs of the avoidance response to danger and threats, and the need for the tensions generated by inquiry; curiosity is satisfied and safety assured. Such systems begin as revelations and end as traditions. At first, they are sanctified by authority but later strengthened and even justified by age. What so many generations have accepted as true, it would be folly to question. The very source of a system may seem like a reward to the faithful and its duration is a reinforcement. The major reinforcement, however, comes from the extent of anxiety reduction.

An absolute security system provides freedom from fear, and thus has a high survival value. The evolutionary development of absolute security systems has seen them move from the concrete objects relatively near at hand (thunder, lightning, mountains, sun), to abstract objects having no specific location within nature (a god or the gods, or even the whole of nature itself). Thus the need which was once terminated by contagious magic is later terminated by sign-behavior. The salvation is an exchange for the complete surrender of the self. Reason is surrendered to a particular rational structure, feeling is surrendered to a particular emotion, and action is surrendered to a particular liturgy.

Religion is the response made when persistent far-away objects stimulate in man the need for security. When there is no reward involved in need-reduction, it may be because an appropriate response is blocked. An intense religious emotion may be the result of a response of the whole organism to the blocked behavior of the need to be. The fear of death elicits an emotional response which consists in supplicatory prayer, mysticism, union with God, or recognized religious frenzy. Such emotions may in turn stimulate further behavior, usually, in terms of existing customs, outrageous behavior.

REINFORCEMENT

We can see now more clearly what the stage of reinforcement looks like in the circuit of the need to be. It involves the transformation of the conditioned stimulus of the need to know to another conditioned stimulus to which there is a different response. The response this time is to the artifacts peculiar to the need to be, to holy objects: abstractions (such as a creed), cities (as for instance Mecca), or relics (like the thaumaturgic arm of St. Francis Xavier), and such like material objects employed to move other material objects. Action in such cases has the function of supporting the faith; that doctrine by which he can live appears in all its aspects to be true. He who deliberately acts as though by his actions he were to insure life everlasting will believe in everlasting life, even though there be little or no empirical evidence for it. The more work one does for a security system, the more one becomes committed to it. This much we have known since Pascal recommended ritual as a support for faith. Thus while belief leads to action through the will, action leads to belief through inference. It is not possible to perform an action without by its very performance implying the presuppositions upon which it rests. Such beliefs are usually adopted inadvertently; they creep upon the individual unaware; and, unnoticed, accord a new status to faith.

There are advantages and disadvantages to be found in the establishment of a security system. We have been talking only about the advantages. The disadvantages are by-products of the establishment. It will be recalled that the stimulus produced by a need does not evoke a response but terminates it. The point here is that the acceptance of a security system shuts off inquiry and so ends the increase of knowledge.

The reinforcement resulting from ritual observance is a mutual interaction of individual and absolute security system. The interaction and interpenetration of individual and absolute security system by means of ritual observance constitutes reinforcement of the drive to be. The gradients of reinforcement are furnished by the similar faith of others, by the construction of institutions, and by the establishment of societies. As the consolidation of feeling traces makes the individual secure, the individual by his strengthened belief supports the foundations of the security system. The increasing availability of the security system, however, makes the individual less available for the appeal of other permanences. The greater the supportable delay between receptor and effector activities the stronger the reinforcement, which means in the case of the drive to be that the strength of the feeling of security is a function of the magnitude and remoteness of the permanent object and the delay between the need-terminating response of faith and the reinforcement of activation by ritual observance. Thus there occurs a final identification of individual with absolute security system with its devotion and dedication leading to the extinction of the individual.

REVERBERATING CIRCUIT

There is a periodicity to all events. A security system is the result of a complex interaction between the organism and its total environment. It is an ecological structure. Every security system is eventually attacked by environmental variables and subsequently diluted; as a result, the stranglehold of dependents is weakened and they are set free. The susceptibility of a security system to alteration is measured by how rigidly it is maintained. Thus a security system which is absolute is stronger but also more vulnerable. For security systems too must suffer the consequences of an encounter with some of the elements which are not included in them; they must, in short, eventually fail.

But the deprivation of a security system not only restores the tissue-need, it also increases anxiety. Illness increases the pressure or revives the drive, as does the approach of death. We are back at our starting-point, where we found that indiscriminate arousal reactions were insupportable, since the animal is incapable of adjusting to an input of total disorder. There is a periodicity to sositropistic behavior. The activation of consummatory behavior in the case of the more importunate basic tissue-needs: hunger, thirst and mating, allows for the functioning of inquiry. Curiosity set free is governed again by the selection of stimuli made possible because of the rank order of the drives in which inhibitory functions play a role. There is once more the phenomenon of approach and exploratory behavior. Animals when moving about will encounter elements which can be worked over by thought, once again to reduce the tissue-needs of knowing and being, thus setting the cycle once more in operation.

The repetition of the cycle, which the elements of the cycle call for, is a reverberating circuit in which the cycle is a component with others; for the cycle alone cannot account for the alteration of the object through responses or of the subject through stimulations; as each is changed, it has the effect of changing. The dedication of a man to his religion strengthens that religion, and the strengthened religion increases his faith. The more a man is satisfied by his faith because of his identification with the persistent elements in which it is placed the easier it is for him to be content with such satisfactions; he settles in with them and looks for no extension of them or substitutes for them. Thus there is constructed an organization, an institution even, to which his cycle of responses is confined. The intensity and amplitude of the material object receiving the response is measured in finite terms, and the transcendental or super-natural appeal has been conditioned by a ritual cycle which has displaced it.

In an earlier chapter, the function of the compound conditioned stimulus was discussed in connection with the product of a continuing reverberating circuit. A material object altered through human agency by means of a series of conditioned responses is an artifact. In the need to be, as we have noted, the response is an operant response, that is to say, it takes place with no stimulus immediately present. Thus the compound conditioned stimulus is represented merely by means of institution-encrusted symbols, and it is the contents of the institution which serve in place of the CCS rather than the CCS-object itself. By definition, a far-away object can be represented only by a nearby symbol. The interaction between organism and environment is in this instance between human individual and symbolic artifact.

But the alteration of animals and objects involved in the reverberating circuit ensures that the situation shall not be fixed. The security system is never destroyed all at once. It is a gradual occurrence, as habit leads to extinction. The movement of security is the ritual of religion; the ritual is not changed after establishment, but that is a change: it had changed before. The loss of novelty exacts the extinction of stimulation as the price of repetition. Thus, the reverberating circuit which offers some continuity contains the elements of its own reduction. Unless the object is altered the circuit is broken, and unless the construction continues the object is not altered. Thus the reverberating circuit of the need to be, the drive to assure the continuance of being, can account for the origin of a religion but not for its unobstructed continuance.

PART TWO
ADAPTIVE BEHAVIOR

Chapter 9

NERVOUS NETWORKS

INTRODUCTION

ADAPTIVE BEHAVIOR—as we propose to call the more advanced type of behavior in the human individual—is the name for continuously revised self-conditioning, meeting or producing modifications in the special ways in which man sets about obtaining the reduction of the needs which he shares with the animals. Adaptation means adjustment to existing conditions. Adaptive behavior is behavior intended to bring about such adjustment.

Need reductions are always to be found in some material object (in which class are to be included both human individuals and other animals). Adaptive behavior alters man himself and the material objects in his immediate environment in such a way as to make his survival more likely. Thanks to the appeal of the material object, the individual operates on it; thanks to the operations, the material object is altered; thanks to the alterations, adaptations are called on from the individual. Hence the adaptive behavior is that behavior required of the individual if he is to meet the conditions imposed on him by changes in his immediate environment—including those for which his own actions are responsible.

Adaptive behavior enables the human individual to interact with material objects in the environment in ways which best serve his own needs. Any activity which tends to fix his behavior in a permanent mold stands in the way. Instinct accounts for many behavior patterns which continue to hold from culture to culture (9). Even though such instincts may themselves be the result of ancient adaptations, they are themselves non-adaptive. Habit, which is the attachment of cues to movement, is also involved in a complex pattern of behavior, and may be an early stage of instinct in the making. Although rigidity of habit is less than that of instinct, it, too, is non-adaptive.

Responses which can be altered to meet the altered stimulus have adaptive value. But the most adaptive are those responses over which the respondent is able to exercise some measure of control. Every response is an adaptive reaction. It improves the capacity for the next response. Fineness of discrimination is a matter of repetition of stimulation. The human individual learns with reactions to distinguish the stronger of two very similar stimuli. With deliberation his discrimination can be increased. For sub-human animals sheer frequency increases discrimination (15, p. 4).

Yet seldom is the individual sure of what his response will accomplish in the way of need-reduction. There is an element of probability in most animal reactions. Will the response which is made to a stimulus result in need-reductions (7, p. 375)? The chances of success are increased with every trial because of the ability of the individual to adjust his receptors to assure a maximum of stimulation. Although the chance of success increases, the probability of success in need-reduction is still a fraction in which success is the numerator and success-plus-failure the denominator, whatever the particular type of stimulus.

Since, as we have noted, it is easier to understand the behavior of the animal if we consider it in a state of continuous interaction with a material object, the explanation of adaptive behavior in the human individual will be extended by means of two sets of descriptions. We shall have to account for the operation of the central nervous system in its various transformations, and we shall have to suggest how the transformations of the material object are influential. The first we shall undertake here, and the second in a later chapter. The behavior of the human individual cannot be accounted for entirely in terms of the central nervous system. The mechanism is more complex than that. No doubt the endocrine system is also involved; for instance thyroid hormone is necessary for the growth and development of the central nervous system, but the central nervous system can stimulate the adrenal medulla. There are many relations between the two systems which are as yet imperfectly understood. Other organs, too, are involved, and finally the entire somatic organism.

In the operation of a well-integrated organism, all distinctions are of limited descriptive value. Nevertheless we shall find it necessary to discriminate three separate reverberatory or reentrant circuits. These are: the neurophysiological, centered on the animal needs; the psychological, centered on the individual human needs; and the cultural, centered on the social needs. There is good precedence for this in the science of physiology. Hughlings Jackson was the first to suppose that there were levels of integrative activity in the central nervous system (8), while Sherrington recognized a hierarchy of receptors (13). Studies in the phylogeny of the central nervous system assign a higher function to those divisions of the brain which were the last to develop. Stereotyped behavior seems to be dependent chiefly upon the ergotropic system, while adaptive behavior involves nonspecific forebrain areas to a much greater extent. All three circuits are of course imbedded in the central nervous system; together they constitute a hierarchy of integrative levels. Each is more complex than the one below, and adds elements which increase functional capacities. Thus for example the psychological circuit contains mediating processes not present in the simpler neurophysiological circuit whereby imprinting is made possible. It will be helpful if the discussion of these is undertaken one at a time.

THE NEUROPHYSIOLOGICAL CIRCUIT

The first type is described usually in Pavlovian terms as a stimulus-response reflex arc. It is assumed that receptor and effector mechanisms are directly connected. It includes sensory feedback of both the exteroceptive and proprioceptive varieties. Central connections are of the simplest and lead back to the periphery with little variability. Here we are confronted with the lowest level of activity possible to an animal nervous system, utilizing sensori-motor connections which exist between receptors and effectors to make possible a conditioned response, a simple exchange of energy barely able to convey information and allowing for a minimum of control, although no doubt affecting ascending projections from brain stem to cortical areas.

This type may be considered a circuit because the response to a stimulation initiates a second stimulation through an alteration of the material object which was the source of the original stimulus, and the second initiates a third in the same way, and so on. There is a series of interactions between the object-stimulant and the animal-respondent which is responsible for alterations in both.

Additions to the Pavlovian structure include the recently discovered facilitating and inhibiting functions of the brain stem reticular formations, influencing through their ascending and descending projections both the proprioceptive input and cerebral hemispheric control of wakefulness and arousal (11, pp. 32, 64) and even perhaps controlling in this way the entire nervous system (3, p. 365). To the neurophysiological circuit also belongs the non-specific projection system from sensory end organs which allows for the occurrence of motor responses. The unconditioned response is the archetype of response at this level. The bombardment by a wide variety of indiscriminate sense stimuli of low level excitation maintains in the cortex a state of arousal which keeps the animal receptive to more specific stimuli. Thus, the neurophysiological circuit has a reactive function and also a facilitative function. It connects the animal with the material object directly, and also makes possible specific responses of a more complex nature belonging to higher levels of reverberating circuitry. Learning of the simple, conditioned response variety also belongs to the neurophysiological circuit. The susceptibility of the individual to such conditioning is made possible by the crudest of associations, those which linger briefly in the circuit before fading and without the storage facilities of the mediating processes. This is what Hull has named "the perseverative stimulus trace" (7, p. 385).

THE PSYCHOLOGICAL CIRCUIT

Perhaps the most fundamental characteristic of the psychological circuit is the addition to the receptor and effector mechanism of an internuncial conduction path. Between afferent and efferent neurons there are internuncial neurons interposed in a mediating process. They make possible the after-discharge of motor neurons when afferent impulses have stopped. At this level, there is increased flexibility provided for by the phenomenon of humoral and neural sets: functions controlled to some extent by glandular secretions or by specific attention. Stimulations occur in relays so that the first merely prepares the animal to respond to the second; responses can be delayed or held.

A number of new factors, new entities and processes, are in evidence in the psychological circuit. Discriminations have become markedly finer and reactions more specific. Cortical association areas come into play, with new paths for more complex pathways for the flow of information. When an artifact, more specifically a tool, triggers responses which result in further alterations, we say that a psychological circuit has been fired. Sensory stimulation now leads through complex mediating processes. The individual acquires some control over the choice of stimuli and over the character and timing of his own responses because behavior can no longer be entirely determined by ongoing environmental stimulation ("voluntarism"). To this level belong the psychosomatic phenomena, with the control of physiological responses mediated by mental stimuli, as for instance when anxiety precipitates diarrhea. At this level, too, we find the development of a specific projection system and localization of function. There is a feedback from the cortex making a closed circuit with the arousal system.

The additional properties of the psychological circuit make possible a new flexibility and a new repertory of response resources. The circuit is no longer a simply mechanical affair in which both stimulus and response are stabilized; with each reentry the stimulus is slightly altered and the response adjusted to meet it. This exigency cannot always be anticipated, and so there arises the phenomenon of self-conditioned responses. The individual has acquired the ability to arrange in advance for preparatory responses, and is now in a position to estimate the probability that a given stimulus will provide a given measure of need-reduction. The differential reinforcement which consists in irregular combinations of reinforcement and extinction provides for discrimination learning through trial-and-error.

The most confirmed evidence for the existence of a psychological circuit as distinct from the neurophysiological circuit on which it is constructed is the appearance of consciousness. We have seen how non-specific sensory projection systems in combination with ascending facilitative functioning of the brain stem reticular formation are responsible for arousal reactions. These in all probability constitute the neurophysiological concomitant of consciousness.

At the psychological level, however, the function has to be redefined; it has become a matter of attention or discrimination. Consciousness at the psychological level means the awareness of perception. This has its qualitative side which defies description, but it can be described partly at least as the perspective of a quasi-second person, a perceiver whose attention is fixed upon the on-going perceptual process.

The psychological integrative level has not yet acquired a fully developed plasticity, however, despite the appearance of consciousness as an enormous step in that direction. A further step will be necessary. Meanwhile, as evidence that the flexibility of the psychological level is only a halfway stage there is the phenomenon of displacement activity in man. Lorenz cites the lighting of cigarettes and the straightening of ties at moments of crises as examples (10, p. 298). The substitution of one antagonistic drive for another would argue for the residue of a certain rigidity which is retained from a lower integrative level where the neurophysiological circuits are more primitive.

To the psychological circuit belongs also perhaps the motor level of thought and emotion, that ideation is occasioned by a series of stimulus-response cycles (6, pp. 58-63), and that emotion involves interoceptive reflexes and even may be interoceptive in origin (2, p. 393). The feedback in this case comes from the interoceptors and the delay between stimulus and response is accounted for in terms of a series of feedback cycles. In simple thoughts, such as the direct attempt at problem-solving or the control of learned responses, the motor account of thought may be sufficient. But there are more complex mental processes which must be explained in other ways.

THE CULTURAL CIRCUIT

Pathways at this level are longer and have grown considerably more complex. The holding process in the central nervous system now involves those vast and largely unanalyzed association areas in the cortex, such as the prefrontal areas, which are probably responsible for the series of mediating processes known to exist. The conduction of impulses is no longer linear but diffused. The cultural circuit is here given this name because it involves speech areas and hence is active in sign-communication, and its more elaborate extension, symbol-communication. When the artifact which triggers responses resulting in further alterations is a sign, we say that a cultural circuit has been fired. Aphasia, as Hebb points out, is evidence that thought processes are involved in the use of language (6, pp. 84-85). Verbal behavior requires the maintenance of a strong arousal level, and there is some evidence that this exists, and indeed continues to exist even during deep sleep (4, p. 1486). No doubt the reticular formation of the brain stem is also involved, since the arousal level of attention has to be maintained if the circuits are to operate. The cultural circuit is the reverberating circuit extended to artifacts. It involves a large measure of control. But in all events the cultural circuit cannot be explained in terms of immediate input; there are complex central processes operating, even though the content on which they operate may have been sensory in origin. The mediating processes, as we shall presently note, exist primarily in the cultural circuit or are controlled from there.

The individual is fully self-conscious and is aware of his own perceptions as such. Indeed the extended chains of the cultural circuit involve long-delayed responses which make possible abstract thought. It is here that we find what Skinner has named "operant behavior," which is behavior with no stimulus present and observable but only the frequency of occurrence (14, pp. 19-21). The association cortex is most likely involved in the elaborate learned behavior patterns, such as the motor and verbal skills, and especially recall. Such patterns provide the background for the thought processes underlying voluntary behavior. An arrangement roughly resembling the tuneable homeostat within the central nervous system makes possible the decisions about values. Such decisions are under the control of symbols, and hence are not graded by just noticeable differences. Consciousness at this level may be described as the awareness of perception, perception conducted in the full knowledge that it is being conducted.

With the existence of the cultural circuit the individual is now in a position to anticipate the probabilities of need-reduction in any given environmental situation; to anticipate, and, what is more important, to prepare for such an eventuality. This is the deliberate interposition of a considerable time-interval between stimulus and response. The drive now involves a search for a material object operating an appropriate tropism, a process which may be long delayed; and with the success of the search the discovery of a potentially tropistic object which may be voluntarily delayed in exercising its effect on an individual who may have drive-conflicting reasons for not wanting an immediate reduction of his needs. An example would be: storing food during a month of religious fasting, or stock-piling a harem while fighting a military campaign.

THE CIRCUITRY OF NERVOUS NETS

We have been discussing in the foregoing pages three sets of re-entrant circuits all of which lie within the central nervous system and together are expected to account for human behavior. This is physiological speculation at its most hazardous, but there is no stopping short of an elaboration of the picture until there is a complete theory of the multi-dimensional system of nervous nets which can account for the plasticity and the large resources of the repertory of responses available to the human individual in his encounter with the world. There is the necessity of accounting both for the repository of those inherited but elaborate patterns of responses and for a mechanism capable of acquiring and retaining equally elaborate learned responses.

It is important, somehow, to posit the integration necessary to coordinate the specific energies within a single sensory system.

The Three Circuits

Element	*Neurophysiological*	*Psychological*	*Cultural*
artifact	tool	sign	symbol
behavior	stereotyped	developed	adaptive
neurones	maintenance	conduction	integration
area	brain stem	cortex	frontal lobes
need	direct	diffused	transferred
reaction	general arousal	awareness	self-consciousness
receptor	interoceptor	exteroceptor	central arousal
motivation	simple response	singly motivated	multiply-motivated
memory	reverberation	alteration with use	retention
response	unconditioned response	conditioned response	operant behavior
control	mechanical	selected	determined

For this we need both the more elementary parallel conduction and the more advanced diffuse conduction. Generally speaking, the structures of the various circuits we have been describing have interconnecting paths. Evidently, between the laminated integrative levels of closed circuits lying within the central nervous system there may be relays, so that the activity of one circuit can open or close another. Thus no one circuit is altogether independent but all operate together in a complex fashion. It is clear, certainly, that there exists a hierarchy of need-relationships, such that to terminate one by means of a consummatory response means only to touch off another. In this way the continuity and fluidity of behavior can be explained.

The joint operation of facilitation and inhibition ranging over the network can make available many alternative combinations having a great diversity of properties. The capacity of the nervous network for containing, recombining and utilizing information depends upon the presetting and resetting the controls of complex channels of association and conduction, and even the ability of the system to maintain established responses, in a manner suggested by the tuneable homeostat. Here, at selected points on the scale a graded response rather than the all-or-nothing response is the rule. The graded response is a subtle response to a complex stimulus, but still a response by the entire individual; for it is true of organs, limbs, and glands, that they are the agents of the entire organism.

Despite the variegated contents of compound conditioned stimuli, at the higher level of human individuals, the integrative action of the nervous system discriminates a single impression from them. Whether the individual is confronted with the stimulus compound issuing from a material object of complex nature or from those of another individual, adaptive behavior requires that the reaction be organized. Wholes operate in terms of wholes.

The organization of nervous activity is exceedingly complex in the human organism. From a number of developments, it is clear that interactions with the environment affect the animal in ways which have reverberations. *First,* the central nervous system regulates the activity of the endocrines. In the preponderance of cases psychic phenomena set in operation by environmental factors furnish the route taken by stimuli. The endocrines themselves do not initiate any new biochemical reactions; instead they influence the rate and intensity of existing reactions. But there is evidently some humoral feedback, and it is certainly true that to some extent the endocrines influence the central nervous system. *Secondly,* the involvement of the central nervous system with the other organs, chiefly through the interoceptors, such as the mesenteric, the gastro-intestinal, the urogenital (2, ch. 13). *Thirdly,* there is the involvement of the brain stem with the higher centers, through the ascending projections of the brain stem reticular formation (11).

Nervous activity is an on-going process which takes place within the animal separately but as a result of its previous and continuing interactions with the material objects in the environment. Outside, there is a pole, which is resistant, if not fixed: the artifact. Inside, there is one, too, and it consists in the memory trace. The interaction between animal and environment takes place as a dynamic event between quasi-static structures at two poles: within the animal the memory trace, and within the environment the artifact. Both are artificial productions.

This much is demonstrable, but it leaves many questions open. Like most investigations of an empirical sort, what are discovered are not so much new entities and processes as new unknown areas and new problems within them. We know that human individuals alter material objects and become themselves affected by such alterations. We know also that within human individuals there is retention and recall. The artifacts are readily accessible to examination, but what about retention and recall? Is there a homeostasis of the higher centers? Or could it be that the memory trace maintains itself more or less intact by riding upon the surface of arousal reactions, where it is susceptible to stimulation by similarities in the environment impinging upon it from pathways lying through the exteroceptors (5, p. 12ff.)?

The account of the circuitry of nervous nets suggested above reckons without disorder. The network of circuits in the central nervous system is complex and delicate in its operation. The equilibrium it supports can therefore easily be disturbed. But the plasticity of the central nervous system was an evolutionary development resulting from the exigencies of environing conditions. Under these conditions, stable states, such as are found in connection with the secondary drives: living with established need-reductions and drive extinctions, are extraordinary and not provided for by the circuitry of nervous nets. Again, it can be recognized that there are rarely less than two opposed drives, and often more. Behavioral oscillation is an observable phenomenon (4, p. 304ff.).

Behavior is usually multiply-motivated. Motivation itself is rarely single. This fact is complicated by the individual's dependence on the environment (12, pp. 14-15). The needs may combine to strengthen a drive, as for instance when aggressiveness is found in surgeons. Responses may conflict, as indeed they do in the neurotic. Otherwise responses are singular and particular and occur one at a time. Ambivalent behavior oscillates, and this situation is aggravated when it is prompted by conflicting response systems. Otherwise there is an orderly procedure, involving the transfer of dominance from one need to another.

Two further developments of the elaborate structure resulting from the interconnections of the laminated networks may be recorded here. One of these is represented by an over-determined drive, the other by a lessening of drive.

One development is that of the over-determined drive made possible by the autonomy of drives under an assumed dominance. When drives become their own goal-objects, then the purpose of the drive is—to drive, thus throwing an emphasis upon the reactions of the animal rather than upon the attainment of the goal-object. An example might be that of material accumulation for its own sake, such as raising more food than can be sold or collecting more food than can be eaten. The drive in these cases extends over the tropism and becomes associated with it, so that need-satisfactions do not lead to need-reduction, or when they do are not extinguished as a result.

The second development is that of the lessening of the drive due to what Allport called "functional autonomy" (1). The circuitry of nervous nets is capable of operating in the absence of the needs or drives entirely in terms of self-rewarding secondary reinforcement. Considerable extensions of this phenomenon will be necessary in subsequent chapters to account for the containment of speculation within the boundaries of a security system.

Chapter 10

TOOLS AND SIGNS

THE CENTRAL PROBLEM in current psychology is learning, which has been described earlier as acquiring from responses the ability to respond. Every animal lives and moves in an environment of material objects (including other animals) to which he is attracted, repelled or neutral, according as he finds in them need-reductions, security threats, or neither. He learns how to react in accordance with his sensations, but what does he learn? Presumably, how to alter material objects in order to gain an objective; and this is as true of the human individual who has learned how to build a hospital and practice medicine as it is of the rat which has learned how to obtain a food pellet by depressing a bar. The building materials and medical equipment have been constructed of less organized "raw" materials and the food pellet digested; the objects at both extremes have been altered as a result of the animal's actions. In order to understand what use the animal makes of his learning as well as what it is that he has learned, we must devote some study to the kinds of objects which exist in the immediate environment of the animal and what happens to them as a result of his learning and his subsequent behavior toward them.

But the sub-human animals live in a world whose limits are set for them by their unaided senses. The human individual lives in the same world but from this perspective endeavors to ascertain others, particularly the world of the very small and the world of the very large, for which his senses require considerable additions. One thinks immediately of the aid rendered to vision by microscopes and telescopes of course, but there are others equally designed to aid other senses. The technique of making instruments to extend the senses is a common enough affair. For instance for the visual receptors, in addition to the instruments mentioned, there are photographic emulsions and photon tubes; for the skin receptors, thermo-couples; and for the proprioceptors, transistors. These instruments, it develops, have properties of their own which do not depend upon the use for which they were originally designed.

It is important to remember that human individuals, like all animals, exist in a world in which there are other objects, chiefly material objects and diverse varieties of organisms. Many of these objects and some of the organisms are indifferent to the individual; certainly others of the same type existed before him and will continue to exist after him. They have other relations to which they are committed and on some of which they are dependent. They do not depend upon him for their existence, but he does depend upon them. He must understand how to approach the objects which can help him to survive and how to avoid those which threaten his survival. The individual engages in no activities which cannot be traced eventually to some stimulation from a material object; whereas the reciprocal relation cannot be posited for the objects: they are not dependent upon him. And this last statement even holds true for those objects he has fashioned for himself.

We are at this point in the argument engaged on the study of human behavior, but we may recall that in certain cases of the behavior of other animals interaction with the environment resulted in the alteration of material objects in a constructive fashion. The ant hill, the bee hive, the beaver dam, are constructions. In these cases, a new element has entered into animal behavior. The animal seeks to make an adjustment to something capable of sustaining interactions in order to anticipate and prepare for the reduction of his own future needs. He must behave in such a fashion as to prepare objects in his immediate environment for his own repeated reactions to them.

We have seen in the last chapter that adaptive behavior is more complex than the simple stimulus-response reflex arc and consists in a structure capable of sustaining plastic reactions. But the same holds true for the material objects which are the sources of the stimuli: they are not simple, either, but are what Pavlov called "compound conditioned stimuli" (3, pp. 141, 145, 269). Pavlov had in mind stimuli operating on more than one sense organ, as when a tuning-fork is reinforced by a lamp. No doubt in every stimulus-response situation there always are a number of stimuli operating from the environment, and just because one has been singled out for notice is no reason to suppose that it has been isolated from the others in any significant way. Whatever stimuli-emitters exist in the neighboring environment are having their effects on the individual (2, pp. 205-206).

But it is also possible for a number of such stimuli to occur in the same material object, as for example in a badly functioning fluorescent tube, which can be seen as a bright light, heard as a humming, and felt as a warm surface. The material object, then, may be a compound stimulus-emitter. Further, it may have been altered in order to be so through human agency, in which case it is a compound conditioned stimulus (CCS) in another sense. For it is not the reflex arc of simple stimulus and response we now have in mind but the CCS and the cultural circuit. The CCS is a product of a history of interactions between individual and material object and embodies them. At the same time, it can be considered apart from them.

The CCS is a material object altered through human agency in such a way as to emit stimuli of various desirable sorts. It has been altered with a view to its effects on the individual, but it possesses its properties in independence of him. The CCS is an object existing in the world, having its capacities as stimuli potentially when there is no individual present to apprehend them, like the rock painting in the Calahari Desert which have remained for millennia unnoticed. Intentions do not always match effects, but the CCS is a material object altered through human agency to achieve certain results. It is the way in which the external world is induced to assist in effecting its own changes. In this way, adaptive behavior occasions changes not only in the individual but also in the object with which he interacts, anticipatory responses only approximately in accord with anticipatory stimuli.

The CCS, then, is a plastic object. It is what a material object produces when a set of stimuli from it vary in space or time or both. Variability in space means that the stimuli issuing from different parts of the object exhibit differences. Stimuli in an object can be lined up in such a way that one blocks out another, or a stronger takes precedence over a weaker, or occurs before another. The degrees of complexity exhibited by CCS objects are enormous, as for instance with a moving vehicle or a musical composition. Variability in time means that there are slight alterations as stimuli from the same region of the object succeed each other. Objects changing location and shape are exhibiting differences of both varieties and hence giving rise to widely variable stimuli. Such eventualities are to be found in the effort at need-reduction in the case of the simplest of primary needs, such as raising, transporting and cooking food before it is eaten. In the case of the satisfaction of the primary needs by the human individual, this conventionally takes place against a background which is cultural.

Now suppose that at highly integrated levels of behavior complex interactions take place between the compound conditioned stimuli which have been produced in the immediate environment and the conditioned responses of the human individuals who have produced them. The result is an altered individual whose survival is secured but who in the process of securing it has become reliant upon material objects which have been altered also and in certain specific fashions. Those individuals with special peculiarities, such as the superior ability to adapt themselves to artifacts, will tend to survive with greater frequency, so that when their advantages are passed on to their progeny it will effect permanent changes in the species. Natural selection operates also on man in his artificial environment. In the course of rendering his environment reliable so far as his primary needs are concerned, he has become a ritual-dependent who can survive even in short-range terms only by behaving in certain prescribed ways. A civilized man would perish quickly if left to his own devices in a wilderness, whereas a dog would not. For the dog's needs are hooked up directly with the objects capable of bringing about his need-reductions, while the man has interposed devices. Smashing a complex object does not immediately produce simple components; it produces only fragments of the complex object. And so it is with elaborate behavior patterns. The cultural cycle leads to complex constructions of the material objects as the advanced set of stimuli, and ritual-dependence in the human individual as the advanced set of responses.

The complex effects of the CCS on the individual are cumulative, but not to the extent to which they can become in the object itself. Objects can be more stable than individuals and they can retain the built-in reactions which he is able to construct in them. The development of a material object into a CCS is a result of the activity, or the operation of a sequence of activities, of the individual. For instance, there is clay by the water-hole. He projectively connects the clay with the water. By making a cup of clay, he no longer has to lie down to drink but can now carry the water away. He has altered a material object, conditioned a stimulus, and by this means achieved a self-conditioning; but henceforth he will be compelled to alter his own behavior in accordance with the requirements of the cup. He has to some extent to follow the pattern of action which the cup of water allows to him.

Thus the material object becomes through its alterations a record of the individual's adaptive behavior. The objects by which he is surrounded and which bear severely the marks of his responses are not accidents; they were designed by him specifically to exercise certain effects upon his own person; they are devices he has discovered for assisting himself in his own self-conditioning. By their means he can become what he wishes and more than he could without their aid. They are the quasi-permanent landmarks of his intentions and accomplishments.

Our task will be made somewhat simpler if we consider the alteration of material objects in terms of the individual's needs. As we have noted, he has the primary needs: drinking, feeding and breeding, and he has the secondary needs to know, do and continue to be. These two sets of needs will have to be treated somewhat differently here. Although for both sets there are CCS objects, they are of different sorts; for the same CCS objects could not meet the diverse requirements of need-reductions of the two kinds of needs.

For the primary needs man constructs constitutive institutions consisting of material objects (artifacts) and particular ways of behaving about them (customs), for instance, agriculture, animal husbandry, the family, as well as regulative institutions designed to make the periodic reduction of the animal needs possible, such as the postal system and banking (1).

For the secondary needs he constructs systems of ideas and institutions to maintain them, for instance, concrete philosophies which are maintained by such leading institutions as universities or religions.

Both kinds of needs involve dealings with selected objects in the immediate environment.

It will be useful to remind ourselves at this point that what is peculiar about human behavior at the level of the specifically human needs, such as the needs to know and to be, is that it is an adaptation to those properties of the environment which went undetected by other animals. Human individuals under sensory guidance have elicited from the environment many properties that would otherwise not have been known to be there. Specifically, two have been treated here, although no doubt many others do exist. The two are: recurrent relations, and relatively persistent material objects. Knowing deals with permanence-as-recurrence, being deals with permanence-as-persistence. The individual does not always deal with permanence directly but requires the aid of mediating material objects. In general, assistance is to be obtained from the CCS.

The compound conditioned stimulus has already been given another name when it was described as the initiating construction of a complex sequence of reactions. The artifact indicates the transition from non-human nature to human nature—which is to say, culture. It furnishes the dividing line between animal behavior and human behavior. For despite the tool-using sub-human animals the cumulative use made by man of his artifacts marks him as something else. When we call material objects which have been altered through human agency 'compound conditioned stimuli,' we are using the framework of psychology because we are speaking of the effects of individual behavior. But the CCS remains as a material object often long after it has been altered, and in this way can become a stimulus to other human individuals, even to successive generations of such individuals. This is the framework of anthropology, and for this context another name for the CCS was required. The archaeologists speak of artifacts when they uncover from a previous culture such altered material objects. When referring to the CCS as a quasi-permanent culture-object, we have been using the term, artifact. An artifact is a quasi-permanent element of culture which arose as a CCS in a single planned material object. Artifacts are the results of the efforts of human individuals to manipulate some segment of the external world of material objects in order to make them more amenable to the reduction of his various needs.

We have noted in earlier chapters that there are two kinds of artifacts: tools and signs. A tool is a material object employed to move other material objects, and a sign is a material object employed to refer to other material objects. Spades, buildings, clothing, are examples of tools. '+,' 'horse,' '$,' are examples of signs. Characteristic frameworks of behavior, customs and instituitons, are simply established ways of using familiar artifacts.

The origin of tools as artifacts is unknown, but it can be hazarded that it was probably an accidental insight. Such insightful learning could only have taken place in the presence of the appropriate material objects; the first time that a man comprehended that the stone at his feet could bring down the deer he could not catch.

The origin of signs began in all probability when a man was first stimulated by a material object similar to a previous object which had stimulated him earlier, and made the connection by means of a common name. The process is similar to the one described by Hull as "stimulus generalization" (2, p. 389): extending the connection involved in a reinforcement situation to a whole class of stimuli lying along the same continuum.

The use of tools and signs together involves behavior of the most complex sort: combinations of simple acts, such as pressing a button or uttering a sound, which have large-scale effects, such as winning an earth-wide war or initiating a new type of industrial production. The multiplication of types of artifacts is always present when the activities of human individuals are intended to reduce the pressure of the higher artificial hungers. It is always necessary to employ artifacts of both types in aid of the reduction of the specifically human needs of knowing, doing, and being.

But a long historical development interposed itself between the simple kind of artifact employed by early man and the complex artifact of modern culture. The former was available to everyone, the latter selects its operators in terms of talent, and then dictates the long preparatory process necessary to the acquisition of the requisite learned behavior.

Artifacts are cumulative compound conditioned stimuli, and the behavior of the human individual required by them adaptive making. The requisite learned behavior may be extremely complex. Before an individual can react properly to a piano, a bank, or a cathode ray oscillograph, he may have to learn how. In some cases—that of the piano, for instance—such learning may take years. The artifact is selective of individuals; only some can ever learn how to play the piano well. Thus the behavior required by an artifact is anticipated only in general in the construction of the artifact; for it can never be altogether anticipated. The consequences of an action are never entirely predictable, and this is no less true of the construction of an artifact.

It should be easier now to understand the independence of the artifact, both as entity and as process, to go its own unplanned and unanticipated way. No anthropomorphic notions are implied, only the intractability of material objects which whatever they are resist to some extent all efforts to make them other than they are, so that the use of force is always involved. The artifact makes demands upon those who occupy some one of its many perspectives merely in virtue of its own structure and function. In this sense it leads an existence of its own, and exercises an influence upon human individuals who to this extent at least fall short of leading lives of *their* own.

It is possible to see this development more clearly in the improvements which have been made in machinery designed for industrial production. The earliest tools were hand-operated, such as a bow and arrow or a spade. Hand-operated tools gave way to power-driven machines, a gun or a bull-dozer. Subsequently, the human operator was replaced by another machine, so that now there are machine-operated machines, for instance the thermostat-operated heater or the automatic steering mechanism that guides a ship or an airplane on its true course without the assistance of a pilot. The latest development has been to hook up machines in series, so that the operation of an entire factory from raw material to finished and packaged product is automatic. All these are properly classified as tools, but the similarities which the generic term thus emphasizes hides the emergence of a revision which lies in the direction of self-dependence.

In this work, tools have received less close consideration than signs. Signs were discussed in Chapter VI, and they will be discussed again in Chapter XI. Signs participate in human behavior through speech and writing, communication takes place through signs by means of sounds or inscriptions. Their object is to convey information with a view to influencing human behavior either as regards the human individuals themselves or in their relations to material objects. Behavior is based upon amount of information—and both are able only to approximate the true situation. A man may be given a responsible administrative post because he possesses the kind of training and stability which it requires, yet lack the initiative to make decisions, equally a requisite but one which nobody had considered. Or he may come to be regarded as an important scientist when he does not have the imagination necessary for discovering successful hypotheses or provocative facts.

A large part of the use of signs is as rules of direction for the operation of tools. When it is said that a captain at sea ought not to desert his ship, or that a crew ought not to leave the vessel until the women and children have been saved first, the behavior of the human individual toward a tool is what is referred to. Men order their behavior with respect to other men but also with respect to the tools employed, and such order is recorded and transmitted conventionally in every profession, which is to say, with respect to every separate set of tools. Men and material objects are always involved when signs are employed, however much we may suppose that we deal with them separately. For when we do, it is for the purpose of dealing with them at all, and not because we regard their function as a separate affair. Speech must be learned in independence of manual skills. But they are not unrelated, and the technological handbook which seeks to instruct in skills is inscribed in signs.

The example is a plain one, but it is not too difficult with a little imagination to see the analogy with scientific monographs and musical scores, yes, and with philosophical systems and theologies as well. If every theoretical work eventually issues in conduct of a certain sort, then every composition of signs has as its application the operation of tools. Signs and tools are equally artifacts, and it is as artifacts that they work together.

It would not be too broad to assert that the whole of human culture—all the civilizations that man has constructed, including the customs and institutions which seem so peculiarly human—are the results of the discovery of the techniques of adaptive making which result in the artifact. Every element of culture is an artifact. In a certain sense it is possible to assert that culture consists in altered material objects which remain, after they are once fashioned by human individuals, independent of those individuals; in the sense, namely, that they have persistence or recurrence in their own right and not as a result of their relations to human individuals. It is no more possible at the present time for artifacts to envisage the end of their collaboration with individuals than it is for the individuals themselves to do so. Possibly, however, there is an end that neither has discovered, one which eventually may be furnished adventitiously by the exigencies of organic evolution.

What is the range of these artifacts and how are we to classify them? They are what Lewis Carroll called them, "shoes and ships and sealing-wax, and cabbages and kings." Philosophy has the task of making an inventory of the world, but the discussion of such an undertaking belongs in another place. Suffice to say for the moment that when we attempt to answer these two questions we encounter the difficulty of exhaustively describing the contents of man's immediate environment. Moreover, that part of his environment which he is capable of modifying is itself modified from time to time. In 1950, we should have said that the surface of the moon was part of the environment which he was incapable of affecting, yet in less than a decade this was no longer true.

The attachment of knowledge-as-such or of being-as-such to an artifact exhibiting the appearance of inquiry takes precedence in times when artifacts exhibiting the appearance of permanence have lost such appearance. Churches have been bombed by the same kind of rockets by which exploratory recording equipment has been sent into orbit. Elaborate artifacts carry a heavy freight of symbolism, and are often the reasons for human sacrifice. Tools are means but such artifacts as the culture depends upon in crucial ways become ends. And the process which began as a method of facilitation is continued as one of regulation. The human individual comes to live *for* instead of *by* the artifacts he has helped in inventing.

Now that we have elaborated the theory of the artifact as a result of human behavior, it will be necessary to turn to an examination of how the human individual has managed to adapt himself to the altered circumstances. It will be necessary, in other words, to account for the advanced stages in a response behavior pattern, specifically those containing the steps outlined by Hull: reinforcement, generalization, motivation, inhibition, oscillation, response, and evocation (2, p. 383).

Chapter 11

ADAPTIVE KNOWING

WE TAKE UP NOW the problem of knowing, beginning where we left it in Chapter IV, namely, with the possession of knowledge. In Chapter IV we saw how the need to know is reduced. Here we shall study the consequences of the reduction of the need to know and its effects upon the individual, having in mind only theories of pure knowledge apart from all practical applications.

GNOSEOTAXIC BEHAVIOR

By 'adaptive knowing' is meant the special ways in which man sets about obtaining the reduction of his need for knowledge. 'Knowing' means 'being in a condition corresponding to some situation which is recognized as separate from the condition of the knower.' Knowing further means establishing contact with a material object through its class. Adaptive knowing means becoming part of a whole of which a class of material objects is through its members also a part. Such a state is far from static, and its alterations are not indeterminate. Under different conditions, the same stimuli initiate different reactions, and, conversely, the same reaction may be initiated by different stimuli. What a verbal communication means to an individual, for instance, is dictated to some extent by the emotional condition he is in when he receives it, and the same emotional condition may be provoked by widely different verbal communications.

With man as with the other animals there is the predicament of an adaptive animal in a changing world. Adaptation for the other animals can be reckoned only in evolutionary epochs, whereas adaptation in man is a matter of civilization and therefore of the order of thousands and perhaps even of hundreds of years. Changes in time and space have stimulated the human animal to look for unchanging, permanent things. One of these is the type of naturally occurring relations, to which the need to know has been adapted.

Man changes the world in accordance with what he knows about the world, and in accordance with the changes he has made what he knows about the world also changes. For instance, as he learns how to make better instruments of observation, he makes better observations; and as he makes better observations his ideas about the world are changed, and as they are changed they suggest new instruments and new observations. The world itself together with the knowledge of it are engaged in a continual round of interactions and sequential alterations.

There are difficulties attendant upon this process, however. If knowing, along with trees and stones and houses, are the things that the human individual knows, then adjustments are required for this new kind of knowing which is the knowing of knowing, the knowing that he knows. The secondary drives with this step assume the stature and authority of full-scale requirements. Psychological adjustment has had difficulty in keeping pace with evolutionary development (12). The human individual has never become adapted to his dependence upon the secondary drives. His hope of adjustment, which in his terms means leading a full and satisfactory life of accomplishment, requires the adequation of behavior with such dependence.

One tends to think of the effects of change in terms of disequilibrium, unless it is a constant change, in which case the response is a habit. But the summation effects of a series of diverse change can be an adjustment to change itself. The maximum of adaptive postures in the human individual is that required by searching and exploration procedures. However primitive in animals, it is a strain in human individuals, who have grown more accustomed to the twin certainties of memory trace and artifact which arrest the flux of events even if only for a little. Thus, the innovator with his novel and unknown conditioning is feared by the conservative for threatening the tidy world of familiar and calculated responses. The mixed procedures of reinforcement represented by repetition and of extinction represented by novelty have elaborate effects upon subsequent behavior. These effects may be divided into stages constituting a later sequence following reinforcement, namely, generalization, motivation, inhibition, oscillation and response evocation (4, p. 383).

GENERALIZATION

We begin then with a consideration of generalization, which is the step following immediately upon reinforcement. Stimulus generalization has meant the tendency of a response to spread outward from its original receptors to others in the organism (4, p. 183). But in the human individual such spreading can penetrate further than the sense receptors, unless the cortex be considered, as we shall presently see, a distance-receptor. Perceptual generalization (2, p. 14), the abstraction of forms, is perhaps the key. Behavior as the response to abstract ideas is really behavior as the response to retained stimuli. The memory image is a stimulus trace and its sign the associated artifact. But in this case the releaser must be triggered by the tropism of a material analogue. For example, a man will respond to the learned idea of loyalty, only his action must be triggered by the spectacle of a friend in trouble. Sherrington's work on distance-receptors (11) and the role they have played in the development of the brain is pertinent here. If we can count as distance-receptors the retention of remembered abstract ideas, on the ground that generals through their class-inclusion of material individual members reach beyond the date and place of the event of recalling, then we are in a position to argue that operant behavior is also stimulus-bound, the stimulus to which the response is made being the retained or remembered signs.

We know from recent studies in neurophysiology that consciousness is not non-specific. The non-specific projection system for arousal is, for the human as contrasted with animals in general, highly selective. The variety of input from the various receptors contain elements not available to animals other than human. Thus even at the level of anlysis of the simple stimulus response reflex arc the conduction system contains information of a peculiar type. We may suppose it to be the knowledge of abstract relations, the similarity of shapes and of quantities, for instance. Psychologists recognize the generalization which is suggested by the similarities of concrete particulars or of abstracted forms: the shape of two pennies abstracted from the pennies or the number of two groups abstracted from the groups.

That relations as well as events are of the furniture of the external world and hence must be taken into account as part of the input into the sensory system is attested by what the psychologists call the "phi-phenomenon," the illusion of movement where no movement exists, such as is experienced in watching motion pictures or lights close together turned on and off successively (7, pp. 406-407). Evidently, what is perceived as well as what is sensed is determined by what exists. An overly simple interpretation of sensory input neglects the complexity of the world by overloading that aspect of it which is pushed into subjective interpretation.

Neurophysiologically, the depth of imprinting is the mechanism for what is, psychologically, belief, the feeling that a proposition is true. Mammalian behavior is a response to external stimulation either directly, or indirectly through the memory trace lasting or revived with delay, or a response to internal stimulation through disorganization or disintegration (decay or tissue damage). The cortical adaptation, which is belief at the psychological level, is at present unknown; psychologically, it consists in various degrees of feeling and acting; and culturally it consists in the social assimilation of the individual. Knowledge exists within the individual as a result of conditioning, *i.e.*, learning. From the point of view of its power to stimulate behavior it may be called the response reserve of knowing (13, p. 26). Warranted beliefs are knowings, beliefs there is some reason for holding, whether or not they are true.

Perhaps the measure of imprinting can be gauged by the resistance to forgetting. Any belief that is forgotten through mere disuse could not have penetrated deeply into the organism. If belief in a general statement is not revived by some occasion whereby the environment can become relevant as a particular exemplification, then belief in the statement has not become incorporated in the organism at deep psychological levels. Some of the beliefs about behavior learned in early childhood and practiced sufficiently to affect posture and even musculature are of this character. Temporary extinction systematically produced indicates a strong imprinting, while retroactive inhibition shows that the belief could only be supplanted by another of equal strength (2, p. 146ff.).

Neurophysiologically, the next step consists in feedback circuits which are available at this level rather than the simple stimulus-response arc. Mechanisms higher than the proprioceptive feedback are involved. The analogue is to be found in machine information processing, the association-dissociation-reassociation of received information, of accepted ideas. Input is not entirely indiscriminate, yet it must be sorted and arranged in some sort of order. The psychological term this time is thought: problem-solving. What is the mechanism by which animals use their sensations to construct categories (6, p. 131)? How are the naturally occurring relations, the knowledge of which has been newly acquired, to be themselves related? This is obviously a feedback function, depending upon the force of the standing waves of excitation, and we shall note shortly the elaborate systematic consequences to which it leads. When a piece of abstract knowledge is assimilated through learning, it is arranged in its proper place among the stockpile of already existing knowledge, and it is this arrangement, and perhaps the consequent resetting of the entire inventory, that constitutes knowing.

Consider the predicament of the human individual who wishes to understand the world. Most of it lies beyond his reach in remote regions of space: the microcosm and macrocosm, and remote epochs of time: the distant past and future. What is absent can be made present only symbolically, and what is present can be regarded as a sample of what there is. The interpretation of the available sample is a form of adaptive knowing. Thought may be considered the sequential outcome of distance-reception and the cerebrum the most effective of the distance-receptors (11, p. 325). The decerebrate animal can react only to the immediate environment, whereas the cerebrum belongs to the olfactory, visual and auditory distance-receptors with which it evidently evolved (9, pp. 16-17). There is further neurophysiological evidence for such statements (5, p. 42). Jasper thinks that some of the changes in electrical activity which occur in the cortex are due not to sensory stimuli but to the meaning of such stimuli. Internal organs are built to deal with environmental factors at second remove (15, pp. 215, 218). Let us suppose that distance-reception is in terms of time as well as space. Human brain development makes greater distance-reception possible by using abstractions, the representations of absent objects. Thought however is not only the extension of the available environment by means of increased knowledge; it is also the anticipation of possible action (11, p. 326) by means of verbal behavior.

Originality of thought is a function of the effect of the external world upon the individual capable of a high state of arousal. Abstractions make possible the free association of relations without the necessity of the corresponding manipulation of material objects. Naturally occurring relations are imaginatively projected into artificial assemblies in possible material objects. If the originality is then carried out, the possible material objects become actual material objects, "new" objects. Thus actual constructions plus imagined geometries may result in the blueprints for the design of a building, and if erected a new building. The original thinker simply projects into a future of artificial relations from a present of naturally occurring relations, the image of the former imposed upon a perception of the latter.

Retention of learned material is a matter of the perseverative stimulus-trace. The depth of imprinting is determined by the force of the environmental impact on the receptors and the state of the cortical areas. The ideas which have made the strongest impression are the longest retained, although at the time of their reception this may not have seemed to be the case. Strength of retention is a matter of association: how good are the connections of any new knowledge which are established during the stockpiling process? The ethical good is a matter of the quality of consistency; such quality emerges only when there are powerful connections between ideas. Also, well-connected ideas are not easily erased or extinguished. The aesthetically beautiful is a matter of the quality of completeness of the ideas: systems are beautiful.

Retained material is available for the process of programming, the making of plans respecting behavior. Any expectation of particular behavior in view of a specific event is a plan. Plans are made when retained material becomes peculiarly relevant to some external situation, and awareness of plans only when action is immanent, or when the control of an artifact is required. In general, abstract knowledge contains implied tendencies toward particular behavior. Ideas are plans of action. "When I know, I am acting," said Royce (10, p. 27). If one "knows" for instance that all men are mortal, one will expect the death of the very old or the very ill, and such expectation includes a plan of behavior on such a future occasion. Since future events are uncertain, plans must be continually modifiable. Adjustment to environmental variables requires a plasticity of behavior based on ease of functional variation. Then, too, motives are seldom atomic. The carrying out of plans must reckon not only with environmental variables but also with multiple motivation. The resultant action consists in a compromise or—as we shall presently note—in conflict and ambivalent behavior.

Habit with respect to the possession of abstract knowledge is a direct function of the length of time and depth of impression. Depth of impression means security of impression, but it means also distance from the foreground of attention. What the individual has long accepted as true calls on less attention. Metaphysical beliefs accepted without awareness by human individuals correspond in strength with depth of imprinting in young animals. There are two opposed influences operating; for on the one hand habit-strength is determined by the number of reinforcements, while on the other there is a lack of responsiveness to simulation and a tendency to fade. An increased rigidity is accompanied by an increased sense of unimportance; old truths are hardly the occasion for agitation. Habituation is a kind of negative adaptation as well as a kind of entrenched assurance. Under motivation, however, the positive response is one of patterning, and there is the result known as operant behavior. When the motive is the need to know, then the response of patterning is intensified and dominates the organism.

MOTIVATION

We have noted that the motivation in the case of abstract relations is to be found in the first of the secondary drives, the need to know. The response to the impinging of abstract relations is exceedingly complex. Single propositions, if they could be understood apart from their background context, would call out no strong immediate reactions in the form of behavior. However, in combination with other propositions under the influence of patterning, the behavior is the peculiar one of adaptation to knowledge.

Some individuals are more susceptible to such adaptation than others. Reaction thresholds and response evocations vary widely. There are even voracious and rapacious knowledge-seeking individuals, a result no doubt of human cortical hypertely. There exist what might be termed "empirical revelations," tiny insights into the nature of things through the perception of things in nature. These adapt for the most part to already-existing structures of knowledge. Insightful learning is much more rare, but there are insights into the arrangement of acquired knowledge of abstract relations, occasions when an existing threshold has been surmounted suddenly by a summation series. The Italian philosopher Croce once wrote, "My friends knew far more than I did, but could not see the connection between the things they knew." (1, p. 58).

Such occasions witness the building of a philosophy. By a philosophy here is meant a system of ideas more general than any other. A philosophy is an orienting response system, a kind of doubly-condensed set of knowings, condensed once by the process of abstraction and again by the systematic relating of the abstractions (14, pp. 107ff.). Differences in philosophies are accounted for by culturally-conditioned differences in stimuli. Philosophies are not adopted as such but only as the connectives between otherwise unrelated abstractive sets, the consistency-rules between divergent sets of empirical data. Consistency is the ground for the feeling of security. Philosophies behave in psychological contexts like security systems. The holding of a philosophy is the acquisition of a security system as the goal-object of the need to know. In the ordinary course of relative events, it is followed by need-reduction.

Philosophy is an activity, not a static set of beliefs. When it functions implicitly as the directive of a set of behavior-patterns, it is an orienting response. It is the name for the consistency which enables us to speak of a set of compatible behavior-patterns as a system. Each human individual knows only a part of what is known, due to the specialization compelled by the immensity of knowledge. The security system, then, involves the human individual with others. Such association requires the employment of tools and signs, in short of artifacts.

Philosophies are associated with artifacts when both are incorporated in an institution. The institution furnishes the housing for the security system. The artifacts are selected or devised in terms of their usefulness in the maintenance of the philosophy. Thus for example the Constitution of the United States is kept under glass in the service of the established philosophy of liberalism. Institutions bring together artifacts, philosophies, human individuals and customs (habitual behavior) in a single organization.

The larger the structure the more determinate of the individual in whom it is imbedded. A system of philosophy is the most determinative, but its effects are not always obvious, particularly if it has been around for so long that questioning it would seem more like a challenge to common sense. Adaptation to security systems makes of them retention schemata. A retention schema is a philosophy held for its security. Every individual maintains two such schemata: a public one and a private one. The public retention schema is that security system which the individual holds in common with his fellows in a particular culture. The private retention schema is one that he holds alone as a result of his own peculiar experience. To a certain extent the individual selects his schemata, but thereafter the schemata determine him.

The discrete elements of retention schemata are the naturally occurring relations which were the original content of the input into the central nervous system. How do such relations act as stimuli? How do they get the individual moving? Again, how do abstract relations act as the stimuli to cue functions? How do they help in the choice of channels through which the arousal function operates? There is an interval between the sensory event and the reduction of the need to know. Goal-directed here means anticipated in terms of need-reductions. Naturally occurring relations not only have to be abstracted, they also have to be assimilated. As with drug addiction, there is a stage between injection and the beneficial feelings which result from it (3, p. 203). In adaptive knowing, an intermediate stage exists between learning and the feeling of wisdom, or of having found the secret.

In the adaptive phase, behavior is compounded. Artifacts in effect make such compounding possible. For instance tools are employed to build more complex and powerful tools which could not otherwise have been constructed. Power tools are necessary if we are to have the kind of tools which make automation possible. Again, signs are employed for the discovery of other signs which could not have been located logically without the use of the first set. For instance it is by means of mathematical systems that other mathematical systems are sometimes discovered. Without Euclidean geometry, it is doubtful whether non-Euclidean geometry would ever have been found. Number theory was made possible by the prior discovery of numbers. Complex numbers could not have been used before the integers were known.

The maintenance of a security system inevitably brings with it sign-behavior. A single proposition can be imprinted without signs. The burned child does not have to verbalize his shunning of the fire. The complex interrelations of a security system cannot be represented without signs. The chief sign system is of course a colloquial language. It must be remembered in this connection that all words are names; not only names for particular concrete objects, such as 'Charlie Chaplin' or 'Paris' but also names for general abstract objects, such as 'triangle' or 'equality.' The words of a language are themselves abstract general objects represented by particular concrete objects in the same way that a class is represented by its members. For instance, an abstract object which is defined by any three points not on a line may be represented by any one of the following signs: 'triangle,' 'das dreieck,' 'triangolo,' 'trigonum.' (The material carriers of the sign are themselves particular concrete objects: physical marks on paper, or physical sound vibrations.) The words put together in sentences represent more complex signs, which refer to material objects or events.

Language is a form of adaptive behavior; objects of all kinds exist and some method had to be devised for dealing with them if they were to be manipulated to satisfy the needs. For the individual, thought concerning objects is facilitated by language, and such thought is necessary in dealing with them. The purpose of language is cooperative behavior. But as the most complex of all compound conditioned stimuli, language runs the spectrum from simple types of self-stimulation to social organization. Socially, communication concerning the artifacts as an aid in dealing with them is also made possible by language.

Sign-behavior is the recognition that there are types of situations calling out the behavior, situations separated in space and time but bearing marked resemblances, so that behavior adapted to one situation of a particular type could well be repeated in dealing with another situation of the same type. The most familiar of these resemblances occurs in the phenomenon of communication. Social conditioning by means of individual sign-behavior is one variety of adaptive knowing. Further adaptation results in the construction of artifacts essential to sign-behavior, artifacts for sign-recording and sign-storing: typewriters, libraries, etc.

INHIBITION

In general, human behavior can be accounted for by assuming that the individual is usually engaged in acting out the consequences of a security system within the allowable limits as determined by the immediate environment. The human individual in cooperation with his fellows builds such artifacts that he becomes a slave of the machine, and can no longer alter the S-R cycle, that is to say, no longer struggle. Fixture is a living death.

As we should expect from such behavior, there gradually is established the effects of what Hull has called "reactive inhibition" (4, p. 278). A kind of side-effect of such actions is the accumulation of very small tendencies toward their cessation, which resemble the effect of fatigue. The effect is the same as it would be were artifacts inducing the reflex described by Pavlov as conditioned inhibition (8, pp. 77ff.). As reactive inhibition continues to operate, there is a feedback falling-off of adherence to the security system, and a kind of stereotyped behavior results. Individuals continue to believe because they have always believed, and they continue to act accordingly because they are accustomed to acting accordingly.

It should be recalled here, however, that the acceptance of a security system reduces the need to know. As adherence to it fades, belief in it fades also; but the security system is still present, blocking all new efforts to drive toward fresh satisfactions of the need and thus constituting a frustration. The security system exists, and so do the stereotyped responses; but, underneath, the need to know continues to exert pressure.

As the adherence to a security system drops, the awareness of ignorance rises; and such ignorance, like doubt, is painful. There are reinforcing effects of need-arousal; the fear of ignorance is a necessary consequence of the evaporation of belief.

An artificial method of bringing about the restoration of knowing has been discovered. The contemporary philosophy of ordinary language is based upon the attempt to circumvent the blocking of inquiry by means of a temporary displacement. If the fundamental response-system of a philosophy is deeply imbedded in the language, then it must be recovered before its limitations can be dissipated. The requirements of effective communication can be met by preparing an inspection of knowing, and the degree of distortion that language entails subsequently recognized. Only in this way can there be a successful resumption of inquiry as a method of reducing the need to know. Such a procedure has the support which the disparity between any response-system and the corresponding environment it purports to represent must always constitute.

Thus we come to a step which can be described as advanced

extinction, the extinction of the drive under the influence of habit and the absence of need-reduction. The response is called out without the concomitant of the usual need-reduction, thus extinguishing the response. Extinction leads to deterioration; there is adaptation to failures in need-reduction also. To the extent to which the drives are extinguished, the animal deteriorates. Alerting responses go unattended, and tonus is lost. Failures in need-reduction mean failures in feedback replenishment, and finally even resistance to inquiry.

The drive of curiosity has a facilitative effect upon learning, but we have seen strong inhibitory forces at work also. And there are others. First of all, instinctual behavior patterns are blocks to learning. What is done on instinct: suckling a child, hunting, sheltering from the weather, in themselves offer no opportunity for novelty, even though novel ways of doing them have been found: nursing bottles, slaughter houses, modern architecture. Novelty in these cases would mean finding substitutions for the instinct.

Further, we have noted that belief constitutes the holding of knowledge. We have noted also that the certainty of knowledge shuts off learning. The belief in a system of ideas stops the craving for knowledge, curiosity is temporarily abated. The individual settles down to the required behavior, and his behavior in turn reinforces belief in the system of ideas.

But arresting learning before the goal of complete knowledge has been attained has its effects also. Knowing is never fully satisfied, there being always more to be known than is known; and security is never wholly attained. Thus whether the higher nervous activity leading to action has as its goal knowing or being, it is sure to fall somewhat short. Even actions aimed at conformity with approximations must result in performances partially incorrect. The stated ideals, absolute or statistical, are not carried out; and the degree of failure will have its effect in the altered stimulation of the subject. A retrograde feedback cycle will have begun.

Thus there takes place a consequent alienation and a subsequent readjustment by means of false knowledge. Man has never become altogether reconciled to the hard facts of his existence, but he does have to exist. And so he has been compelled to invent systems of ideas containing limited truths to account for widespread phenomena.

There is one dodge taken by the organism which ought to be mentioned here chiefly because it is so common an occurrence. When a security system is threatened it is either abandoned (a phenomenon which we have been studying) or adherence to it desperately increased. Desperate adherence is easier to accomplish with compact systems. Now a compact system is a limited system, one whose limits have been demonstrated. When inquiry is inhibited by limited knowledge, the knowledge is assumed to be total knowledge. Accepting a security system as limited means acting from it as absolute. But absolute knowledge calls for absolute action, uncompromising action. The idealist is thus one who wishes to apply a limited philosophy in a merciless fashion. The more absolute the belief in the security system, the more unmitigated the behavior to which it leads. Thus the activity of resistance to reactivating the cycle of inquiry may take destructive forms.

A good example of the absolute application of limited security systems is to be found in the behavior which follows when a primary drive is substituted for a secondary, as when food or drink is substituted for knowledge or security, when a means-by-which is substituted for an end-for-which. The self-punishment entailed in such a substitution is not sufficient to eliminate from the individual's repertory the proper responses. It is characteristic of secondary drives that punishment does not lead to a reduction in the number of responses but may instead act as a reinforcement. Insufficient inquiry is what prevents the martyr from knowing that he died for a limited system.

OSCILLATION

The habit of responding to a CCS is one involving continual change. We introduce another dimension of response when we introduce into the CCS an element strengthened or missing. This is the situation with many artifacts where the degree of complexity can be varied by varying the consistency or completeness. Consider for example a book in which the meaning is obscure, or one in which the sentences carry a double meaning.

The probability of reaction means that inquiry must be kept open and the individual sensitive to changes. There is an advanced mechanism for this: the habit of seeking need-satisfactions which persists after satiation. Need-reduction does not always terminate the drive, it terminates only the consummatory response. The habit of approach-and-exploration may continue for some time after the consummatory response has ended.

Such a held-over drive does not come to an end suddenly. The oscillation of a reactive potential (4, p. 393) is what is described here as the hysteresis effect of subsidence. It approaches zero as a limit but never reaches zero in the live individual. Life is action, and so long as there is life there is motion. A kind of random scanning procedure is typical of the inert animal under conditions of arousal.

Oscillation is, one might say, the very model of adaptive behavior. The human individual must learn how to avoid deprivation and satiation, and this involves crossing the border into each condition one at a time. Deprivation is so to speak a starting-condition. But there are constraining excesses, too, as with the man who does not want to know the news when it is bad or the little boy who was given a huge treatise because he said he wanted to know about frogs and who then exclaimed, "There is more in this book about frogs than I want to know." The practice of combining sense impressions in order to make the necessary adjustments is the only way in which the individual can bring himself into conformity with the exigencies of the environment sufficiently to make his own survival possible; and the same mechanism can be turned into preparing the proper reception for abstract relations to become knowledge. Who can say in advance what we shall have to know? Unique particulars so often have proved to be members of classes and abstract objects so often have proved to be names for classes having members. Such surprises must be met with rolling adjustments.

One familiar way in which inhibition leads to oscillation is through the transfer of training by which old knowledge inhibits learning and so forces curiosity into other channels. There is for instance the phenomenon of play, and the boredom of those who "have nothing to do." Play is a variant of displacement activity. Extremes of displacement range all the way from "creation": the exaggeration of pathological claims of discovery, to the persecution of non-believers. There is an effort to defend a security system at all costs when it is no longer possible to accept it on rational or factual grounds; the romantic attachment to lost causes and impossible ideals.

Thus there are in the individual with respect to his immediate environment all sorts and grades of responses taking place simultaneously. Some are rising, others are falling; some decisively stimulating to effectors, others are so faint they barely manage collectively to keep up the alertness to decisive stimuli. The individual in his response is a complex of statistical averagings, a sensitive set of receptors and recall mechanisms played upon by the relative frequency of similar external events. Within this complex there is room for a considerable degree of self-determination, and this is made possible by the elaborate hook-up of mediating processes which prevent the individual from being involved in the sort of direct stimulus-response behavior to which the sub-human animals are almost exclusively confined. Oscillation is evocation.

RESPONSE EVOCATION

The accumulation of fatigue of inquiry has the effect that the full evocation of response can never be restored. The artifact has been too well apprehended, the security system exhausted of its consequences. The reaction threshold rises to the full height of the CCS, and no response is made other than the aforementioned low-grade arousal. The amplitude of stimulus necessary to evoke a response is missing, and latency takes over; improbability of response replaces probability.

Presumably, the object of knowledge is always present, but in most advanced adult cases it does not act tropistically upon the human individual. Adaptive knowing belongs essentially to the past. Normally, the average adult lapses into a latency with respect to the acquisition of knowledge. The need has been all extinguished, and its satisfaction, which was gained earlier, accepted. In the instance of knowledge, the goal is reached and the object consumed but not destroyed. Unlike water or food, the knowledge remains intact after it has been assimilated. Thus it acts to preserve the extinction and to prevent a fresh arousal of the drive.

Now it so happens that periodic reactivation of the drive is essential to mental health. After rest and recovery, a new approach to the CCS will evoke a new response. The need is not merely to know but to increase knowledge. The craving is recurrent. The recovery is sometimes spontaneous (4, p. 270); extinction was, after all, only a special case of inhibition (8, p. 60). But there is another side to the problem. Despite the amount of response reserve which may have accumulated and the consequent generalization of the respondent, the resumption of inquiry encounters obstacles, such as the intractable material objects which resist alteration or the disclosures of false knowledge.

The conditioned response is weakened through extinction, not destroyed; it recovers with rest. Now in the case of knowing, of activation and rest in the reaction to a security system, other processes are going on, notably rest and recovery of inquiry. Eventually, the stability evinced by the imprinting of a security system is misleading when it appears permanent; for it is a period also when inquiry is being restored. Capacities in and of themselves call out special needs. An athlete needs to exercise, an intellectual to work out abstract problems or to make discoveries. Similarly, the ability to think calls out the need to know; and a strong hold on existence calls out the need to (continue to) be.

But still, on behavioristic principles, a tropistic stimulus is required to trigger the renewal of inquiry. It is not possible to resist the impact of an internal breakdown of the security system (as with the revelation of contradictions in it) or the challenge of some other security system supported by stronger evidence.

It is so easy to forget that the direction of neurophysiology and most of psychology since the work of Pavlov has been to the study of the cortex as the mediating mechanism dealing with the complex set of relations between the animal and the external world. It is clear, even in the case of man, that the animal does not change the world nearly so much as the world changes the animal. More specifically, responses are often modified progressively in order to discover which ones will produce the desired alterations in the artifacts. The results of repeated stimulation, each time with novelty and increasing complexity, are that the animal advances in capacity of responses and also in external accomplishments—in artifacts. The two kinds of artifacts become extremely complex as the result of the continuity of human behavior. Signs complicate into languages and knowledge systems. Tools complicate into capital cities—civilizations. It is no mere coincidence that those societies which have produced the greatest philosophies were those with the most elaborate mythologies: chiefly Greek and German but also Indian.

The independent individual is one of the social group needs. The dependent individual is one who needs the social groups. The independent individual holds a philosophy as such. The dependent individual holds his philosophy from a social group.

But the culmination of adaptive behavior is in cooperative activity, cooperation to eliminate ignorance or to avoid destruction. In man the behavior necessary to gather information and to survive are combined in cooperative efforts, making possible group reductions of the primary animal needs and of the secondary human needs: economic and agricultural opportunities for food, marriage and family opportunities for sex, military opportunities for defense and avoidance, scientific opportunities for knowing, religious opportunities for surviving. Thus being is doing and knowing no less so, whatever subordinate forms they may take.

And knowing, in the last analysis, is doing. Activity is initiated at the choice point just as clearly as it is when the choice point is a cue in a maze for a rat. There is more in the world than is known, and that is why the activity of knowing is a movement toward the encroachment on being.

Chapter 12

ADAPTIVE DOING

WE TAKE UP NOW the problem of doing, beginning where we left it in Chapter VII, namely, with the activity of construction. In Chapter VII we saw how the need to do is reduced. Here we shall study the consequences of the reduction of the need to do and its effects upon the individual, having in mind only theories of pure doing, apart from all practical applications.

PRATTOTAXIC BEHAVIOR

By 'adaptive doing' is meant the special ways in which man sets about obtaining the reduction of his need for making. 'Doing' means being active in relation to some material object. It means further establishing contact with a material object through its alteration. By means of the will there has been a translation of decisions into actions. Also, as in the case of adaptive knowing, being goal-directed here means being aware of object potentials or anticipating, however dimly, expected need-reductions. Contact is now interpreted objectively, the alteration in material objects is to be undertaken not using the self as tool but constructing other tools specifically for the purpose.

With man as with the other animals there is the predicament of an adaptive animal in a changing world. Adaptation for the other animals can be reckoned only in evolutionary epochs, whereas adaptation in man is a matter of civilization and therefore of the order of thousands and perhaps even merely of hundreds of years. Changes in time and space have stimulated the human animal to look for unchanging, permanent things.

One of these is the type of resisting material objects to which the need to do has been adapted.

Man reacts to the world in accordance with what he does in the world, and in accordance with what he does in the world his reactions to the world also change. The alterations he effects in artifacts transform the material object into a compound conditioned stimulus (the CCS), and the CCS as itself a stimulus-emitter effects alterations in him. Occupational diseases exemplify aberrations so produced by marking the failure of his adjustment to the novel elements he himself has brought about in his environment. He is strongly object-oriented and object-identified, dependent upon the object for his meaning. He is altered by it as himself a dependent variable.

The individual is under the necessity of making the requisite adjustments to meet the new set of conditions thus imposed upon him. He has to learn how to live with—to get along with, so to speak—the new and increasingly complex artifactual society which he has helped to bring about without anticipating exactly what sort of environment it would provide for him. At the same time, the old need to do remains and must be reduced, the ancient Adam coping with the situation as he finds it outside the Garden of Eden. An equilibrium established under these circumstances looks like a remote and monumental achievement. Indeed an equilibrium established under any circumstances which manage to include the aggressive aspect of the need to do seems difficult.

Thus we are here obliged to study the effects of prattotaxic behavior upon the individual. As in the instance of adaptive knowing, these effects may be divided into stages constituting a later sequence following reinforcement, namely generalization, motivation, inhibition, oscillation and response evocation.

GENERALIZATION

First, it will be necessary to consider adaptive doing in its relation to adaptive knowing.

Adaptive doing is derived from adaptive knowing but differs from it in the following respects:

(1) Adaptive doing is an extension of adaptive knowing; (2)

adaptive doing produces in its turn new conditions to be known; (3) adaptive doing verifies (to some extent) the truth of the content of adaptive knowing.

(1) Action in so far as it is not entirely random is a general proposition. Not all that is known is done. Many things can be known at the same time even if not consciously, but only one thing can be done at a time. What is done therefore is a selection of what is known. But not all that is done is known, either, not at any rate so long as we are not entirely deliberate in our actions. There is an element in every action which had been unplanned and of which we are not entirely aware. Thus knowing and doing overlap. But for the most part doing follows from knowing as a consequence. What we know we tend to put into practice if we can.

(2) The consequences of knowing are doing. The consequences of doing are new areas to be known. An individual performs an action. But what does he know in advance of its consequences? If he has accomplished a construction, how will it fit into the world of other constructions? What effects will it have on its maker? What will it lead to of itself, simply in virtue of the fact that every new existing thing has to crowd out a place for itself and in so doing have effects upon other things? If what the individual has accomplished is a destruction, does this too not leave him in ignorance of its effects? What will be the results of the gap it has left? What will move in to take its place? What will be the effect on the individual that his need has been reduced by a destructive action? New actions, then new areas of ignorance. No finite batch of experience is self-contained. The object of any experience is more experience in terms of which the earlier and more limited experience can be rendered intelligible. All overt behavior accounts for new conditions into which there have to be new inquiries conducted.

(3) In adaptive knowing we are dealing with tentative propositions, probative truths. The content of adaptive knowing includes general propositions. In addition to containing no contradictions, a proposition must be shown to be capable of corresponding with at least one exemplification. Pragmatic evidence does not prove the truth of a statement but does support it. There are

no empirical proofs at all but there are empirical indications. Practice is capable of offering concrete material confirmation of the truth of propositions developed in the course of adaptive knowing. The death of a man does not prove the truth of the statement that 'all men are mortal' but it certainly is a tiny step in that direction. Degree of belief tends to be strengthened by the evidence of action. The effects carried out which the individual witnesses is one degree stronger, but the actions which when carried out exercise effects upon him are considerably stronger still. We tend to believe more firmly what we feel than merely what we have learned indirectly.

Adaptive doing derives from adaptive knowing but enjoys an autonomy in its own terms. The making of objects, like any other kind of being, can also be generalized. The generalization of adaptive doing is the mass production of artifacts, the designing of methods of production which insure the endless repetition of reproduction. Mass production introduces a novel element at its very inception. This is the actualization of the archetype, the ideal in a material object. In industrial mass production terminology it is known as the "pilot model." After that, the actual examples follow the pilot model as the member approximates its class. The ideal automobile is a logical possibility, and it is exemplified in the pilot model of the automobile which in turn is exemplified by automobiles which reproduce its form. There are of course as many pilot models as there are newly designed automobiles, so that the actual pilot model stands to the ideal pilot model as the automobile manufactured by the belt line method stands to the pilot model. There is one difference: the pilot models differ among themselves more sharply than do the manufactured automobiles.

The shifts just described and illustrated show the pliability and capacity for adjustment inherent in the methods of production peculiar to the generalization of adaptive doing. 'Generalization' here means, then, the establishment of a class actually exemplified by first constructing the model of a class which it is proposed to bring into existence, retaining only the method and neither the model nor its copies. This is the inner meaning of the method of generalization in adaptive doing, that a technique has been invented for production which is itself capable of endless revision.

Mass production is of course not the only kind of generalization of adaptive doing. Another prototypic form is the generalization of experience through the extension of areas of experience. As we have noted in a previous chapter (Chapter 8), from the mesocosm, the world of the average size available to the unaided human senses, man has extended his experience into the microcosm, the world of the very small, and the macrocosm, the world of the very large. It is not possible to "go" to any part of the microcosm but it is being demonstrated currently that it is possible to visit certain small areas of the macrocosm, possibly for example the other planets in the solar system. Experience can be generalized in both directions, however, by means of instruments to extend the senses or to obtain information which can then be translated into the terms of ordinary sense experience.

For every new advance in technology, whether in the mass production of marketable products or in the construction of orbiting satellites, there is a price in human adjustment to be exacted. Something in the behavior which is evoked as response will have to be changed to meet the new knowledge and the new conditions brought about by the new activity. For physical technologies whether in aid of practical benefits or of scientific theory are planned actions and call out in the human individual the appropriate plasticity of behavior to deal with it.

MOTIVATION

In connection with the generalization of the need to do we must consider the thesis of the generalized drive. It has been argued earlier that the generalized drive is one of aggression, the drive to dominate the environment. This can take constructive or destructive expression. Thus a skyscraper or a battle is equally an expression of the generalized drive of aggression and results in its need-reduction. Thus as we have noted the need to do is the archetypal variety of the generalized drive. Animal making serves animal survival through need-reduction. In some cases in addition to feeding and breeding procedures there is also the factor of concealment from predators. The human individual makes the same set of responses to his environment. He, too, has need-reductions which can be effected by means of adaptive making, including in all probability the refined human version of concealment from predators. We shall note in the next chapter that this generalized drive of aggression can be interpreted as having for its goal-object the survival of the individual, so that adaptive being becomes especially significant. But here we shall adopt the first interpretation and consider prattotaxic behavior primary.

We have laid down the principle that all adaptive behavior is multiply motivated. Motives are seldom atomic, and the motives calling out prattotaxic behavior of the advanced adaptive variety in which the needs are anticipated are no doubt mixed. The resultant plasticity of behavior is responsible for some important differences as we shall presently note.

The essence of adaptive doing is planned construction or destruction. But in adaptive doing the response can be so determined that it takes more subtle forms than those evoked by the need to do in its primitive form. Men acquire the ability to respond to a certain class of stimuli in a way which has had to be learned. The physical posture required by a culture is pervasive and fundamental. Thus the preparatory responses shape the individual in many ways, from the physiological to the psychological. Alertness is primitive (2, p. 339). Now, just as we saw skills serve the preparatory response of the need to do, so originative talent serves the plastic requirements of adaptive doing. Originality is ultra-adaptiveness, it is that capacity for following closely the changes in the world. Not the skill of the pianist but that of the inventor of new musical instruments, not the skill of the airplane pilot but that of the aeronautical engineer.

Complicated forms of adaptive doing are to be seen in the phenomena of possessiveness and acquisitiveness. These are in man the development of territorial behavior which confines activity to a particular area and a particular number of material objects, including aggressive behavior toward other individuals who encroach upon the area. Property rights mean to an individual that he has made some material object his own and subsequently behaves accordingly. He has become the collector of real property, of power over men, up to absolute monarchy with its power of life and death, or it may be of money, of women, or of works of art. The generalized stimulus here would be the aggrandizement of the ego, and it would be the response to the challenge constituted by the existence of a material world—or of those parts of that world—with which the individual had not been in forceful relation. Material objects unassaulted present a certain aspect of potential resistance which is felt as an affront by the aggressive animal. It must be met like any other challenge—with force.

The prattotaxic response to the stimulus of independent material objects is to alter them in some way and thus to indicate possession: "I have made this mine, or at least I have made it what it is." The constructive side of prattotaxic behavior is to make over some material object in a form which facilitates need-reduction. The result is an artifact and adaptive doing the activity of dealing continuously with artifacts in a way more prolonged than is usual in meeting the need-reductions of the primary needs. Thus for example the fine arts are the highest expression of human making, the grandest variety of need-reduction of the need to do, although as we shall note in the next chapter the contents of the work of art serves to reduce the need to be. The construction may be a building, it may be the planning of a city, or it may be an industrial empire. The destructive side is equally effective and may be an individual fight with an opponent, a murder or participation in a war. The destruction of material objects (including human persons) is equally need-reducing so far as adaptive doing is concerned.

Physiologically, the musculature has been employed in the interests of the organism's individual self. Territorial behavior in excess of primary needs represents an over-response to stimuli resulting in alteration of the environment and the reduction of specifically individual ego-needs. A man is able to eat only so much bread at a single meal, but it satisfies a quite different hunger when he is able to corner the wheat market. The activity of construction is one which receives its rewards in quiet contemplation of achievement. The activity of destruction is more intense and immediate. Those who have been in battle often tell us that with the single exception of sexual intercourse there is no other emotion as strong.

One of the unspoken but powerful elements of motivation in prattotaxic behavior is that of survival. We have often noted that each of the needs supports the others, but the relationship in some cases goes further than that. We shall see in the next chapter that the primary drive of aggression is also to insure persistence. When the individual seeks the aggrandizement of his ego through territorial behavor, by means of possessiveness or acquisitiveness, this too is an effort at survival. From the activity in response to the need to be it has been learned by the individual that size bears some relation at least to persistence: the largest objects seem to be those which last the longest. Thus material possessions by increasing the individual's physical size, as he does when he extends it over other material objects, seems also to indicate a longer life for him. And even if he cannot live himself it may be that he will 'live' in some other form, if only by writing his name on the things he has made or put together. This holds even for the destructive drive, for the 'scourge' wishes also to be remembered as the scourge that he was. A conqueror would not otherwise make a pyramid of the skulls of the conquered.

Thus contemporary prestige in strict terms of ego-expansion based on essential connections with material objects territorially bound is the qualitative goal-object of adaptive doing. Where being known as wise (adaptive knowing) or holy (adaptive being) is appropriate for other needs, being known as rich or powerful, as the multi-millionaire is rich and the statesman powerful, is appropriate for adaptive doing. And those last two states constitute the aims of the largest class of human individuals in most societies at most times and places, even though perhaps not all.

There are areas of adaptive doing not characterized by ego-expansion. Like the detached search for knowledge for its own sake, or like dedication to ultimate being, adaptive doing has its counterpart. In the scientific method of investigation, the hypothetico-experimental method, the three human capacities, which are for thought, feeling and action, are united now for the first time in the external world where they appear as mathematics, instruments and experiments respectively. Thus the scientific method externalizes as it completes the human effort to know and be through doing.

The search for reliable knowledge has but lately emerged from the earlier and more primitive search for practical knowledge. That science has replaced technology means only that man has discovered a way in which to broaden his powers by establishing first the principles from which a practice can be derived. Science has its technology, but a technology without science, as was the case before the seventeenth century, is far more limited. Knowledge cultivated for its practical benefits continues of course to exist and to flourish. And so, as we should expect, the first rewards and reinforcements of abstract knowledge are to be derived from its practical side-effects. Reliable knowledge is not any the less pure, *i.e.*, theoretical, because some useful applications have been found for it and put into practice.

INHIBITION

There exist well-defined limits to ego-expansion. They are necessitated by the existence of the needs of other egos. Individuals must be protected from harming each other, if only in the interest of partially meeting individual needs. Hence the existence of regulations of all sorts, of brakes to freedom of action, in a word, of governments.

A government is a security system designed for relative security within the limits of action absolutes. That is to say, it guarantees relative security (rather than ultimate security as in religion), and it provides for action by restricting action within certain allowable limits. The allowable limits are not those of the total environment, non-human as well as human, but only those of the human environment, the social milieu with its cities and cultural conditions. The acceptance of government by means of promised obedience to its laws involves the surrender of action outside the domain of legal permissiveness. Action is narrowed and thus deepened and behavior altered to some extent at least in the direction of the stereotyped variety. The inclination of action which is prevented from spreading is to repeat. Action is necessary, and if it cannot be changed, cannot be allowed to seek new channels, then it merely grooves the old ones over again.

In this way, regulation inhibits construction. Or it insures that all new constructions shall be copies of established types of construction. It seeks to conserve itself through convention. Thus origination is seen as a threat to the established order and hence to the more conservative individuals. The political revolutionary is the strongest threat, but it is a challenge which carries over into literature and the arts. Violence in the arts is curbed by means of an emphasis on style. Thus ritual is introduced into art in order to channel destructive activity, as in the Spanish bullfight. But all art inhibits action by sublating it. It is usually the case that the innovator and the *avant-garde* artist is considered if not dangerous at least definitely unsafe. Similarity reinforces, difference decomposes. The 'ought' is dictated by the 'is' interpreted as the 'always was.'

The inhibition of action does not dissipate the energy which has been made available but preserves it in the physiological circuits. Emotions may be understood as the result of inhibited efferent discharges reverberating through the neurophysiological circuit. Blocked off from access to the stimulating object, the impulses turn inward as it were and seek to expend themselves in cyclical motion. The sensitivity of the diffuse excitatory system insures that the extended involvement of the re-entrant circuit under such forces as were intended to activate skeletal muscles shall be destructive in their effects. If the channels to overt action are never opened, the destructive effects of this particular set of impulses are final. But if now suddenly the channels are opened the build-up within the circuits makes it probable that the consequent behavior will be violent and irrational.

There is no standing still with respect to the forms of action. When forward progress is inhibited, retrogression takes its place. The ideal is the behavior of ancestors, or, more accurately, the supposed behavior of ancestors so far as it can be reconstructed from the remaining records. The 'age of chivalry,' the age 'when knighthood was in flower,' but minus the ignorance, the filth, the disease, and, of course, minus the brevity of the life expectancy. At the same time, the energy which provided for the advance, an energy always in excess of that required for maintenance, is not available for retrogression. Conservatism in cultural forms always lack punch; there is no novelty to furnish excitement, no unexpectedness to insure fresh breezes. And the result is a slowing down, an arresting of the very forces that make the difference between mere existence and human life.

The forward movement of progress and novelty, however, has its own limitations. What are foreshadowed by cultural changes are not the advantages of a new order and not indeed an order at all but a necessary interval of intervening chaos and confusion. Change brings with it, temporarily at least, disorder. And so there is seen a threat to all order. The individual at this stage cries for government or death; what he finds himself unable to withstand are the strains of uncertainty that a threatened total disorder brings with it. Such an atmosphere is destructively disorganizing. Irrational behavior can result, the randomized action which results from blind impulse, the urge to do anything rather than nothing, to hurl oneself at any target rather than remain without a well-defined aim.

Thus, irrational behavior may find the channel of destruction more suitable than construction. The alteration of the material object in ways designed to effect a reduction of the need to do in the phase of adaptive behavior is more apt to be destructive than constructive. It requires only emotion, not reason; only blind impulse, not planning; only ungovernable action with outcome unknown rather than action anticipating certain results. The equilibrium provided by established channels of action within the limits of action absolutes is an unstable equilibrium but a necessary one. An uneasy variety of a desirable situation is greatly to be preferred over an easy variety of an undesirable situation. Thus government though far from perfect is necessary, and its authority can be distributed only at an enormous cost to the individual.

OSCILLATION

Where the inhibition has not permanently turned action into

another direction, it tends to restore itself. But the restoration cannot be entirely effective once it has been disturbed and for a while lost. Thus there is set up a movement of oscillation occasioned by an ambivalence in the choice of goal-objects.

> O what a rain of ashes fall on him
> Who sees the new but cannot leave the old

says E. A. Robinson. But a worse rain of ashes falls on him who pursues alternately both the old and the new, interminably oscillating between them. There are of course many other types of oscillation in the adaptive behavior called out by the need to do. Learning how to avoid deprivation and satiation is one, and it often consists in the achievement of a balance by an insistence upon the extremes. An old method of house training dogs consisted in rubbing the dog's nose in his faeces in order to teach him not to defecate in the living room and then by forcibly ejecting him upon the slightest indication that such undesirable behavior was about to be repeated.

The very rhythm of effort aimed at achievement, be it constructive or destructive, calls for oscillation. Sustained effort is not possible at a steady pace. There are well-recognized rest periods in all constructive effort, and even pauses in battle.

One source of oscillation is the result of operant behavior, another the result of increase of information. Behavior with no stimulus present and observable but only the frequency of occurrence is not apt to be as steady and persistent because not as insistently focused. There are definite unobservables existent but although real they are also easily interchanged and thus lend themselves to the oscillation of adaptive behavior. One immortality is like another in this mortal life, and the promise of one type of infinite goal can so easily be substituted for the promise of a different type.

Then, too, increase in information tends to weaken the strength of action. The more an individual knows of both sides of an issue the less he is inclined to take sides, that is to say, to act at all. *Hamlet* is a beautiful example of the paralysis of the will by knowledge. Degree of certainty of conviction is inverse to amount of information. The less an individual knows the stronger are his convictions. Thus, men of action actually cannot afford too much knowledge, and men of knowledge cannot be men of action. To be only 51 per cent sure may be all that the facts will warrant, but it is not enough to justify action. If action is taken on the strength of such evidence, it will tend to turn on and off, and thus exhibit the phenomenon of oscillation.

RESPONSE EVOCATION

The drive of aggression, the drive to dominate the environment, which early in this work we saw as the archetype of the need to do, in adaptive doing is sure to fail. However brilliant its first successes, they are destined to come to an end in the lifetime of some individual. Activity, in so far as it is directed toward achievement, is bound to terminate. Nothing actual lasts forever, and cultures like individuals disappear eventually. Thus from one point of view the doing is wasted.

But adaptation to failure is also an effect. The individual responses to defeat is a reshaping in terms of it. Adaptation to doing eventually resolves itself into a question of the style in which the individual proposes to fail, since fail he will. Thus style becomes life-style and eventually a posture in the face of death. But meanwhile there are adjustments to make to the new factual situation. An appropriate conduct is invented, and habit turns into habituation. Externally the individual makes his efforts and externally they fail, but internally the effects of the failure are felt. Thus the positive challenge and the negative results are forces to which he is compelled to respond and by which he is made. Thus the need to do eventually issues in the need-reduction of being done. It is the same individual who does what he does and who, by means of the effects of the energy which courses through the channels of the re-entrant circuit, is also done.

The recognition of failure which comes to the individual when first his efforts cease is received with something of a shock. If to accomplish something is to be in the framework of adaptive doing, then to give up doing also is to give up being. This the individual cannot acceptably countenance, and so he raises himself for the making of one last supreme effort. The period of latency has been a period of rest. But it is near the end. The reactivation needed for health does not respond with the same degree of muscular reserve. But there is rest and there is recovery to some degree. And there is a certain measure of the renewal of effort.

It is in the last stages of adaptive doing that we can see most clearly the approaching end of the human effort. Adaptive doing consists in behavior called out by the necessity of responding to the feedback from artifacts. The most imperishable form of response consists not in constructions or discoveries but in the development of sets of abstract formulas for the methods of construction and discovery, the necessary techniques, procedures and rules for construction in the arts and sciences, everything from architectural design to musical counterpoint and harmony and the scientific method. This is the way in which the human limitations in so far as they are the limitations of the individual can be transcended: by handing on to a successor surrogate generation the methods of doing which have been learned but insufficiently employed. For art is long and life is brief. The series of individual responses falls off in a curve asymptotic to inaction. It is not that the material object no longer furnishes the resistance necessary to sustain human effort but only that eventually the muscles tire and the will falters. For the individual the adversary has proved too strong, the world too much with him. Mercifully, as Peirce has pointed out (1) in place of failure we have death. The battlefield, like the ruined cathedral, stands longest, a mute witness to the magnificent effort and inevitable failure of human ambitions. Adaptive doing belongs essentially to the present as adaptive knowing belongs to the past, for what is not done now never will be done and whatever is done will have something else in its place. The individual can say and is in fact now prepared to say, in the words of the *Tao Te Ching*, "the best way to do is to be."

Chapter 13

ADAPTIVE BEING

WE TAKE UP NOW the problem of being, beginning where we left it in Chapter V, namely, with the possessing of being. In Chapter V we saw how the need to be is reduced. Here we shall study the consequences of the reduction in the need to be and its effects upon the individual, having in mind only theories of pure being apart from all practical applications.

SOSITAXIC BEHAVIOR

By 'adaptive being' is meant the special ways in which man sets about obtaining the reduction of his need for existence. 'Being' means 'the condition which makes possible interaction with material objects.' Being-as-such refers to the self-identity property, since anything which can affect or be affected must retain its identity. It can readily be seen, therefore, that such a condition is far from dynamic, and its alterations are indeterminate. To be is to have the power to react but not necessarily to react. Admittedly, the same stimuli initiate different reactions, and, conversely, the same reaction may be initiated by different stimuli. What the spectacle of considerable persistence—of the solar system, for instance—means to an individual will vary with his mood and state of physical well-being; his feeling could be one of awe, of fear, or of boredom. Let us suppose that his feeling is one of awe. But this could have come as well from other sources: from the study of nuclear physics, from listening to the music of Bach or from a reading of Plato's philosophy.

With man as with the other animals there is the predicament of an adaptive animal in a changing world. Adaptation for the other animals can be reckoned only in evolutionary epochs, whereas adaptation in man is a matter of civilization and therefore of the order of thousands and perhaps even merely of hundreds of years. Changes in time and space have stimulated the human animal to look for unchanging, permanent things. One of these is the type of persistent material objects, to which the need to be has been adapted.

Man reacts to the world in accordance with what he feels about the world, and in accordance with the feelings he has had his reactions to the world also change. For instance, his reaction to persistent material objects, such as the solar system, is to become aware of himself as a short-range self. Thus, there comes about the phenomenon of sositaxis, and the reaching out beyond the self to a remote goal.

There are difficulties attendant upon this process, however. But need-reduction for the need to be means self-surrender; adaptive being means existing-for-other. Here the need to be runs counter to the primary drives, and psychological adjustment has difficulty in keeping pace with evolutionary development. The human individual has never fully adapted himself to dependence upon the secondary drives. His hope of adjustment, which in his terms means leading a full and satisfactory life of accomplishment, requires the adequation of behavior with such dependence. For the individual at this point chooses to interpret the short-range self as a long-range self, to identify himself as one of the persistent material objects he encounters. He discriminates the condition of being from that condition as a property of material objects.

One tends to think of the effects of permanence in terms of equilibrium. But the summation effects of a series of reactions to permanence can be an adaptive posture of a rigidity maladapted to the exigencies of the short-range self. A permanent whole can be constructed of changing parts, and it is to these parts that the short-range self must adapt. There is, moreover, more than one persistent material object. The conservative effects of adapting the self to one such object is in conflict with the revolutionary effects of the encounter with another such object. The mixed procedures of reinforcement represented by repetition, and of extinction represented by novelty, has elaborate effects upon subsequent behavior. Like the divisions in the studies of adaptive knowing and adaptive doing, these effects may be divided into stages constituting a later sequence following reinforcement, namely, generalization, motivation, inhibition, oscillation and response evocation.

GENERALIZATION

First, it will be necessary to consider adaptive being in its relation to adaptive knowing.

Adaptive being is derived from adaptive knowing but differs from it in the following three respects:

1) Adaptive being is an extension of adaptive knowing; 2) in adaptive being, in addition to having a security system consisting in abstract relations of ideas, the security system itself is attached to a material object by means of its qualities; 3) in adaptive being, the security system is not placed at the service of the individual as it is in adaptive knowing, but instead the individual is placed at the service of the security system.

1) Adaptive knowing is a form of detachment from something in the external world in an effort to extract its permanence for the individual. Adaptive being is a form of attachment to something permanent in the external world in order to share its permanence with the individual. Adaptive knowing is in terms of parts, adaptive being in terms of wholes. We have noted that for adaptive knowing the form of permanence is recurrence; whereas, for adaptive being it is persistence. The need to (continue to) be exists in the case of knowing but is further extended in the case of being. The general structure is equally complex in both drives, but in the drive to continue to be involves the entire organism in a way in which it does not in the drive to know.

2) In terms of orientation, it may be said that human life is based on variation expressed as a function of the independent variable of security, of which knowledge constitutes a subclass. Knowledge consists in the awareness of (and the belief in) recurrences: abstract laws, principles, invariants, which remain over long after the concrete instances which were their members

have passed away and been replaced with new instances. Adaptive knowing abstracts from the material object its logical relations which are imbedded in them; but adaptive being requires also their qualities, and these are not so easily separable. Being (in the sense agreed) consists in the awareness of (and the belief in) persistences: identification with material objects such as mountains, immortal men, the cause of the cosmos conceived as material. To know a principle is mentally to come into contact with something recurrent and so to acquire safety by association; to feel an identification is physically to come into contact with something persistent and so to acquire security by association.

3) Knowledge can be assimilated because it is an abstract property. But survival is not a property which can be assimilated. Knowledge yields a certain measure of security. But ultimate security requires surrender to an absolute security system, a religious commitment, a dedication, complete devotion. The individual cannot persist as an individual but only as a part of some larger whole. The absolute security system is conceived as attached to some huge material object or the whole collection of material objects which is the cosmos. Men have often sacrificed themselves for a cause, but usually by removing the goal from one of security to one of ultimate security. The knowledge remains, but transformed in the service of ultimate security.

Adaptive being is derived also from adaptive doing but differs from it in the following three respects:

1) Adaptive being is an extension of adaptive doing; 2) the positive version of the avoidance of pain becomes the activity of conversion by means of pain; 3) in adaptive doing the individual seeks to remake the environment, whereas here he seeks merely to accept it.

1) We have noted in Chapter III the model of the servo-mechanism in which there is a feedback from the goal—more specifically, to the animal from the artifact. But when the goal is a material object remote in space or time, or a conceptual sign representing absent objects, the situation is somewhat different. The human individual reacts by representing in a nearby object an artifact which is itself the sign of his goal-object. He

constructs a ritual archetype of behavior around a material symbol of his far-away need-reductions.

2) If the human need to be is a positive development of the animal need to avoid pain, then a regression of the positive need would mean a return of the negative one. The avoidance of pain of this sort, which is anguish, takes the form of an active defense of the system of being, a "defense of the faith": the spread of religion by means of frustration and aggression, strict adherence, the punishment of all deviations, and the demand for conversion by means of the sword. When there occurs no alteration of the information available within the re-entrant circuit with respect to the reduction of the need, then the drive retrogresses.

3) Here for the first time man has stopped trying to remake his environment and is simply trying to surrender to it. He is like a disorganized soldier in a defeated army who is trying to find the most disciplined arm of the enemy to surrender to because he does not wish to be destroyed and is looking for someone who will accept his surrender honorably and preserve his safety. He wishes to find the greatest power over things-as-they-are and then to identify himself with it to the greatest extent possible.

MOTIVATION

In connection with generalization of the need to be, we must consider again the thesis of the generalized drive. It has been argued that the animal has only one drive, which is to escape from pain, manifested by arousal (1, pp. 158-59, 170-71). Needs are painful: there are thirst-pains, hunger-pains, for instance, but the single motivation for all of them is avoidance. It should not be too surprising, then, that each separate action is a result of mixed or multiple motivation, even though goal-directed here means anticipated in terms of some one expected need-reduction. Since the greatest threat to the organism is death, the strongest drive to the animal is to avoid death and so to continue to be. It is further supposed that the generalized drive is differentiated by cue functions, so that for instance, fear or sexual desire could be the response of the aroused animal depending entirely on what stimulated the arousal reaction. Thus, the drive for ultimate security which dominates the human individual is the generalized drive to which all others are subservient.

This thesis is accepted here, with certain reservations. It will be assumed that the characteristic performance of the human individual can be explained on the basis of sositaxic behavior alone. However, the activity elicited by the separate and distinguishable cues is markedly differentiated. The loading of the circuits which results from the stimulation of objects which can be eaten changes the object in ways which are so specific as contrasted, say, with the stimulation from objects which can be mated (other animals of the same species), that the turn away from similarity of drive manifestation indicates that sositaxic behavior is only a class name, the name of a class having members whose particular properties are in some ways crucial.

Sositaxic behavior considered as the response of a generalized drive would require also a generalized stimulus. The qualities of the external world are part of the input into the sensory system which concerns us here. The tropistic object attracts the feelings of the individual in adaptive being rather than his curiosity, as in adaptive knowing. The tropism in such a case could be furnished by the world-quality, a quality which emerges from the commonalty of parts in the whole, that everything in the world is equally part of the world. It has two aspects, which can be designated respectively goodness and beauty. Goodness is the quality between wholes, the quality of completeness, whereby everything in the world reflects the quality of belonging together. Beauty is the quality between parts, the quality of consistency, whereby everything in the world has something of the quality of the whole cosmos.

The sositaxic response to the stimulus of goodness is the moral code, that ethical system which is adopted by a society in order to bring it into the behavior of its participating individuals. By moral behavior is meant the conduct toward confronted objects, in consideration of all other objects. The moral quality is the quality of completeness. A distinction must be recognized here between the code professed and the one practiced. The code professed is the inherited code, while the code practiced is of course the believed code because it is the code tied into the accepted theory of reality.

The sositaxic response to the stimulus of beauty is the work of art. By aesthetic behavior is meant the sensitivity to confronted objects, in consideration of their perfection. The aesthetic quality is the quality of consistency. Art is an effort to deepen feeling as another way of understanding the sources of being, self-conditioning by means of symbolic artifacts making possible a deeper penetration of the external world.

Parenthetically, it should not be too surprising to find that there is in every religion a moral code and a set of aesthetic objects. Both have their role to play in adaptive being as surrogate expressions of the need for far-away objects. The need for them exists, and if the individual is to survive there must be some organized form of need-reduction. Thus through special entities and processes—works of art as objects and moral acts as events—is symbolized that wide sweep of the immensity of existence which otherwise lies beyond individual reach.

Neurophysiologically speaking, the need to be, then, will be considered here simply arousal raised to the highest pitch of intensity of which the human individual is capable, against a cortical background of continual sensory stimulation. Organisms are plastic objects which can maintain themselves only by constantly interacting with the environment. Thus the expenditure of energy is a necessity, and the singly-motivated drive only another description of it. The power of the drive can be seen dramatically in its pathological manifestations. Optimism and pessimism are characteristic drive-states, euphoria and depression exaggerations of the same. The manic wishes to live at the top of his voice, the depressive to die. Sositaxic behavior is the life of the organism demanding its place in the universe, and willing to sacrifice for that purpose all petty lesser aims and goals. The need to be may be so strong that it cancels all lesser specific drives, such as the drive for economic security or for group approval, even the drive for power; and sometimes reaches as far as the powerful primary drives, as in the case of religious fasting or sexual asceticism.

The occurrence of conversion called out in an individual by

his encounter with an absolute security system is not an all-at-once phenomenon. The threshold may be surmounted suddenly, but only as a summation of events of a lesser nature which have been occurring for some time. There is an interval between the sensory event and the reduction of the need to be. Identification with the goal-object has to be worked out, and the steps may be painful. In adaptive being, an intermediate stage exists between confrontation and the feeling of security, of having been "saved."

Faith is absolute belief. Beliefs less than absolute belief have to be supported by evidence, whereas faith is belief without evidence. All faiths are comforting, and tend to reduce the anxiety of the need to be. The truth of such beliefs does not have to be known to the believer. Indeed they may be stronger when they are not known. One believes in something, not in the knowledge of it. Belief is a feeling that looks straight through to the object of belief, without the evidential intermediation of knowing.

We have noted earlier that sositaxic behavior means identification with a material object which has exhibited some evidence of persistence. The individual hopes to continue his existence by identifying with an object larger than himself which appears destined to continue its existence. As a result of the operation of the cultural circuit, which continually produces effects upon both the individual and the artifact, a religion eventually accrues. Many revolutions of the circuit are necessary before the material object operating as a compound conditioned stimulus (the CCS) can produce in the individual the existence of retention schemata, and the individual can combine an absolute security system with a set of ways of behavior (ritual) around a large enough material object to constitute a religion. This is what happens, however. For, as a result of some act of insightful learning, a permanent material object does become combined with a philosophy, and eventually an institutional housing does get constructed over them. A religion is a work of art. Like opera and architecture, it is itself an art as well as one embellished with other arts. Only, it is large enough for the individual to live within it and to feel secure, and to find an analogy between this sort of security and ultimate security, *i.e.*, the survival of death. Such a religion represents to the individual adherent a guarantee of ultimate security. As a result of adherence to an absolute security system, the emotions provide him with a sense of having been pervaded by a feeling, specifically the feeling that the security system is true. For this reason he follows its prescribed ritual, dedicating himself to it and even making an absolute commitment. His sositropistic behavior becomes stereotyped, and his fears of non-being allayed.

Adherence to ultimate security systems involves emotions and inevitably brings with it the signs appropriate to the emotions: symbols. Symbols may be defined here as signs charged with the intensity of qualities. Symbols are always concrete objects and they are seldom combined in the way abstract objects are combined in sign-behavior. Symbol-behavior is ritualistic, consisting of certain sequences of actions in which more than one symbol may be involved. Symbol-behavior is the recognition that there are qualities in the world of a more powerful character than those which can be manipulated; the qualities are passive, and the individual behaves according to the ritual which is held to be proper to them. Thus the peculiar character of symbols is that in place of the operation of symbols by individuals there is the operation of individuals by symbols. Symbols are more than names attached to material objects; they are qualities attached to artifacts: the circuitous route taken by individuals in order to affect themselves in ways similar to the ways in which they would be affected by those absent objects which necessarily lie outside the immediate environment. Emotions are self-reflected effects driven by enormously powerful sositropistic motives, and symbols are those objects which can stimulate the emotions. Within the institution of religion absolute security systems are stored as theologies; within the individual they are stored as retention schemata.

INHIBITION

A theology is an absolute security system, the goal-object of the need to be. It is followed by need-reduction: a discharge of the feelings. Acceptance of a security system means cessation of attention. The maintenance of responses to sensory stimuli involves processes of a far more complex nature than the simple repetition of afferent impulses. Habit in the case of conformity to security systems means subsiding to a lower integrative level of energy. There is deterioration of higher nervous activity and so of attention. The equilibrium of organism and environmental forces has been disturbed and restored but under less favorable circumstances to the activity of the organism.

In general, human behavior can be accounted for by assuming that the individual is usually engaged in acting out the consequences of a security system within the allowable limits as determined by the immediate environment. The human individual in cooperation with his fellows builds such artifacts that he becomes their captive, and can no longer alter the S-R cycle, that is to say, no longer struggle. Fixture is a living death.

Corresponding to every drive, there is a negative reflex and an inhibition. The positive drive is to novelty of permanence through inquiry into being. The negative inhibition which arises from living out the consequences of an accepted security system leads to fading and extinction. As Sir Thomas Browne said in *Hydriotaphia,* the long habit of living indisposes us for dying. The aim of human life is ultimate security: the promise of life everlasting, with its freedom from fear of death and all annihilating consequences.

It happens, however, that ultimate security systems never become sufficiently grounded. The death of others leaves ourselves as well as them in the dark. Inhibitions result from doubt, when the drive encounters frustrations. The residue of the old craving for knowledge is still an ingredient; the need to be was only an extension of the need to know, as we saw earlier. It has to be reduced if the need to be is not to be inhibited.

The prospect of total extinction is difficult to accept. Those who cannot accept it cultivate the promise of continuance of existence incorporated in a security system and fostered by a religion, conditioned by established ritual as an avoidance response. The fear of danger takes precedence over the love of permanence. Retroactive inhibition blots out all imprinting of earlier efforts at identification with infinity. The repeated reinforcement of an avoidance response can only mean, however, that the substitute satisfaction for a need is dimensionally smaller than the conventional need-reduction.

Aggressive action taken for the avoidance of pain usually consists in the destruction of the threatening object. The human individual, like all other animals, may destroy the object in reducing his need, or at least change it. But in attempting to reduce the need to be he cannot change the object. It is too large or too remote. Therefore he substitutes for such effective destruction by inhibiting some one of his other needs, through fasting, for example, or chastity. In this way, he seeks to reinforce belief in the security system as a form of protection for it.

Asceticism is a variety of displacement of the inhibited drive for survival. A failing concentration on the need to be is reinforced by inhibiting the primary needs. Practices of fasting or the preservation of chastity, retreat and vows of silence, are examples. There are other varieties. The inhibited drive may for instance be displaced onto two related behavior patterns.

The first of these is the need to encounter death. The dangerous games, which have never gone begging for participants, include a wide variety, from bullfighting, jousting and fencing to stunt flying, auto racing and border skirmishes. The heroes of possibly fatal sports have always seemed exceedingly romantic, and this is true whether they have performed and perhaps died in the bull ring or on the northwest frontier of India over against the Pathans. We can look up to him who has had the courage to escape from our petty concern with mere personal survival because he has demonstrated that he does not care. The encounter with death, survived or not, is a kind of escape from the intolerable strain of insecurity; it means either that the struggle to be is over or that it has been demonstrated worthless. Flirting with death, in short, is evidence of the strength of the need for ultimate security which absolutely dominates the individual, even though it be expressed in obverse fashion.

The second behavior pattern of the displacement of the drive to be is represented by the reversal of the drive. The inhibition of the drive to be shifts the energy into a drive to not-be. Like matter in space, being is a rare occurrence in the vast extent of non-being. An individual who contemplates his existence as it might be after his death in terms of what it must have been before his birth is sure to understand that being lacks the pervasiveness and the persistence of non-being. And he would conclude that ultimate security lay in the identification with non-being.

More than one 'world' religion is founded on the acceptance of this argument, for instance the Hindu doctrine of karma, the 'eternal return' in a series of terrestrial existences. Hinayana Buddhism, the Buddhism of the Pali Canon, or the Little Vehicle, another example, is a doctrine according to which the necessity to escape from the need for existence and immortality is the religious life.

OSCILLATION

One form of oscillation is represented by displacement.

We have seen oscillation at work in the operation of displacement in adaptive knowing, and in the pull of different goal-objects calling alternately on constructive and destructive behavior in adaptive doing. In the examples given above, however, there is no oscillation. The effect of the inhibition is a permanent alteration of direction.

However, oscillation is very much in evidence in adaptive being. Its most obvious form is the result of spontaneous activity (2, p. 362). Activity alternates in an organism with inactivity, under the influence of a neurophysiological state of arousal. Non-directed energy will take any direction, and none for long. Before there is struggle, there is at least motion.

But when there is struggle, there can also be alternation. It is possible to see in the act of flirtation with a death which is only partly desired an ambivalence of approach-and-avoidance. There is comfort to be found in the viewpoint *sub specie aeternitatis* advocated by Spinoza. Death is a call to resume identification with eternity. To affirm unity with the cosmos is under any set of circumstances to be forever a genuine part of it however small. But there is also life *sub specie temporalis* and the viewpoint of time. Adaptation meets the conflict with oscillation.

Time and eternity, these correspond with the extent in the

security system of the elements of novelty and ritual, of searching and establishment, or of revolution and conservation. The novelty stimulates inquiry and the ritual inhibits it. A security system is never destroyed all at once, but there is instead an oscillation between maintenance and extinction. A religion at first relies upon novelty of insight, but duration is the prime religious reinforcement.

In addition to approach-and-avoidance, the acceptance of an absolute security system requires response-and-reinforcement. Periodically, the need-reductions are themselves symbolically reduced. Continuity of existence before and after death calls for a deprivation before to bring about consolation after. Heaven is what is not available here; the Moslem heaven is full of flowing fountains not accessible to the desert Arabs who founded Islam. It would be difficult to frighten Eskimos with the hellfires of damnation, or to have promised the Polynesians a Garden of Eden. As an indication of the oscillation between the two elements of living: enjoying the pleasures of this world and hoping for those of the next, it is necessary to observe the deprivation of some satisfactions as a symbol of their future plenitude. Abstentions remind us of the bounty to come.

The same ambivalence the individual finds in a security system he finds also in society. Other human individuals aid survival and extinction as friends and enemies. Consider for example business partners and business rivals. Human individuals share with all other material objects in the individual's environment the threat of danger and the promise of security, among which it is essential that he make his decisions correctly. Thus his life presents him with a series of extreme emergencies, the last of which is sure to be fatal. He learns to remain quite calm about it either when he thinks that the necessary steps to meet the absolute emergency have been taken or that nothing effective can be done.

Those who are too desperate or too alarmed to accept the truth calmly are able to reduce their own anxiety by sharing it with others. The philosophical movement named existentialism which has arisen in the last century in continental Europe, beginning with Kierkegaard and continuing through Heidegger and Sartre, takes off from Hegel's doctrine of alienation and emphasizes the anguish contained in the contemplation of the end of individual existence. It marks the breakdown of current security systems and substitutes an acceptance of despair. The intensity of being which is to be substituted for duration of being is to be found in the very state of emergency itself, according to the existentialists. Existentialism is an attempt to bring to a halt the intolerable oscillation between hope for the continuance of being and despair at the poverty of its prospects, and to hold at an insecure point the tensions which cannot be controlled in either direction.

RESPONSE EVOCATION

Fear of annihilation makes adherence to a system promising ultimate security a virtual certainty. Old people for instance tend to shrink from personal extinction by falling back into the tradition of the culture from which they had first emerged. It is as though by becoming immersed in social history they could escape their individual fate, by stronger identification with the class they could avoid ceasing to be an individual member. Thus they are converted to religion, or take it seriously for the first time, follow its ritual and liturgical practices more conscientiously, and in general rely upon tradition and past beliefs. Feelings of belief exist within the individual as a result of conditioning, *i.e.*, the making of a commitment or a self-dedication. From the point of view of its power to stimulate behavior, it is a response reserve of being. But such certainty is never in accord with the facts, ascertainable fact never being more than approximative. The assumption that the goal-object of the need to be is there and will remain as it is until we reach it is unfounded. The task the individual has set for himself is to survive; the efforts of the individual to continue to be must be deduced from what the individual does, his drives discovered from his actions. An inadequate task may be recalled; but attention-value is decreased by the shock of interruption, and tension results. The rigid posture of belief may long survive the genuine belief. There is in such behavior a resistance to the resumption of inquiry.

Let us suppose that a system constructed to provide for the

need to be no longer furnishes the necessary security. As we saw, doubt gives rise to inhibitions, and drives encounter frustrations; and the decision to retain or abandon the security system oscillates with increasing tension. At the same time, the alternative, which is the evocation of response, meets with considerable resistance. Displacement behavior finds another outlet: aggression. The rigid posture of belief combined with the avoidance of inquiry then leads to aggression: whatever threatens the precarious balance must be eliminated. Hostility is merely aggression transformed into a drive and functioning as a goal-response. Thus there are forced conversions, wars of religions and defenders of the faithful.

It will be useful here to elaborate an earlier point about the concern of the existentialists with the relation of consciousness to being. They seek to explore this relation by looking at being from consciousness. It is more to our purpose here to look at consciousness from being. Human individuals are subjects, and introspection comes easily to them, but the more scientific view is not necessarily the easiest one. The behavior of human individuals is a sequence of events and the individuals themselves are beings. They can be viewed as beings caught up in events, explicable only if the larger context of the whole of the events be taken into account. Thus there is the world as seen from man, but there is also man as seen from the world which influences him more than he influences it, considering that from the beginning he was part of it and himself composed of its elements.

What the human individual has to face while he has being is the permanent possibility of his non-being. Thus adaptive being in ultimate terms means simply: reconciliation with non-being. It is marked by the absence of struggle. The universe, we now understand, is so immense both in its age and expanse that it can begin to be encompassed only by a few men's thoughts and by no men's fortunes. Dying is serious enough but not death. Death is merely the end of life. There are many ways of being but only one way of not-being: we are all one in nothingness. What we have noted in early Buddhism is negative: the avoidance of being because being is painful and non-being non-painful, is in actuality positive. It is the pursuit of security through the pursuit of being itself. Pain ends being; the avoidance of pain preserves being.

The religious impulse so-called is a distance-receptor, scanning out beyond the reach of any object with which it is capable of establishing contact. Distance-receptors have an anticipatory character. The human individual has to take his readings from here and now, from his present state, his material existence. And when he finds that his existence will come to an end at a prescribed limit, after that there is what? To say that being is terminated at non-being is only again to refer to the limit. But *beyond* that, beyond the *limit,* non-being becomes positive, a condition, if we know about it at all—and we know about it only through feeling—in which universality prevails.

Little can be said about non-being except to place it. It occurs as the *terminus a quo* and the *terminus ad quem* of existent being. Before the individual was as he is, he was not; and after he is, he will not be. In life his being is concentrated at a spatio-temporal point, but limited, existing only in virtue of the loss of universality. In death the universality is restored, and in this way his being is widened. It reaches out to the universe and spreads over it, as equally true of one place and date as of another. Thus the *terminus ad quem* of being is being self-fulfilled.

As the control exercised by the individual over his behavior has increased, he has devoted more of his efforts to serving the interests of the long-range self. What kind of being is it which holds in common with what is both that which has been and that which could be? They share a common non-presence, yet absence does not indicate nothingness. The time is now for most beings; yet absent being indicates that present being is not all. The individual inherits the past and he prepares the way for the future, yet *qua* present he behaves in accordance with eternity. Every piece of present behavior is a valid and inherent part of genuine being. What is, is no more, but also no less, valuable than what was, what will be, or even (and more generally) what could be. The past is absolutely determined, but chance enters into the present and the future. Adaptive being struggles with the present but must adjust primarily to the future.

Adaptive being finally means the acceptance of a surrogate successive generation. For eventually the need to be must fail and the individual die; but his efforts at ultimate survival do not ultimately fail. For in dying he achieves positive otherness and leaves a residue of artifacts and of patterns of behavior to his successors. The need to be is reduced when the individual is assimilated to its consequences. The failure of the individual is in a certain sense the success of society.

Chapter 14

ABERRATIONS OF BEHAVIOR

ABERRATION MEANS the action of wandering away, more specifically of deviation from the normal type (Oxford English Dictionary). Aberrations of knowing, doing and being are the all too common instances of wandering away into deviations. We shall consider first aberrations of the need to know, next aberrations of the need to do, then aberrations of the need to be, and finally the interference each imposes on the others. Our illustrations of aberrations will be little more than illustrative. For corresponding to each type of behavior correctly aimed at reducing a need, there are many more ways of missing the mark. A considerable number of aberrations are quite common and therefore may be viewed as standard deviations. Average aberrations are as species-predictable as normal behavior.

ABERRATIONS OF THE PRIMARY DRIVES

Aberrations in the case of the primary drives consist in excesses or defects of need-reductions. Excesses of thirst, hunger or sex may be due to physiological or psychological causes. For instance, obesity may be the result of an increase in food-intake due to anxiety or it may be due to an endocrine disturbance, as in reactive or metabolic obesity. Excesses in sexual activity may result from similar causes, such as infantile obsessions or abnormal gonadal activity. In the confrontation of the needs with material objects promising need-reductions, the organism takes no account of previous and quite adequate need-reductions and behaves as though the needs had been aroused afresh by a protracted deficiency.

Defects in need-reductions may be due to the feedback of noxious effects from the prattotaxic activity of the individual in relation to his chosen goal-objects. Such for instance is the situation when there is adaptation to destructive stimuli: drug addiction, for example, and alcoholism. Acquired motivation when it takes the form of artificial hungers such as these can hardly be denied the classification of aberrance. Behavior is designed to reduce needs, not to promote welfare. When the need is self-destructive, need-reduction acts against welfare. An example is masochisms in which the erotic aggression of the individual is turned upon himself. Defects are more commonly due to interferences from other drives, usually from some drive of the secondary group. We shall discuss these later in the chapter when we come to the considerations of the phenomena of interferences.

ABERRATIONS OF KNOWING

It will not be possible to follow too closely the lines of the original stimulus-response cycle and reverberating circuit as employed in earlier chapters, but a rough approximation will be made.

The grossest aberration concerns the location of the original material object, when it is supposed for instance that the object is located internally. The difficulty here is due to an error in confrontation. When an individual in normal behavior finds that his need is confronted with a tropism, he behaves accordingly, namely, by moving toward the source of the stimulus by means of a response to its emitted cue. In the aberrant behavior of the need to know, the individual mistakenly supposes that the cue was internal and that the original material object which was the source of the tropism was in his own consciousness. Accordingly, he tries to move inward upon himself and seeks there for the satisfaction of his need for knowing. The result is a concentration on the needs themselves rather than on their reduction. It can happen too that the generalized drive of aggression can itself become the goal-object, and the concentration can be shifted to the drive stripped of all need-reduction, as in obsessive or fanatical concerns.

But there can be another type of reaction. Instead of concentrating on needs the individual may withdraw altogether from the external world into a stupor of the kind familiar in catatonic schizophrenia, in extreme cases even with cataleptic symptoms. For the psychotic no knowledge is receivable from the external world and no impulses acceptable from within: a world, including that portion of it which lies within the individual himself, too difficult and too dangerous to recognize. It might be added parenthetically that all pathological cases encountered in psychiatric experience can be interpreted as an aberration of one of the needs.

Objectivity is the posture proper to the individual; he must be faced outward toward his goal-object, that which can best reduce his needs. Consciousness of the non-deviant type is the condition of arousal which makes possible alertness toward the goal-object; consciousness is consciousness *of* something external and outward. The healthy individual active in pursuit of some one of his objective goals is a happy individual, an individual in use as he should be used.

Consciousness presents the individual with an unique advantage. For the individual himself is the only material which he is ever likely to experience from inside. Therefore, consciousness can and often does mean the view from inside a material object.

There is, however, in this perspective a danger lurking. It consists in the possibility that the individual will consider his own consciousness as itself the unique object and so fall into the aberration of subjectivism. In the attempt to find in the inventory of the world one type of object more important than the others, the choice of the self is an error. But this happens more often than not. The avoidance of subjectivism is made possible by the steadfast maintenance of the structure of the reverberating circuit. Consciousness may be an element certainly, but the important question is what function should it be assigned. For there must also be a material object at one focus; and so if consciousness is at the other focus, a circuit can be maintained. For it is the view *from* the consciousness of the material object which is the self that we want, and not the view *of* consciousness from itself. The problem, then, is, will consciousness help us to understand a typical material object or not? And the answer is yes, but only if we consider the self a material object among material objects.

But when consciousness is aware of itself, when subjectivity is the posture assumed, then there is no goal-object, only a subject reflecting upon itself, a single, unsupported, self-reflecting consciousness. This is a misuse, and unhappiness is the result. The unhappy consciousness is a consciousness in which the subject has become its own goal-object.

Since the term employed here, the "unhappy consciousness" is the same one used by Hegel, some comparison is in order. The use is similar but it is not the same. Hegel used the term to describe the divided self (3, p. 251), whereas the term is employed here to stand for a self-sufficient self. However, in a later passage in the same work Hegel seems to take account of this other meaning (3, p. 752). There, however, he called it the "unhappy self-consciousness."

A rampant self-reflecting consciousness is one type of subjectivism. Another familiar type is what may be called inadvertent subjectivism. This occurs when need-reduction is effected by means of false knowledge. The reduction of the need to know begins in such cases with a mistaken tropism. The individual turns toward particular instances of naturally occurring relations on the assumption that he is eliciting the material for general propositions which will accord with the facts. It proceeds by the usual channels through the repetition of a stimulus-response cycle into a reverberating circuit. It is treated, in other words, conventionally, but it does not have a conventional ending. For it often happens that the need to know ends with a consummatory response when the individual has experienced learning.

The need to know is a craving for knowledge which is no less powerful for being pervasive. The individual lives in its atmosphere just as he lives in a strong gravitational field. Yet it is a craving which is sure to be partly aberrant. There are a number of reasons for the aberrance. These are: 1) that knowledge is partially false; 2) that the human equipment for its acquisition is inadequate; 3) that truth is often unacceptable; 4) that partial truths are more easily understood; 5) that knowledge is general while events are particular; and 6) that false knowledge is comforting.

1) We have noted in earlier chapters that knowledge means acquaintance with propositions having a correspondence with the concrete events to which they refer, and also that the function of knowledge is to make possible through the use of abstractions the representation of absent objects. Only some of the members of a universal class are ever present. But of course, only the members which are present are available for examination; the others are not. Hence inaccuracies of representation are bound to occur. And when there are consequences in the applications of knowledge, either to understanding or to practice, such inaccuracies may lead to conflict.

2) If the craving for knowledge is led astray by the fact that available knowledge is false knowledge, it is no less frustrated by the inadequacy of the human equipment for its acquisition. The likelihood of false knowledge is increased by the fact that the human faculties for learning, reasoning, feeling and acting are notoriously crude and much escapes them. The senses in particular are not fine enough to discriminate the differences in the world with which they come into contact. Perception cannot err but it can fall short, while action can be misinterpreted and reasoning mistaken. Again, knowledge as such is general; it is stated in general terms and, in extreme cases, in universal terms. But events are particulars; and so if knowledge in order to be true must consist in a correspondence with events, then it must always be partly false. The discovery of truth occurs, as shown by the efficacy of its applications, but it is never the whole of truth and always limited.

3) A third reason for the aberrance of the craving for knowledge is the unacceptability of truth. Although the satisfaction of the need to know is pleasurable, as we have noted, it is abstract knowledge of which this is true. The prospect of applications or practical consequences is particular and so either pleasurable or painful. For instance, the contemplation of death considered as annihilation, with its concomitant damage to ultimate security, is so painful that it is often rejected as a possibility. Truth is a simple logical relation, without regard for its

injuriousness, but individuals often exhibit aversion (or avoidance) behavior with regard to injurious truth. The security afforded by partial truths is attractive; they require no hard intellection nor any loosening of traditional loyalties. Few have the strength to seek the truth directly, nor the stamina to sustain it when acquired.

4) A fourth reason for the aberrance of the craving for knowledge is that partial truths are simple and hence easily understood. They are the truth seen from a peculiar perspective and thus can be made dramatic. They are incisive without being comprehensive, and thus can be seen as profound. Single ideas complexly reinforced have considerable emotional appeal. The explanation of human life on the basis of single motivation is popular; on the basis of the sex drive alone (Freud) or of hunger alone (Marx), for example.

5) Knowledge, then, knowledge-as-such, is identical with true knowledge. False knowledge is the possession of propositions which do not have such a correspondence. Most propositions are mixed; they are partly true and partly false. And since they contain some falsity, they increase the likelihood of false knowledge. Some propositions are easily disclosed to be true or false, while others are difficult. "All men have red hair" is easily shown to be false, but "Mars is inhabited" is not. Truth as such—logical truth—is absolute; and because it is absolute it is never actual but only approximated in any instance. Empirical truth is a matter of approximations. The statement "Men are safe crossing the street" is empirically true just in case more men are safe crossing the street than are unsafe, and otherwise false. It is absolute if and only if all men are safe crossing the street. Thus what are encountered in existence are usually probabilities, fractions which are at least partially false. And because the moiety of false knowledge is so prevalent, it has to be reckoned with. Some false knowledge is a permanent feature of the human environment, it has its effects.

6) We do not have any definite and well founded knowledge with respect to what our state is to be after death. We may continue to be or we may not. We do not know, the evidence either way is insufficient. But if we assume either a continuance

or a renewal of life after death, we are going further than the facts warrant and our unjustified certainty constitutes false knowledge. Now false knowledge is more comforting than uncertainty. Those who have faith die happy. However, there is always the danger that too strong a belief in a security-system may lead to obsessive-compulsive behavior, the abnormal behavior of the "fanatic." In view of the absence of true knowledge the faith can only be considered an aberrance.

The need to know, then, must inevitably encounter false knowledge; and to the extent to which it does there is damage. But knowledge is only partly false; it is also partly true. And only to the extent to which it is true does it properly satisfy the need.

False knowledge means that no lack is felt in the need to know when in fact there is a lack. There is also the situation in which no lack is felt when there is a substitution or displacement.

One kind of substitution is deliberate recourse to a delusional system. There are two kinds of delusional systems: those the individual frankly recognizes as such and *visits,* such as are found in literature and works of art; and those the individual lives in as though they were more real than the conditions surrounding his animal existence.

The generic type of displacement has to do with the need to know naturally occurring relations. The goal-object of the need to know is pure theortetical knowledge, the abstract knowledge of relationships. But the drive to knowledge is often satisfied by the substitution of concrete, applied knowledge, the knowledge of practicality. For instance, the man with a deep desire to know what there is, why we are here, and how there can be time, has often been put aside with stock answers of a more immediate usefulness. There is primarily the immediate community in which he lives, he is here to support a family and raise children, and time is something of which we do not have enough. The practical problems exist of course and must be solved, and the lives of most human individuals are devoted to these ends, as well they may be. Yet these are the satisfactions of the primary drives, the means-*by*-which; and they are meaningless except for sub-human animals without the subsequent satisfaction of the secondary drives which are peculiarly human, the ends-*for*-which.

There is another and more specialized instance in which no lack is felt because there has been a displacement. This is when the goal-object of the need to know is assumed to be the need-to-know itself. The drive to know is displaced onto the mechanism by which it operates, in place of a proper goal-object. The need to know is then reduced by means of the knowledge of knowing. A good example is to be found in technical philosophy, when epistemology preempts the functions of ontology, when, in other words, the theory of being is displaced onto the theory of knowing and being is assumed to be almost entirely a matter of knowledge, so that what-we-know is asserted to be all-there-is-knowable, as with the Kantian philosophy, or, in a more extreme case, as with solipsism, for to be fair to Kant he did allow for a thing-in-itself beyond knowledge, which, however, he declared to be unknowable.

The reinforcement of response which follows from destructive behavior takes the form of a reversion to the repetition of a more primitive cycle. The stimulus-response pattern largely unadapted and with no effect on the material object means also an end to inquiry. When knowing is repeated, as with the individual who recalls a piece of knowledge or who reminds himself of something that he knows, it acts as a negative or inhibitory response to the need to know. One who knows has nothing to learn; and one who has nothing to learn has no need to investigate. Thus knowledge produces an inhibition to inquiry.

What is not so well known, however, is that inquiry is equally inhibiting to knowledge. The activity prompted by curiosity looks forward to new knowledge and blots out the knowledge which represented curiosity satisfied on some past occasion. As Pavlov pointed out, exciting the investigatory reflex means inhibiting the action of previous conditioning (5, p. 44). Aberrant knowing is a deviant of the primitive and very fundamental drive of approach-and-exploration. The consciousness which lives on the edge of inquiry is considerably more forceful; that which is compelled to be content with a repetition of an established cycle without any change is the lowest level of consciousness entitled to the name, and close to the absence of consciousness. It is a kind of negative adaptation, a habit of responding to planned stimulation according to a program of fixed conditioning. Species-predictable behavior calls for an elementary patterning of some sort; where all human individuals belong to cultures in which there are settled beliefs and prescribed behavior, every human individual must have some settled beliefs and some prescribed behavior; but in the fixed patterning due to false knowledge accepted as absolute these can be aimed at the minimum required to remain human, and so not be of serious import to the individual.

There is a variety of aberrant behavior which does not lead to the destruction of artifacts but only to their misuse. It is equally a deviation. As there are two kinds of artifacts: tools and signs, so there are two kinds of aberrant behavior in regard to them. We shall be concerned with them here in relation to knowing.

The misuse of tools in reducing the need to know can be easily illustrated. The newspaper was invented for the dissemination of information, not for the control of public opinion. A degree from a university was intended to be an indication of education, and neither a status symbol nor a guarantee of proficiency in some technology.

The misuse of signs in reducing the need to know is just as easily seen. Language was intended as an instrument of communication of meaning, not as a method of concealing the absence of meaning. It was intended also to convey truth, not falsehood, as for instance in the making of a verbal promise which the speaker does not look forward to keeping.

ABERRATIONS OF DOING

The behavior of subhuman animals occurs chiefly in terms of reflexes, a stimulus-response cycle operating directly, as we have seen in earlier chapters. The behavior of human individuals has in addition the intermediate processes which delay the response to the stimulus, and also the reverberating circuit which provides for an alteration of the material object and for the adaptation of the individual. The adaptations of knowing, doing, and being allow for a construction of the material object and its consequent reinforcement of the individual's responses. The aberrations of doing would take the form largely of the destruction of artifacts. Confrontation in aberration phenomena always exerts a distorting effect.

First as to the need to do, itself. There is a certain sense in which the generalized drive of aggression, the drive to dominate the environment, when unspecified and undirected toward the reduction of some particular need, is itself a form of aberrant behavior. Sheer, unadulterated aggression without the extenuating circumstance that it has as its aim some need-reduction is undoubtedly aberrant, a variety of behavior which may lead not to the destruction of some object nor to the benefaction of the individual if it succeeds but rather to the destruction of the individual as well as the object whether it succeeds or fails.

The aberration of the drive to do which is most characteristic is the exaggeration of the drive to dominate, namely the drive to dominate at all costs. Racketeers, criminals, political dictators, are good examples. When an individual acts as though no price were too high to pay for his own aggrandizement and he is willing to exchange the respect he would normally receive from his fellows for the exactment of their fear of him, then he—and they—become victims of the aberration in him of the drive to do.

In all animals deprivation intensifies a drive while satiation extinguishes it. In the human individual and with the secondary drives this is not always the case. The deprivation of activity if carried to excess may render the individual indisposed to activity and perhaps incapable of it. The failure of achievement, which is a variety of deprivation, may turn the individual against making any further effort to achieve and he becomes non-productive. Many an alcoholic represents the escape taken by a thwarted or disappointed ambition. Again, satiation in the instance of the need to survive may mean only an increased effort in that direction. Those who devote full time to a religion become less and less inclined to be active outside it except in its cause.

The purchase and maintenance of more expensive equipment than it is possible for an individual to use in his or her lifetime, motors cars, houses, estates, furs, jewelry, represent the aberrance of excess with respect to artifacts. This is the activity Thorstein Veblen described as "conspicuous waste." The aberrance of the defect is illustrated when the drive is hung on a particular object or class of objects no longer capable of functioning as intended. The love for antique furniture too frail to be used as furniture or for old motor cars too decrepit to be driven on the streets, the love for old houses not comfortable to live in or for ruins with no function left at all, these are instances of defect.

Another example of aberrant behavior in connection with the need to do is occasioned by the conflict which ensues when a single human individual subscribes to two or more response systems. So long as the behavior appropriate to each is emitted upon different occasions and under different social conditions, there is no difficulty (7, p. 286); but they may be emitted upon the same occasion and then there *is* difficulty. A scientist who adheres to a dogmatic religion may find that his scientific activity calls for the performance of certain experiments which the religious authorities forbid. What happens when a man's obligations to his family and his country conflict? Sartre reports one such case, when during the occupation of France by the Germans in World War II, a young man had to choose between remaining with his mother who lived chiefly for him and escaping to join the Free French forces in England to fight for the liberation of France (6, p. 28ff.).

What is true of the other secondary drives is true also of the need to do, that its possible aberrations are many, far more than it will be possible to enumerate here. The aberrations of a drive can occur at any point: an over-determination, such as the Freudians have discovered, as for instance when the unconscious multiple determination of a proliferation of factors, can together produce a neurotic symptom by converging from several directions (2, ch. VI); the aboulia which results when an individual is unable to choose between stimuli and therefore unable to act; the randomized activity when an individual finds himself incapable of self-direction; and many more.

ABERRATIONS OF BEING

As with knowing and doing, it is necessary to follow roughly the guide lines of the reverberating circuit, and to consider the aberrations of being accordingly. In the aberrations of being particularly the errors begin with misinterpretation of confrontations.

A familiar aberration of being is one in which the goal-object is less stimulating than its background and there is a defective response to an ordinary stimulus from the external world. It is conventional for the individual to find himself in either an enclosed space or an open space, a city room, say, or a country field. Such an environment is ordinarily the background against which the individual receives more specific cues. In the room or in the field there are material objects which attract or repel accordingly as they promise need-reductions or threats to security. One aberration of behavior is his reception of impressions from such backgrounds as though they themselves constitutes threats. The aberrations are so familiar that they have been given names in abnormal psychology. The first of the two aberrations is called claustrophobia and the second agoraphobia.

Another aberration of being is the appearance of non-being: there is no goal-object, only the absence of one. What in the case of the ordinary drives is felt objectively as a desirable object: the inherent attractiveness of food, a mate, wisdom, or security, is felt subjectively as a lack. The human individual in such a case feels incomplete, and anticipates that the object toward which he would move but which does not exist could have satisfied the craving. The missing object could have offered completeness, either by being assimilated (*e.g.*, food or knowledge) or by assimilating him (*e.g.*, the nation or God).

One variant of subjectivism in the aberrations of being is to be found in limited conceptions of the goal-object: either it resembles the subject himself or it is very near in space and time. Identification becomes projection, in the Freudian sense (2, ch. II). From association with a goal-object the individual turns to imitative behavior and himself draws near to just such a goal-object. In the case of the need to be, the aberration is contact with God by means of resemblance or proximity. Two familiar conceptions exist in religion: the conception of an anthropomorphic god, and of a nearby God.

One way to bring security closer is to attribute to God an human form. If the chances of continuing to be seem to hang upon identification with God, such chances are increased should it prove that God is a man like ourselves, only perfect, eternal and more powerful, but a god of love who will wish us well and be in a position to do something about it. The similarities of man to God must increase the sympathy of God for man and so make our case appear somewhat better than it might otherwise. Another variant of this is the terrible God: God as a formidable figure requiring appeasement and exacting vengeance. The god of love and the god of power have this in common, that they offer security and bring it into our neighborhood where it is accessible.

Another aberration of being of the same sort but less familiar (at least in these terms) is the aberration of the nearby God. God is assumed to have surrogates the human individual can touch and see: Lares and Penates, the gods of the hearth, the Christian deity on the dashboard of the automobile, or the Bodhisattva in the bedroom. Identification with deities which lie within the reach of human perceptions is easy of attainment and appropriately comforting.

A more elusive aberration of being is one which may be called the aberration of false being. It is best illustrated, perhaps, by the work of the existentialist philosophers earlier referred to, in particular Kierkegaard, Heidegger and Sartre. This misconception of being is noted by the existentialists as the encounter with non-being. If the experience of nothingness produces dread, then the security which comes from identification with being is best accomplished by a reconciliation with nothingness. Such an encounter results in a shrinking back in horror, a turning away revolted, the refusal of a reconciliation. In the end the ultimate security which is sought for by the self, the existentialists would urge, is to be found only in the self itself. The far-away goal-object is identified with the short-range self. Man has been surrendered to his own custody, and feels the loneliness of his responsibility. Thus the naked self can find an identification with the nothingness which it had at first refused.

This particular aberration lies in the misunderstanding of

being itself. To understand being, we must first look at the nature of the unit class in logic. Let us assume that the unit class is that class whose only member is identical with itself (1, 17.42). Then 'being' is the ontological equivalent of the unit class in logic. Being is the class that has itself as its only member and is identical with itself. 'Being' is a unit-word; 'being' attributed as a property to a fish means merely 'there is a fish.'

Now there has been a subtle corruption of the term by the existentialists. 'Being' for them is a transitive verb without an object. Such being is accordingly felt as a lack. No being where being is expected is false being, and consequently the anguish of the struggle back to true being. The error comes of somehow supposing that being is an attribute not of all beings but only of some beings, namely, those beings endowed with consciousness.

Another and equally serious aberration of being to be found in existentialism is the substitution of otherness for nothingness. This will have to be explained. In the *Sophist* of Plato, non-being is defined as 'positive otherness.' Another word for non-being is 'nothing.' Thus we have to deal with three terms instead of two; we have being, and we have two conflicting definitions of non-being: positive otherness, and nothingness.

The conflict can be resolved if we remember that opposition and contradiction are not the same. The opposite of 'being' is 'non-being' defined as 'positive otherness.' The contradictory of 'being' is non-being defined as 'nothingness.' The human individual encounters being-*qua*-being and non-being-as-positive-otherness in existence, and presumably is confronted in existence with the prospect of non-being-as-nothingness after death. Now if he is an existentialist he tends to commit the aberration of reversing these. For he supposes that he encounters nothingness in existence and faces positive otherness after death.

Existentialism has its roots in Kierkegaard's reaction to Hegel's conception that every individual is some part of the absolute whole. Kierkegaard saw in this inclusion a threat to his need to continue to be as a separate and distinct individual, and hence revolted from it in terms of himself as an individual by cutting the individual self off from the absolute whole of being. But this is an act not possible to the part, and in so doing he felt cut off and alone, life became for him a "sickness unto death" (4). Being as a part of some large whole is not continuing to be as a separate and altogether independent individual, yet being as a separate and altogether independent individual brings with it a continual despair at the lack of connections.

Existentialism is the need to (continue to) be as it is felt when it is turned away from its proper goal of persistent or otherwise permanent objects and directed inward toward the self. When the aim of the self is the short-range self, then there is no prospect of permanence and hence anguish arises. For the need to be is not reduced but only deflected by brief-lived things such as the self, when it is the self itself which is driven to search for association with long-existing things.

He who relies only upon himself and makes no objective and external identification is without hope and is sure to despair. And, as Kierkegaard wrote, the more intense the consciousness the greater the despair, for it means to have lost at once both the self itself and what is permanent in the world (4, p. 360ff.).

MUTUAL INTERFERENCES OF KNOWING, DOING AND BEING

A need out of place may lead to aberrant behavior. The basic tissue-needs operate independently, and it often happens that, in attempting to satisfy the demands of one, another is diverted. We shall take up the topic of interferences next and discuss them one at a time, endeavoring to run through all of the combinations.

The interference of knowing with doing is familiar enough: the paralysis of action following too much thought. To understand the factors involved in both sides of a dilemma is to sympathize with both and hence to become unable to decide between them. The man of action is a "narrow-minded" fellow who perforce sees all of the justice in a situation only on one side. The man who makes a choice of issues, accepting the one and rejecting the other, must have concluded that the preponderance of truth or of value was overwhelmingly with the one he accepted.

The application of knowledge is species-predictable: where

there are human individuals, there will be behavior carried out in terms of what has been learned. If ideas can alter actions, small wonder that false ideas can lead to harmful actions. The aberration of knowing means here the exercise of action on material objects as called for by false knowledge. With knowledge the human individual behaves as a member of the species *Homo faber;* with false knowledge he becomes *Homo destructor.* Conflicting actions may issue from false knowledge which in this way is capable of occasioning the revival of inquiry.

Aberrant behavior leading to the destructive alterations of artifacts does not always appear candidly as what it is, and often may seem a construction. Human constructions are immense: in addition to capital cities, social organizations as large as nations arise from joint efforts. They cannot be destroyed by the simple application of false knowledge by human individuals. What is required for such a mammoth overthrow is a small and efficient construction. This under the rule of false knowledge is often claimed as an absolute. False knowledge is always absolute knowledge, and its application therefore essential, as with the militaristic regime or the religious sect.

The proper adjustment of knowing to doing requires that action be taken on the basis of less than certain knowledge. We must learn how to act on probabilities if we are to act at all, inasmuch as certainty is so hard to come by that action on the basis of certainty alone would be impossible. Feigned certainty for the purposes of action must lead inevitably to difficulties. For when true knowledge leads to action it is surely better than when false knowledge does. Contradictions in knowledge when applied to action occasion conflict.

The interference of knowing with being is occasioned by the reversal of roles. We are, but we do not always know. Usually, knowing is the conditioned stimulus to the unconditioned stimulus of being. But when being is the conditioned stimulus and knowing the unconditioned stimulus, the phenomenon of interference results. A good example can be found in the kind of occasion when what the individual learns is not in accord with what he has been in the habit of doing.

The reduction of the need to be requires faith in a security-system or in some remote material goal-object promising continuance. Faith is belief without reason, whereas true knowledge is belief based on reason and fact. Strength of belief is inverse to amount of evidence. The less convincing the evidence the stronger and more tenacious the belief. And this comes about because of the deep craving for certainty. Thus the more knowledge the less faith. In this way knowing seems to interfere with being. However, that is because the knowledge is not extensive enough. Human individuals being natural animals and natural animals being parts of nature, it would be fair to suppose that nothing which could happen to an individual could be unnatural. Thus, where we know that belief in the continuance of existence after death is a faith, we cannot deny that its opposite, namely the belief that life ends with death, is not unnatural. Very often faith in false knowledge is introduced simply because true knowledge is unavailable.

Another interference of knowing with being issues from the fact that behavior is a form of knowing. The consummatory response of ritual designed to reduce the need to be, such as religious liturgy, reinforces the philosophy which as theology is inherent in the ritual. Claims to superior knowledge gained through mystic rites and practices: eating the body of the god, or getting beyond the body by denying its demands (asceticism).

We have already seen in earlier chapters how knowing is involved with being. Philosophies are capable of serving as security systems, and every religion has a philosophy in the form of a theology. Philosophy of religion is knowledge serving the need to be. This delicate relationship can always be upset with the consequence that the knowledge instead of serving can be turned to interfering. For what seemed limited knowledge under one set of conditions may seem too limited under another. What seems adequate information under one set of orienting conditions may not under another set.

The proper adjustment of knowing to being seems to require the elevation of truth to the condition where knowing and being become indistinguishable. But the complex needs of the human individual at the high integrative levels of knowing and being make interferences almost inevitable. For the most part they lie beyond the powers of the single human individual to prevent.

The resolution of the interference of knowing with being could consist in the shifting of belief from the results obtained by means of inquiry to the activity of inquiry itself. The advanced human individual is dedicated to inquiry rather than to a chosen set of findings. He has become aware that the only constant is the inquiry itself, since findings often prove false or at the very least inadequate.

The interference of doing with knowing is found most commonly in the man of action whose behavior is apt to be precipitate. The man of action suffers from the opposite limitation which as we have already seen besets the intellectual. Whereas the intellectual knows too much to act at all, the man of action knows too little to act properly. To do first and to think afterwards may mean that the action accomplished has only to be undone. In the actions characteristic of compulsive doing, the goals chosen may be conflicting goals. Everything is proximate and positions temporary, ends are lost sight of in the intoxication of action itself, and the degree of violence apt to be exaggerated.

When an individual is too active, he cannot think properly. The man of action conventionally looks down on the thinker, the scholar, the intellectual, as not being quite a man, manhood being identified with action, and preferably violent action. Action, it is held, has a purity which is contaminated by contemplation, "sicklied o'er with the pale cast of thought."

But the fact is that action is involved with thought. Action must have a goal-object, a direction, and if it is to be consistent and not defeat itself the end must be kept constantly in view. Undirected action is worse than thought which never leads to action. For while random action has no qualified place in the life of the adult, thought has. "He also serves who only stands and waits."

The interference of doing with being occurs when activity threatens survival. The human individual often builds such powerful artifacts that he becomes their victim, and so struggle is transformed into the effort to sacrifice himself to them. Extinction is a final death. The tradition of the sea that the captain ought to go down with his ship carries his responsibility beyond the safety of his human passengers. A life of action is potentially more dangerous than one of contemplation. The soldier, the explorer, the adventurer, does not expect to have the longevity of the philosopher or the academician. An active life in the physical sense is not one an individual would engage in as part of the search for security. Then, too, the primary needs, which guarantee immediate security, are threatened. Living conditions for the man on the move are not of the same quality as they are for the sedentary individual.

There are more extreme forms of the interference of doing with being, forms in which the aberrant nature of the behavior becomes painfully apparent. Suicide is the most familiar of these for here clearly doing brings being to an end but then certain varieties of homicide are also. The motiveless murder as portrayed by Dostoyevsky in *Crime and Punishment* is an example.

Doing is involved with being to a certain extent, however. Life, human life, like all animal life is committed to a certain measure of struggle, and when the struggle meets with success thrives on it. The animal was not constructed in order to remain passive, and this is as true of the human animal as of any other. Striving may be costly, it may involve risks, but it is necessary, and, as we have seen, the need to do is a fundamental one. If aggression is the generic type of drive-reduction, then it cannot be supposed that an inactive life has much of a share in being.

The interference of being with knowing is occasioned by the exigencies of survival. The short-range self is the individual who must exist from day to day, the effort of survival taking precedence over pure learning in the order of importunateness. Such precedence constitutes an interference from the point of view of the need to know. Being terminates the need. The individual with the deepest curiosity, eager to approach and explore an unknown, will put it aside in favor of behavior designed for the avoidance of pain. No man with a toothache will continue his reading.

Another interference of being with knowing issues from the substitution of piety for knowledge. In some religions it is supposed that the religious life can be led in ignorance provided all the requirements of the church are met. There have been many ignorant monks and saints who have thought that knowledge interferes with holiness, instead of understanding the holiness of knowledge itself. One message of Socrates was the virtue of knowledge. The drive to continue being can only block the drive to increase knowing at the cost of one kind of contact with being: the kind of contact that knowing is. Thus the interference of being with knowing to some extent at least is the drive to continue being defeating itself.

Being is involved with knowing because it is possible to know only about what there is while remaining outside the confines of false knowledge. Therefore being is in a position always to interfere with knowing. One form of interference lies in just this, that knowing cannot encompass being. Of any material object or abstract relationship, it is never possible to exhaust its being by means of the knowledge process. Knowledge however large is finite, whereas being is infinite; the extensibility of being must interfere with the completeness of knowing.

The interference of being with doing occurs when weak men prey upon the strong. The successful man is usually found supporting a number of incompetents: the mentally or physically inadequate or ill who rely upon him to maintain through his efforts their passive hold on existence. In the life of lower organisms the phenomena of parasites and predators are common, and it often happens that the parasites multiply so much they kill the host organism.

The interference of being with doing is seen also in the passivity of some Eastern religions in which "water-like behavior" rather than struggle is recommended. The Eastern way is the way of acceptance and inactivity.

Still another variety of interference of being with doing comes from the contemplation of the concept of the perfection of being. When perfect being is held up by the individual as his chosen goal-object, it is apt to paralyze action. The individual will not strive when the object of his striving is on the face of it remote and unattainable. Doing seems to turn over into being in nympholepsy, the state of rapture inspired by a violent enthusiasm for an unattainable ideal.

Being is involved with doing, however, for there is no form of existence that can escape inclusion in being. Whatever we are, that we tend to bring out in what we do, and activity is after all only an expression of character. The stage of maturity is for the individual only an opportunity to become more what he is than he ever had been able to do before. The largest category is always to be found present in every one of its subordinate states.

Chapter 15

THE CONTROL OF ADAPTIVE BEHAVIOR

STATEMENT OF THE PROBLEM

IN AN EARLIER CHAPTER, adaptive behavior was defined as continuously revised self-conditioning, meeting or producing modifications in the special ways in which man sets about obtaining the reduction of the needs which he shares with the animals and the complex ways necessary for obtaining the reduction of those additional needs which exist in versions peculiar to him. Adaptive behavior is reflexive, since every adaptation not only adjusts the individual to the reduction of his needs by means of the immediate environment as he finds it but also to his own capacities for such adjustments in the future. But such reflexive behavior is not mechanical in any simple way, certainly not with the intervention of mediating processes. As we shall presently see, an increase in knowledge affects the need to know, just as a protraction of survival affects the need to (continue to) be.

It is sometimes the case that a deep understanding of psychological processes can be obtained by means of a few basic assumptions. As Bellman points out, a simple approximate solution to a problem is often more useful than a complex exact solution (2, p. 35). The aim of this work has been to improve the understanding of the human individual by imbedding human behavior as a process within a group of similar natural processes. It will aid in the exposition of control procedures if we have stated these assumptions briefly and clearly, for then we can move on to the announcement of the approximate solution. As we shall find out, all non-mathematical solutions are of necessity only approximative, but the proper qualitative solution is a stage on the way. The use of mathematics must await adequate conceptualization, as the pleasure-pain calculus of Edgeworth and Jevons so dramatically illustrated. Human relations are also naturally occurring, and their abstraction is extensive, depending upon the environment through which they are related directly or by means of artifacts.

ADAPTIVE CONTROL

Human individuals are natural material objects, and they interact with the other natural material objects (including other human individuals and sub-human animals) in their environment. That they have adapted successfully is attested by the fact that as we have noted they have survived as tool-using animals for something like a million and a quarter years. Such adaptation has been partly conscious and partly unconscious. They have employed consciousness in the process of arranging their own survival both as individuals and as a species, but the process has been partly unconscious because the individuals have not been aware of the implications of their moves. As in any vast social organization, the individuals perform their separate duties uninformed of the effects of the collective effort.

Examples of such procedures might be helpful.

One is to be found in the fact that ignorance of ultimate goals does not actively interfere with the striving toward them which takes place, not even when such striving is a calculated affair. Positive adaptation is largely a matter of knowledge, for if the individual is to select from the environment what is needed he must first find it in the environment; but he is ignorant of the negative adaptation whereby the environment impedes him in certain activities. The final need reduction of the need to know can be accomplished only by the ideal of complete information. Similarly, the final need-reduction of the need to continue to be can be accomplished only by the ideal of eternal survival, which is to say immortality. But the human individual does not have these goals in mind. He strives instead for a little more knowledge, a little greater longevity. He finds that he is able to adapt very nicely to a moderate amount of education and an equally moderate life expectancy.

Another example. The requirements of utility, of day to day

existence, are frequently confused with the requirements of fundamental inquiry, and conversely. It is not easy to separate out the various strands of motivation in the course of behavior conducted at once on the basis of animal exigencies and that of more specifically human needs. The mammalian existence of the sign-using animal with its consequent multiple causation does not allow his hunger for being to be distinguished from his air-hunger. And as his motives are mixed so are his actions. The situation is rendered no less complex by the fact that behavior intended to reduce one need may often have an effect upon another.

A last example. It is recognized that our decisions have definite but unknown effects upon our dispositional states (2, p. 199). A disposition in favor of a particular outcome is the usual accompaniment to the decision to try a particular solution to a problem didactically faced. The decision is deliberate in the sense that the individual knows he is making it. But he never contemplates as a whole the situation which includes the decision. In other words, he contemplates the problem of which the decision is a result, but he never contemplates the decision in such a way that both the problem and the decision together lead to further results.

Since the human individual is not aware of all the consequences of his actions, and since those actions themselves are often dictated by the content of consciousness, it can be said that he is not aware of all the consequences of the content of his consciousness. Put otherwise, consciousness is a channel through which flow sequences of behavior of which he is hardly aware. Thus he participates, and thinks himself in control, of many of the events by which he is surrounded, when in fact he does not have any control at all.

Some contemporary authorities believe that human evolution is over, man having produced an environment which will henceforth serve to keep him stationary. But the artifactual environment in which he is immersed is anything but fixed. It develops rapidly, and what man makes changes him. The feedback from artifacts which we have taken note of in earlier chapters effect considerable alterations in everything human, from anatomy to behavior. In a few generations the animal that rides in automobiles and elevators will not be the same one that formerly walked. We are raising a species whose characteristic posture is seated. It is not possible to predict all of the effects that artifacts will have on man, but it is possible to predict that the total effects will be considerable.

This statement brings us logically to another. Is it possible to control artifacts and with them their effects upon human behavior? The complex artifacts of modern industrial and scientific societies are comparatively new. We have not yet learned how to live with them. Their existence thus presents a tremendous new problem to the human individual. He has little in the way of precedence to guide him in dealing with machines which have only been in evidence for a very short time. New environments present new challenges. It is no easier and no simpler to cope with a new environment when man has had a hand in the making of it than when he has not. An individual in the forest with his bare hands or in a complex modern civilization with his skills is in the same situation in at least one respect. He has to make the necessary adjustments to ensure survival, and such adjustments may be anything up to the evolutionary kind of natural selection which might single him out because of his particular variations or discard him for another individual whose tiny differences are more favorable.

Man is the animal that will be self-surpassed. Progress continues with those best suited to move beyond the present stage, the artists, scientists, mathematicians, philosophers, productive statesmen, who try to lift society to a higher level of organization and achievement. Certainly evolution does not stop with the present stage of development. Those who suppose that because man has devised an artificial environment for himself evolution is thereby arrested do not understand the nature of feedback. Indeed it is likely that now man will be changed much more rapidly, but in any case he will be changed; and it is a question only of whether and to what extent he can plan for and control his own future development.

There is another aspect to be considered. Adaptive behavior socially speaking refers, in Darwin's phrase, to the survival of the fittest. It is, however, not the fittest individuals that is intended by this theory of evolution, but instead the survival of the fittest types. The fittest individuals carry the types but die like the others, even if somewhat later. The types of which they were the living exponents continue in other individuals *of the same type;* whereas other types made possible by individuals *not* fit are *not* continued by other individuals of the same type. Although each tiny variation is confined to a single individual, the sum constitutes an alteration in type. The variations which prove most suitable are continued in the newly established type by oncoming individuals exhibiting its characteristics.

In the last analysis, then, the control of behavior is a social rather than an individual matter, and so takes us over the borders of this book and into another. The control of behavior is surrendered by the individual to a social group, an institution, a society, a culture, and thereafter submits himself to its dictates.

If there is to be adaptive control in the case of human behavior, then the human individual will have to widen the field of his awareness. He will have to see himself with his own problems and actions as part of an ensemble which includes a segment of the material world. Only in this way can he hope to find his way intuitively to a set of alternatives out of all the possible alternatives which at present we have no way to treat mathematically.

The human individual works with artifacts as an integral part of society. Adaptive control would mean in the case of the artifacts that he understands very well and can employ in his calculations not only his effect upon them but their effects upon him. Such calculations would have to include the highly singular behavior called out by artifacts, by the piano and the chess set and the airplane, for instance, with their permanent influence upon the individual's entire behavior pattern. Witness the distorting effects of the artifact upon the private life and outlook of the piano virtuoso, the chess expert and the professional pilot.

Adaptive control would mean in the case of language that the individual understands very well and can employ in his calculations not only his capabilities of expression but also its effects upon him. The latter would have to include not only the connotative effects of language, such as literary artists are accustomed to employ, but also the denotative language of didactic communication. The individual would understand very well both the possibilities of language and its limitations. For language cannot be exactly controlled on the one hand, and on the other hand not all thought is susceptible of linguistic expression, the large area of qualities which can be named but not described, for instance. It is easy to see in politics language out of control, as in the distorting effects of speeches and writings intended to conceal rather than reveal the truth.

From the analysis of ordinary language it is possible to learn the prevailing philosophy, with a view to supporting, revising or replacing it. It was Wittgenstein's contention that we do not experience the world directly but only through the mediation of ideas we hold so deeply we do not know that we hold them. The individual views the world through a system of ideas he believes without knowing. He thought we could recover the deep-lying metaphysical beliefs which are imbedded in it and so get rid of them through the analysis of colloquial language.

Adaptive control would mean in the case of society that the individual understands very well and can employ in his calculations not only his contribution to (or detraction from) society but also its drastic influence on him. Participation in a social group means becoming a member of the group in many ways only indirectly related to its main aims. In return for his participation, the group exacts a price in the shape of conformity. A man is very largely what his associations have made him. The schoolteacher is not only an instructor of young people, he must also be the model for them that is required of him by their parents, regardless of its intrinsic desirability or undesirability.

Thus it is a very long way for the human individual from adaptive behavior to adaptive control. The distance between them eventually comes down to a matter of the distance between the practical man and the idealist, those who are busy solving immediate problems, and those who wonder what such problems ought to be. We do not yet know much about measuring the metabolic rate of need-reduction.

The most sophisticated version of adaptive control is the one constructed on the feedback model. This is a technique specifically designed to maintain an uninterrupted application by employing deviations to correct themselves (2, p. 19). Once a plan is chosen, the behavior in accordance with it must mean meeting changing conditions which could not have been foreseen. Techniques for keeping the plan in operation under these conditions require a method of continual correction. In the case of the human individual this means that a plan of action intended to bring about the reduction of a particular need must be continually corrected in terms of both the results it achieves and the changes in the location or character of the goal-object.

The name for the animal version of adaptive control may well be "learning," as Bellman says (2, p. 203). For learning is, as we have indicated earlier, acquiring from responses the capacity to respond. In adaptive control, learning becomes acquiring from responses the capacity to improve the efficiency of additional responses. When the human individual with a need to reduce and a plan designed to bring about its reduction behaves accordingly, he may learn that he is not achieving the maximum of need reduction, and he may find that he may have to alter his direction toward the goal-object or improve his techniques for obtaining it. What worked under some conditions may not work as well under others.

In the following pages some attempt will be made to study the control of adaptive behavior as it manifests itself in the human individual in the control of his animal needs and then in the control of the more specifically human needs we have been examining for some while, the needs to know, to do, and to be.

THE CONTROL OF ANIMAL NEEDS

We have considered in earlier chapters that the animal needs are thirst, hunger, sex, approach-and-exploration, activity, and the avoidance of pain. Since we have considered the last three under their peculiarly human versions of the need to know, to do and to be, it is the first three that will have to be taken up again as the animal needs. For it must be remembered that while the human individual has his own versions of the last three, he shares the first three with the sub-human animals unchanged except for the preparatory responses.

Although the human individual drinks, eats and mates like the other animals, there are serious differences in his preparation for reducing these needs from what we can find among the sub-human animals. The preparatory responses for drinking and eating are enormous, and include not only water purification plants and scientific agriculture, but also restaurants and table manners. The preparatory responses for mating include the elaborate ceremonials of courtship and marriage. The human individual has the problem always before him of how to control the animal needs. The revision of methods for obtaining secondary needs often means dropping back to an existence devoted merely to the reduction of the primary needs. Eating and copulating in war time often means dispensing with preparatory responses altogether. A man in battle may eat with his fingers and tear with his teeth, and he may commit rape with no preliminaries. In such cases there is little in the way of the anticipation of need reduction. Yet under ordinary circumstances, the human individual has always before him the prospect of reducing animal needs not only for the pleasure involved but also to make way for the secondary. Thus, plans for the reduction of animal needs in the future are not peculiar to the human individual but they are certainly prevalent though limited.

Another common feature is the extensive use of artifacts of both kinds: tools and signs, in the preparatory responses to the animal needs. We shall have next to consider the advantages and obstacles which these characteristics present to human life as a whole.

As a result of the manual use of tools through evolutionary epochs, man has developed reason. As a result of the development of reason, man has complicated his tools. One consequence of sign-behavior is social cooperation in the construction of larger and more complex tools. Now, where the contribution of an individual is a part of the structure of the entire procedure, he has clearly lost effective control. Even with special individuals assigned to the task, the effort is a failure. A dominant feature of society which everyone has overlooked is that nobody runs it.

While it is true that there are plans, and even charters and declarations, the fact remains that societies more often than not take a course that could not have been predicted. Too many variables enter into the operation, and thus far the functions of many variables lie beyond human powers of calculation. The size of the tables of values which would be necessary to calculate the functions of thousands or even hundreds of variables is staggering, for the complexity of so many variables simply exceed our understanding (2, pp. 197, 244).

Now societies rest on a bedrock of animal needs, and the more primitive the society the more evidently this is true. The most primitive tribes, which is to say, those with the fewest artifacts, such as the Guaharibos (4) or the Nambikwaras (5) of the interior of Brazil, spend all of their time food-collecting or hunting. The immediate survival of the individual and of the species dominates and replaces every other concern. In this for all their possession of cooking utensils and languages they resemble nothing so much as the sub-human animals.

In more civilized societies this is no longer the case. The reduction facilities of the need for food are by this time firmly under control, thanks to advanced methods of production and storage. It is possible to see well ahead so far as the supply of water, food and mates is concerned. The human individual often has the leisure to turn to other matters, for he has, as we have noted in earlier chapters, additional needs which have of necessity been held in abeyance. There is the need to know, there is the need to do, and there is the need to be, the needs of knowledge-as-such, for construction and for survival beyond death. He has now the time and the means to produce institutions of learning and religions.

We have noted now two important phenomena: the tremendous role played by artifacts in the preparatory response for the need-reduction of the animal needs, and the inability of man to control his destiny as lived out in society. As Peirce once described it, we are all putting our shoulders to the wheel for an end that none of us can envisage (3a). Both the collective effort and the wheel work together in a way that remains unpredictable and—what is worse—largely undirected. The human individual adapts as he goes along, and the largest part of his adaptive behavior has to be devoted to the adjustment to the movement of social forces.

But the meaning of all this must be made somewhat clearer. For all of the efforts of the human individual are deliberate, and he is conscious of making them. It is only the whole that lies beyond his awareness and his understanding. It is fair to say that such adaptive behavior is a form of human self-conditioning. It is a self-conditioning that takes place by means of artifacts and by means of social participation. The human individual is constrained to make himself over into what he must become if he is to adjust himself to human existence with its myriad of complex artifacts and the intricate structure of its social organizations.

Because of the concentration required for adaptive behavior in the face of civilization, there is no effective control. It is not possible to say that it was lost, for it never existed. The individual is carried along on a strong tide of events brought about by the actions of artifacts and the exigencies of society. Here we see the phenomenon of species dominance. There is no disposition to stand back, away from the immediate flux, in order to ascertain the advisability of a particular action. A new set of pressures has come into existence, and the individual in a complex society may not have to concern himself quite in the way that the Nambikwaras and the Guaharibos do with the problems of the reduction of the most urgent needs for the purposes of immediate survival, but in another way he does. The needs to drink, eat and mate have merely assumed other guises. They have taken on institutional forms which make different sorts of demands upon him, but essentially they remain the same. If he does not get and keep a job and a wife, he cannot assure himself of continuity in the reduction of his basic tissue-needs. He may have to do something only indirectly related, such as cut hair for a living, or practice law, but the purpose remains.

In the course of meeting the new conditions he sometimes misses the mark and commits the error of excess. He lives to drink, by substituting alcohol for water; he lives to eat, by becoming a gourmand rather than a gourmet; or he lives for sex, by becoming a profligate lover of women. Or he lives to collect the money with which to buy excessive amounts of drink, food or women.

Such excesses obscure the fact that there are other needs which through these procedures must be neglected. For the human individual the animal needs are primarily means, and the specifically human needs—the needs for abstract information and ultimate survival—are primarily ends. Getting control of the animal needs, then, means first of all arranging them in an order of proper subordination. The superordination of any one of the animal needs means loss of control. There can be enjoyment of need reduction in the case of the animal needs without compromising the superordinate needs of knowing and being. Knowing about the preparation of enjoyable food for example is not "knowing" in the sense of the need reduction of the need to know about the nature of things, except in a small way which serves chiefly to obscure the larger ways. There is a facilitation to means which is not possible when means become ends; the pathways to ends are blocked.

The control of the animal needs, therefore, requires an understanding primarily of which way to go with them, and secondarily of how far. Fasting and asceticism, like gluttony and libertinism, are errors. They obscure the goals by becoming the goal. Consider for example the religious exercise of the feast, or the pious duty of intercourse with temple prostitutes.

Arousal is a continual state but attention is single, and there is room in the consciousness for only one thing at a time. If the human individual is to have the opportunity to entertain in consciousness the problems set for him by his very existence, the problems of securing information, remaining active and guaranteeing survival, then he must be in a position to put out of his mind the more immediate problems of drinking and eating and copulating. The way to set aside the animal needs is to reduce them and prepare for their adequate reduction upon foreseeable future occasions.

In such delicate negotiations with nature, artifacts of both the tool and sign varieties play their part. Here once again, the means interjects itself in a way which threatens dangerously to become an end. The desire for exotic foods, the ornate ceremonials of the mediaeval courts of love, the merchandise of the desert caravans and the songs of the troubadours, were apt to attract men whose love for adventure or of art beguiled them into mistaking certain elaborate preparatory responses of feeding and breeding for preferable ways of life.

But here again the matter of proportions is crucial. For actions taken to insure immediate survival can block the execution of plans intended to secure ultimate survival, and the reduction of animal needs can itself interfere with preparations for their reduction upon future occasions, as when for instance food-gathering prevents the development of agriculture. Again, agriculture cannot be developed without the kind of established inquiry that is conducted by means of the scientific method, yet how is utility to be kept from interfering with inquiry when utility presents itself in more pressing variety? The problem presented by the necessity of controlling the animal needs is no simple affair even if we consider such needs apart from the other, more specifically human, needs. Before considering the problems of the totality of human needs, it will be necessary to turn first to consider the control of the needs to know and to be.

THE CONTROL OF ADAPTIVE KNOWING

We have noted in an earlier chapter on adaptive knowing that man has never become adapted to his dependence upon the secondary drives. Consider for instance the first of the secondary drives, the drive for information. The control of this drive would have to be predicated upon a thorough knowledge of what it is and how it operates. The more usual situation is to acquire knowledge in bursts during a period of disequilibrium, followed by the restoration of equilibrium centered on the newly acquired knowledge. The control of adaptive knowing would mean establishing an equilibrium centered on the drive to inquiry, and the drive to inquiry itself predicated upon an adjustment to inquiry.

Inquiry is not and cannot be a steady state. There are other demands on the organism, as we have noted. Thus control in the case of adaptive knowing means recognizing and using the cycle of learning and resting, where the positional attitudes in the resting posture are intended as preparations for the restoration of inquiry.

All such periods, of course, are to take place in a continuum of activity. Resting, in terms of inquiry, means rounds of reducing other needs. Man from birth onwards is immersed in a flux of behavior patterns over which he has little control without deliberation. Even the most deeply-motivated actions may be occasioned through some thigmotaxic episode. Consciousness of aim therefore constitutes the first step in the kind of liberative process which ends in control. It is possible to detect two very different degrees of awareness.

The first degree of awareness is the self-awareness of the knowing subject. He is aware not only of what he knows but also that he knows. He is aware, in other words, of himself as a knowing subject. This is the degree of knowing in which the theory of knowing makes its appearance formally as epistemology, and there is the inception of a philosophical debate around the question of the location of reality. It is contributed by the knowing subject, it lies in the object of knowledge, or it is contributed by the relations between them.

But for the control of adaptive knowing, the attainment of the second degree of awareness is essential. In the second degree of awareness, the subject recognizes in himself a center for the reception of impressions. He has attained that degree of detachment which permits him to occupy the perspective, whereby both subject and object are viewed objectively and even dispassionately. Only when he can imaginatively step outside the locus of forces in which himself as respondent reacts to the impact of external stimulants can there be control. For in such a perspective it is possible to see all of the influences at work, to anticipate the consequences of behavior, and, finally, to understand that the naturally *oc*curring relations involved are instances of naturally *re*curring relations.

The ability imaginatively to step outside the knowing process as a second degree of awareness involves the operation of decision about decisions—imagination brought under control. Imagination except for the self-conscious professional producer, such as the artist or scientist, is involuntary, and to some degree it is in him as well. Those theories of the creative process so-called which encourage automatism or involuntarism as a way of eliciting the aid of the unconscious are self-defeating because focusing the artist upon himself as his subject-matter, which is the very opposite of the effects desired.

Particularly is this true in the case of the wider categories of philosophy whereby societies and cultures found themselves by means of institutional aims and arrangements. There the most preferred goal is the control of the category-constructing faculty on the part of these self-selected individuals whose function it is to exercise in the highest. That the philosopher is also subject to some of the strictures of self-involvement we have been delineating is shown by the fact that it is possible to analyze at some distance the assumptions of those leaders of thought whose entire careers, admittedly successful, were devoted to the isolation of assumptions (1).

Another good example is to be found in the course of development of the experimental sciences. Once having opted for the dominance of the scientific method as a source of inquiry, a society can only watch the progression. Some sciences develop faster than others, and those which do impede the others by affecting the society in ways detrimental to their development. For instance, in recent times physics has developed faster than sociology and so has obstructed the progress of sociology in two ways: in one way, by employing the scientific method so that sociology tries to follow too exactly, and without the extenuating circumstances by means of which alone can any particular science adapt the method to its own subject-matter; and in another way, by affecting the whole society through its applications so powerfully and so thoroughly that sociology can do no more than study the effects.

This in a sense is science out of control. The phenomenon of the lack of control we have just been observing can be extended to any variety of knowledge system. The antidote is difficult to obtain, for it consists in the anticipation of the effects of a knowledge system before the construction of the system. The effects are individual as well as social, and their interweavings in the individual are matters of the relative positions of the private and public retention schemata. The human individual is a member of society, and the society has permeated him through the extent of the beliefs incorporated in the public retention schema. Control, again, consists in his ability to recognize its nature and to contribute to its correction or alteration.

Thus the control of adaptive knowing is a prize to be won only by the most intellectually vigorous individuals, while others can profit by imitating the achievement. Everyone is touched, however, and no one is immune. The aristocracy of adaptive control is self-selective in any form of society.

THE CONTROL OF ADAPTIVE DOING

Adaptation to dependence upon doing is imperative if the human species is to survive, yet at the moment it seems the least likely. Recognition of the cycle of war and peace calls for a periodic revision of established social planning and a regulated abandonment of the old in favor of a new.

The central problem in the control of adaptive doing is of course how to use action to control action. To this end the aid of the will must be evoked. The capacity for sustained response is this time to be exercised upon the control of activity and the need for achievement satisfied by the powerful construction of a state of inactivity. It is not easy to transform a drive toward doing into a condition of not-doing. Nor is the consequent inactivity to be mistaken for that passive state in which there is no need to do.

One important difference is that in the control of adaptive doing, unlike anything in the state of passive inactivity, there is the feeling of a tension established between the individual and the objects in the environment whose cues of resistance constitute a challenge. The self does not lack the proper urgency but contains the proper set of controls over it, and this records itself in the feelings as the tensions by which an equilibrium is sustained.

Under the genus of doing, then, the last thing to be done is an exercise upon the self itself. But the pitting of the self in this way against the profusion of material objects small and large in the environing universe is itself an immense claim with repercussions. For deliberate inaction is a form of widening the claim of the self in another direction. Instead of undertaking to dominate the world, as the generalized drive of aggression at first suggests to every organism, there is the attempt to stand off domination by the world—all of it, to match the world by balancing with the world, thus claiming a greater participation in the world by a substitute method.

There is another possible method of the control of adaptive doing which has not been so well understood. This is the exercise of activity kept fixed upon the goal of the objects themselves, material objects altered only in their own interest and for their own ends, and including physical objects as well as organisms. Such an endeavor has been many times advocated in connection with living organisms and is still part of Buddhism. But with physical objects the case is somewhat different. An ultimate religious interest could not legitimately exclude so large a fragment of being as is constituted by the material universe and still maintain itself as ultimate. In a universe assumed to be a whole, the welfare of every part concerns all other parts; since what things are largely determines the human individual, it is only an analogue of the subjective interest of the long-range self when he becomes devoted to things-as-they-are. The environing material objects of the human individual are the impressions of his autobiography, recorded at the time. He must exercise the greatest care in what he does to them, except as he is willing to have them perpetuate his efforts. For it is a characteristic of at least some material objects that they live longer than individuals and so manage to constitute cultures and civilizations. What a man does is what he leaves behind him, and if he does what everyone else does then it means either that he was content to go by the numbers or that he was less than capable of making an impression.

The control of behavior consists in operations on environmental variables (6, pp. 227, 254). The outcome of the manipulation of behavior cannot at the present time be predicted because of the vast number of unknown variables which are involved both in the individual and in his environment. Consistent behavior is behavior within the limits of a system, and the system is determined by its axioms. Hence the necessity for making an intuitive choice of axiom sets from which theorems can be deduced capable of application to action. Learning the methods of emitted response (in Skinner's sense) in contrast with elicited response, which is for the most part what we have been examining throughout the early chapters, will help.

The admonition of adaptive doing is: learn to need what is demanded of you. Demanded, that is, in the way of activity or of selective inactivity. There is a mechanism for this, and it consists in the intuitive reaching for the appropriate, a feeling for the fitness of right actions. Not to do what will continue doing but only to do what needs to be done. For this it is necessary to comprehend that the state of the present moment is not a solipsism but a concentration of the world. Incised into the delicate boundary between the individual and his present world there is the silent but forceful representation of all absent being.

THE CONTROL OF ADAPTIVE BEING

If man has never become adapted to his dependence upon the first two of the secondary drives, neither has he upon the third. In general it is true that the more fundamental the aim the more primitive the search. Recognition of the cycle of belief and doubt calls for a periodic revision of established doctrine and a regulated abandonment of the old in favor of a new.

The central problem in the control of adaptive being is of course how to use existence to prolong existence. The hard shell of an equilibrium based on conformity must first be broken before there can be restoration of an effort to acquire a greater measure of permanence-as-persistence. Religion is the search for reality under the leadership of inquiry—what Einstein once called the holy curiosity of inquiry.

As with the control of adaptive knowing, we find degrees of being, recognized by the feelings. The first degree of being consists in the feeling of the self for the self. This is the *cogito, ergo sum* of Descartes. It is manifest in the egotism of the religious leader, the willingness to sacrifice his family to the conduct dictated by his own personal sense of what is the good, as did Augustine and Gandhi, for instance. Self-feeling is an extreme form of self-regard. I am and that I am marks the first degree of feeling for me, my own being and its necessity as conceived under the genus of being.

The second degree of being is the degree necessary for the control of adaptive being, the being implied in the conception of a far-away god. A good example is Aristotle's god, abstract, remote, and presently unconcerned (3), a model but not a minion of human will. That such a conception of god makes no demands allows for the yearning for persistence to be brought under control. We shall need to know a great deal more about the nature of theologies, retention schemata, and the relations between them. Two further assumptions are implied: the recognition of the self as a datum, and the dismissal of the nearby god as an illusion.

The recognition of the self as a datum puts the onus of effort on immediate survival and throws the human individual back upon the primary drives. That 'I am' is a simple fact of existence prevents the supererogatory elevation of subjective aims which is so damaging to more disciplined strivings in the secondary drives, an elevation which forcefully and often doctrinally precludes the participation of the pure sciences and the fine arts. This is the state of religious ignorance in which being and knowing are thought to be mutually exclusive (5, p. 395). The abatement of supernatural claims for the self, as in the immortality of the soul, actually provides for a greater share in being, for it abandons a provincial corner of the world in exchange for the world. That 'I am' means to merge its little with the grandeur of the cosmos, is large.

The dismissal of the nearby god as an illusion eliminates local conceptions in the same way as the recognition of the self as a datum. The incense burned to small bronze castings of serene figures or of tortured and suffering ones, the adoration and subservience accorded small wood carvings, amulets and magical pieces of all sorts delivers some men into the hands of others and serves to prevent the development of the pure sciences though it does in a certain sense promote the fine arts. The dismissal of the nearby god allows for the freedom from the far-away god, from the ignorance of the narrowly religious interest which had prevented knowing and being from working together.

The result in both cases is the acceptance of death as a transformation into positive otherness. The control of adaptive being is only possible on the basis of a reconciliation with positive otherness. Death, as we have seen in an earlier chapter, is not non-being, its contradictory, but positive otherness, its opposite. Being cannot not-be, it can only change forms, the substance remaining. Thus in order to achieve reconciliation with positive otherness, the recognition of the self as a datum and the dismissal of the nearby god as an illusion are essential.

The admonition of adaptive being is: learn to need what is inevitable. There is a mechanism for this, and it consists in the control of the generalized drive, the ability to modulate the intensity of arousal. If organisms are plastic objects which can maintain themselves only by means of a constant interaction with the environment, then the energy which it is necessary to expend must be turned into the anticipation of the effects of a security system before its adoption.

The proper proportions of primary and secondary needs would allow for the longest pursuit of what is sought. Suggestions have ranged all the way from the division of labor to the due proportionality of the golden mean, from some variety of Marxism to some variety of Buddhism, including a mixed version of the two working together. Marxism for the primary needs, Buddhism for the secondary. But it has been shown possible to live comfortably on a more modest expenditure of belief, spending very little, and then only when compelled by the evidence, and maintaining at the same time a large banked reserve. Such large-scale commitments elicit absolute belief over which there is no control, only the surrender of the individual.

INTERACTION OF KNOWING AND BEING

The problems of control of adaptive behavior are faced with arduous difficulties flowing from the complex nature of the interactions between knowing and being. There are for instance the phenomena of knowing in order to do, of being in order to know, and of knowing in order to be. Let us discuss them briefly one at a time.

First, knowing in order to do. Ideals have acquired a bad name because most of those individuals who act in terms of them do so absolutely, that is, without regard to whether their actions will further or retard events in the direction of the ideals. Strategy has been misunderstood as pragmatism in the bad sense of time-serving. But there are two kinds of time-serving: that which furthers an ideal and that which does not. Also, not all ideals are equally good ideals. Consider for instance the ideal of perfection established as a guide to action. There is much involved here that could be clarified by analyzing the structure of the act. It is the inability to foresee the consequences of actions which makes the division between motives. That an act is intended does not mean that it was not externally caused and does not imply necessarily that the action itself was free.

The consciousness is a thoroughfare through which the ideas retained in the memory sometimes pass over into action. To say that such ideas move through consciousness means that the individual looks at them and thinks about them but not necessarily that he deals with them. He cannot help observing them in passing, but to reckon with them when he does is something else. Consciousness admits of all sorts of degrees.

The intentionality of the act, then, is the degree of consciousness it receives. A man with Parkinson's paralysis may inadvertently knock a vase off the table, and he knows immediately what he is doing but remains powerless to prevent it. He is conscious of his act but he does not control it. Control requires assigning to each content of consciousness the degree of concentration it deserves.

Next, being in order to know. If we do not exist, then we cannot know. This final end is the retention of consciousness after death in order to continue to inquire and to complete the knowledge, through which, it is hoped, we can be one with being. Here with being as a means and knowing as an end, the subordination is aimed at the acquisition of knowledge. Other drives are modulated accordingly, and the result is the true type of the scholar. He wishes to live and to die rich in the details of knowledge, firm in the possession of wisdom achieved through cortical retention.

However, we shall see that the picture is far from simple. For there is also knowing in order to be. Knowing extends its being by contact with the general. Thus, the acquisition of the knowledge of abstract structures in so far as they are true of the actual world pushes back non-being. The direction of being is clear: that knowledge of the more general is to be preferred to that of the less general. The pure knowledge of the nature of things serves to further the chances of surviving. The more we know, the more we participate in being by assimilating sign-copies of universal, or at the very least of world-wide, natural law.

But such knowledge is a matter of participation rather than possession. It reflects being and possesses it only through representation and by means of images or signs, both in a way pictures. In this way man can be let in on more than he can have. Thus although Sartre is right in saying that knowing is a kind of having, this is not the whole story of knowing. It opens up vistas into which he cannot move and from which he is excluded in every way except that of comprehension.

The interaction of knowing and being thus presents the final problem in the control of adaptive behavior, which is the control of adaptive survival, extending being by means of knowing not as the private possession of knowledge but as the private contribution to the planning for species-dominance. The clearest instance of adaptive behavior is the activity of the practical dreamer: artist, scientist, philosopher, or culture-maker in other forms, who completes the supreme act of self-conditioning by implementing the social conditioning of the future, before departing for his own fate in positive otherness.

REFERENCES

CHAPTER 1

1. Hull, C. L.: *Principles of Behavior.* Appleton-Century, New York, 1943.
2. Neisser, U.: The Imitation of Man by Machine, *Science 139:*193-7, 1963.
3. Pavlov, I. P.: *Conditioned Reflexes.* G. V. Anrep trans., Dover, New York, 1960.
4. Sherrington, C. S.: *The Integrative Action of the Nervous System.* Yale University Press, New Haven, 1961.
5. Skinner, B. F.: *The Behavior of Organisms.* Appleton-Century-Crofts, New York, 1938.
6. Thorndike, E. L.: *Animal Intelligence.* Macmillan, New York, 1911.
7 __________: *Human Nature and the Social Order.* Macmillan, New York, 1940.
8. von Neumann, J.: *The Computer and the Brain.* Yale University Press, New Haven, 1958.
9. Walter, W. Grey: *The Living Brain.* Duckworth, London, 1957.

CHAPTER 2

1. An estimate of 1,750,000 years made by J. F. Evernden and Garniss H. Curtis as reported in the *National Geographic,* 12, 568. 1961. See also Dr. Kenneth Oakley as reporting to the British Association, *The Sunday Times.* London. September 3, 1961. Revised to 1,300,000 by W. Genter and H. J. Lippolt, in the *Sunday Times.* London. November 26, 1961.
2. Clark, Graham: *World Prehistory.* University Press, Cambridge, 1961.
3. *Collected Papers of Charles Sanders Peirce.* 8 Vols. Harvard University Press, Cambridge, Mass., 1931-58.
4. Dobzhansky, T.: *Mankind Evolving.* Yale University Press, New Haven, 1962.
5. Herrick, C. Judson: *The Evolution of Human Nature.* University of Texas Press, Austin, 1956.
6. Howells, William: *Back of History.* Doubleday, Garden City, New York, 1954.
7. La Barre, Weston: *The Human Animal.* University Press, Chicago, 1954.
8. Linton, R. (ed.): *The Science of Man in the World Crisis.* Columbia University Press, New York, 1947.

9. Pannekoek, A.: *Anthropogenesis.* North-Holland Publishing Co., Amsterdam, 1953.
10. Pavlov, I. P.: *Lectures on Conditioned Reflexes.* 2 Vols. W. H. Gantt, trans., International Publishers, New York, 1928.
11. Sherrington, C.: *The Integrative Action of the Nervous System.* Yale University Press, New Haven, 1961.
12. Spuhler, J. N. *et al.*: *The Evolution of Man's Capacity for Culture.* Wayne State University Press, Detroit, 1959.

CHAPTER 3

1. Bullock, T. H.: The Origin of Patterned Nervous Discharge, in *Behavior.* (In press).
2. Crozier, W. J., and Hoagland, H.: The Study of Living Organisms, in *Handbook of General Experimental Psychology.* Clark University Press, Worcester, 1934.
3. Deutsch, J. A.: *The Structural Basis of Behavior.* University of Chicago Press, Chicago, 1960.
4. Gibson, J. J.: *The Perception of the Visual World.* Houghton Mifflin, Boston, 1950.
5. Harlow, H. F., and Woolsey, C. N. (ed.): *Biological and Biochemical Bases of Behavior.* University of Wisconsin Press, Madison, 1958.
6. Hebb, D. O.: *The Organization of Behavior.* John Wiley, New York, 1959.
7. ————: *A Textbook of Psychology.* Saunders, Philadelphia, 1958.
8. Hull, C. L.: *Principles of Behavior.* Appleton-Century, New York, 1943.
9. ————: Knowledge and Purpose as Habits Mechanisms, in *Psychol. Rev.*, 37:511-25, 1930.
10. Jasper, H. H.: Recent Advances in our Understanding of Ascending Activities of the Reticular System, in *Reticular Formation of the Brain.* Little Brown, Boston, 1958.
11. Lewin, K.: *A Dynamic Theory of Personality.* McGraw-Hill, New York, 1935.
12. Loeb, J.: *Der Heliotropismus der Tiere und Seine Uebereinstimmung mit dem Heliotropismus der Pflanzen.* Würzburg, 1889.
13. ————: *The Mechanistic Conception of Life.* University of Chicago Press, Chicago, 1912.
14. Lorenz, K., Tinbergen, N., and others: *Instinctive Behavior.* Schiller, C. H. (ed.), Methuen, London, 1957.
15. ————: *Instinctive Behavior*, pp. 88 n 2, 121, 141, 292-93. Tinbergen, N. *The Study of Instinct.* Clarendon Press. Oxford. 1951.
16. MacLean, P. D.: The Limbic System with Respect to Two Basic Life Principles. Brazier, M. A. B. (ed.). *The Central Nervous System and Behavior.* Transactions of Second Conference. Josiah Macy, Jr. Foundation, New York, 1959.

17. McCullough, W. S.: Cortico-cortical connections, in Bucy, P. *The Precentral Motor Cortex.* University of Illinois Press, Urbana, 1944.
18. ————: The Functional Organization of the Cerebral Cortex. *Physiological Review.* *24*:390-407, 1944.
19. ————: Modes of Functional Organization of the Cerebral Cortex, in *FED. PROC.*, *6*:448-52, 1947.
20. Magoun, H. W.: *The Waking Brain.* Thomas, Springfield, 1958.
21. Meyer, D. W.: Some Psychological Determinants of Sparing and Loss Following Damage to the Brain, in *Biological and Biochemical Bases of Behavior.*
22. Olds, J.: Effects of Hunger and Male Sex Hormones on Self-Stimulation of the Brain, in *J. Comp. Physiol. Psychol.*, *51*:320-24, 1958.
23. Pavlov, I. P.: *Conditioned Reflexes.* G. V. Anrep trans., Dover, New York, 1960.
24. Penfield, W., and Roberts, L.: *Speech and Brain-mechanisms.* Princeton University Press, Princeton, 1959.
25. Sherrington, C. S.: *The Integrative Action of the Nervous System.* Yale University Press, New Haven, 1906.
26. Skinner, B. F.: *The Behavior of Organisms.* Appleton-Century-Crofts, New York, 1938.
27. Sommerhof, G.: *Analytical Biology.* Oxford University Press, London, 1950.
28. Sperry, R. W.: Physiological Plasticity and Brain Circuit Theory, in *Biological and Biochemical Bases of Behavior.*
29. Thorndike, E. L.: A Proof of the Law of Effect, in *Science*, *77*:173-75, 1933; and An Experimental Study of Rewards, in *Teach. Coll. Contr. Educ.*, No. 580, 1933.
30. Tinbergen, N.: *The Study of Instinct.* Clarendon Press, Oxford, 1951.
31. Walter, W. Grey: A Statistical Approach to the Theory of Conditioning, in Jasper, H. H., and Smirnov, G. D. (ed.) *The Moscow Colloquium on Electroencephalography of Higher Nervous Activity. EEG Journal*, Montreal, 1960.
32. Wiener, N.: *Cybernetics.* Wiley, New York, 1948.
33. Woodward, R. H.: *Dynamic Psychology.* Columbia University Press, New York, 1918.

CHAPTER 4

1. Aristotle: *Metaphysics.* 980a20.
2. Elkin, A. P.: *The Australian Aborigines.* Angus and Robertson, Sydney, Australia, 1938.
3. Gesell, A.: *The First Five Years of Life.* Harper & Bros., New York, 1949.
4. Green, J. D., in Williams, R. H. (ed.): *Textbook of Endocrinology.* W. B. Saunders Co., Third edition, Philadelphia, 1962.

5. Harlow, F. H., and Woolsey, C. N. (ed.): *Biological and Biochemical Bases of Behavior.* University of Wisconsin Press, Madison, 1958.
6. Hebb, D. O.: *Organization of Behavior.* Wiley, New York, 1959.
7. ————: *A Textbook of Psychology.* Saunders, Philadelphia, 1958.
8. Herrick, C. J.: *The Evolution of Human Nature.* University of Texas Press, Austin, 1956.
9. Hilgard, E. R.: *Theories of Learning.* Appleton-Century-Crofts, New York, 1948.
10. Loeb, J.: *The Mechanistic Conception of Life.* University of Chicago Press, Chicago, 1912.
11. Lorenz, Konrad A.: *King Solomon's Ring.* Crowell, New York, 1952.
12. Olds, J.: Effects of hunger and male sex hormone on self-stimulation of the brain, in *J. Comp. Physiol, Psychol., 51*:320-24, 1958.
13. Pavlov, I. P.: *Conditioned Reflexes.* Dover, New York, 1960.
14. Piaget, J.: *The Language and Thought of the Child.* Meridian, New York, 1958.
15. *Science, 133*:748, 1961
16. Sherrington, Sir C.: *The Integrative Action of the Nervous System.* Yale University Press, New Haven, 1961.
17. Skinner, B. F.: *The Behavior of Organisms.* Appleton-Century-Crofts, New York, 1938.
18. Steward, J. H. (ed.): *Handbook of South American Indians.* Vol. 3. The Tropical Forest Tribes. U. S. Government Printing Office, Washington, D. C., 1948.

CHAPTER 6

1. Berlyne, D. E.: Novelty and Curiosity as Determinants of Exploratory Behavior, *Brit. J. Psychol., 41*:68-80, 1950; The Arousal and Satiation of Perceptual Curiosity in the Rat, *J. Comp. Physiol. Psychol., 48*:238-46, 1955; Conflict and Information-Theory Variables as Determinants of Human Perceptual Curiosity, *J. Exptl. Psychol., 53*:399-404, 1957; Berlyne, D. E., and Slater, J.: Perceptual Curiosity, Exploratory Behavior and Maze Learning, *J. Comp. Physiol. Psychol., 50*:228-32, 1957.
2. *Collected Papers of Charles S. Pierce.* 8 Vols. Harvard University Press, Cambridge, 1931-1958.
3. Cournot, A. A.: *An Essay on the Foundation of our Knowledge.* M. H. Moore trans., Liberal Arts Press, New York, 1956.
4. Dell, P. C.: in *Reticular Formation of the Brain.* Little Brown, Boston, 1958.
5. Deutsch, J. A.: *The Structural Basis of Behavior.* University of Chicago Press, Chicago, 1960.
6. Feibleman, James K.: The Cultural Circuit in Psychology and Psychiatry, *J. Nervous and Mental Disease, 132*:2, 1961.
7. See the Peirce references in Feibleman, J. K.: *An Introduction to Peirce's Philosophy.* Harper, New York, 1948.

8. Gibson, J. J.: Perceptions as a Function of Stimulation, in *Psychology: A Study of Science. Study I, Conceptual and Systematic.* Vol. I. Sensory, Perceptual and Physiological Formations. Koch, S. (ed.), McGraw-Hill, New York, 1959.
9. Guthrie, E. R.: *The Psychology of Learning.* Harper, New York, 1935.
10. Hebb, D. O.: *Textbook of Psychology.* Saunders, Philadelphia, 1958.
11. Hull, C. L.: *Principles of Behavior.* Appleton-Century, New York, 1943.
12. ———: Quantitative Aspects of the Evolution of Concepts, an Experimental Study, *Psychological Monographs, 28*:123, 1920.
13. Jasper, H. H.: Reticular-Cortical Systems and Theories in the Integrative Action of the Brain, in *Biological and Biochemical Bases of Behavior,* Harlow, H. F., and Woolsey, C. N. (eds.). University of Wisconsin Press, Madison, 1958.
14. ———: Recent Advances in our Understanding of Ascending Activities of the Reticular System, in Jasper, H. H., and others (eds.). *Reticular Formation of the Brain.* Little Brown, Boston, 1958.
15. Lewin, K.: *Principles of Topological Psychology.* McGraw-Hill, New York, 1936.
16. Magoun, H. W.: *The Waking Brain.* Thomas, Springfield, 1958.
17. Marcel, G.: *The Mystery of Being,* Vol. I: Reflection and Mystery. Harvill Press, London, 1950.
18. Miller, G. A., Galanter, E., and Pribram, K. H.: *Plans and the Structure of Behavior.* Holt, New York, 1960.
19. Pavlov, I. P.: *Conditioned Reflexes.* G. V. Anrep trans., Dover, New York, 1960.
20. Plato: *Republic.* 412e-413a.
21. Russell, B.: *Human Knowledge: Its Scope and Limits.* Simon and Schuster, New York, 1948.
22. Skinner, B. F.: *The Behavior of Organisms.* Appleton-Century-Crofts, New York, 1938.
23. ———: *Science and Human Behavior.* Macmillan, New York, 1960.

CHAPTER 7

1. Coghill, G. E.: *Anatomy and the Problem of Behavior.* Cambridge University Press, London, 1929.
2. Dorfman, R. E., and Shipley, R. A.: *Androgens.* John Wiley, New York, 1956.
3. Hebb, D. O.: *A Textbook of Psychology.* W. B. Saunders, Philadelphia, 1958.
4. Pavlov, I. P.: *Conditioned Reflexes.* G. V. Anrep trans., Dover, New York, 1960.
5. ———: *Lectures on Conditioned Reflexes.* W. H. Gantt, trans., 2 vols., International Publishers, New York, 1928.

CHAPTER 8

1. Brazier, M. A. B. (ed.): *The Central Nervous System and Behavior.* Transactions of the First Conference. Josiah Macy Jr. Foundation, New York, 1959.
2. For a good account of the traditional conception of tropisms in animals, see Crozier, W. J.: The Study of Living Organisms, *The Foundations of Experimental Psychology.* C. Murchison (ed.). Clark University Press, Worcester, Mass., 1929.
3. Elkin, A. P.: *The Australian Aborigenes.* Angus and Robertson, Sydney, 1938.
4. Frazer, J. G.: *The Magic Art.* 2 vols., Macmillan, London, 1926.
5. Hebb, D. O.: *Biological and Biochemical Bases of Behavior.* Harlow, H. F., and Woolsey, C. N. (eds.). University of Wisconsin Press, Madison, 1958.
6. Hull, C. L.: *Principles of Behavior.* Appleton-Century, New York, 1943.
7. Magoun, H. W.: *The Waking Brain.* Thomas, Springfield, 1958.
8. Pavlov, I. P.: *Conditioned Reflexes.* G. V. Anrep trans., Dover, New York, 1960.
9. Sartre, J. P.: *Being and Nothingness.* H. E. Barnes, trans., Philosophical Library, New York, 1956.
10. Sherrington, C. S.: *The Integrative Action of the Nervous System.* Yale University Press, New Haven, 1961.
11. Skinner, B. F.: *Science and Human Behavior.* Macmillan, New York, 1960.
12. ————: *The Behavior of Organisms.* Appleton-Century-Crofts, New York, 1938.

CHAPTER 9

1. Allport, G. W.: *Personality: A Psychological Interpretation.* Holt, New York, 1937.
2. Bykov, K. M.: *The Cerebral Cortex and the Internal Organs,* W. H. Gantt trans., Chemical Pub. Co., New York, 1957.
3. Dell, Paul C.: *Reticular Formation of the Brain.* Little Brown, Boston, 1958.
4. Granda, A. M., and Hammack, J. T.: Operant behavior during sleep, *Science, 133*:1485, 1961.
5. Hebb, D. O.: *The Organization of Behavior.* Wiley, New York, 1959.
6. ————: *Textbook of Psychology.* Saunders, Philadelphia, 1958.
7. Hull, C. L.: *Principles of Behavior.* Appleton-Century, New York, 1943.
8. Jackson, J. Hughlings: *Selected Writings.* 2 vols., London, 1931.
9. Linton, R. (ed.): *The Science of Man in the World Crisis.* Columbia University Press, New York, 1945.

10. Lorenz, K., Tinbergen, N., and others: *Instinctive Behavior.* C. H. Schiller (ed.), Methuen, London, 1957.
11. Magoun, H. W.: *The Waking Brain.* Thomas, Springfield, 1958.
12. Pavlov, I. P.: *Conditioned Reflexes.* G. V. Anrep trans., Dover, New York, 1960.
13. Sherrington, C.: *Integrative Action of the Nervous System.* Yale University Press, New Haven, 1961.
14. Skinner, B. F.: *The Behavior of Organism.* Appleton-Century-Crofts, New York, 1938.
15. Thurstone, L. L.: *The Measurement of Values.* University Press, Chicago, 1959.

CHAPTER 10

1. Feibleman, J. K.: *The Institutions of Society.* Allen & Unwin, London, 1956.
2. Hull, C. L.: *Principles of Behavior.* Appleton-Century, New York, 1943.
3. Pavlov, I. P.: *Conditioned Reflexes.* G. V. Anrep trans., Dover, New York, 1960.

CHAPTER 11

1. Croce, B.: *Autobiography.* Clarendon Press, Oxford, 1928.
2. Hebb. D. O.: *Textbook of Psychology.* Saunders, Philadelphia, 1958.
3. ——————: *The Organization of Behavior.* Wiley, New York, 1959.
4. Hull, C. L.: *Principles of Behavior.* Appleton-Century, New York, 1943.
5. Jasper, H.: in *Biological and Biochemical Bases of Behavior.* Harlow, H. F., and Woolsey, C. N. (ed.), University of Wisconsin Press, Madison, 1958.
6. Luce, R. D.: *Individual Choice Behavior.* Wiley, New York, 1959.
7. Munn, Norman L.: *Psychology,* 2nd ed., Houghton Mifflin, Boston, 1951.
8. Pavlov, I. P.: *Conditioned Reflexes.* G. V. Anrep trans., Dover, New York, 1960.
9. Penfield, W., and Roberts, L.: *Speech and Brain-Mechanisms.* University Press, Princeton, 1959.
10. Royce, Josiah: *The World and the Individual,* 2nd Series: *Nature, Man and the Moral Order.* Dover, New York, 1959.
11. Sherrington, Sir C.: *The Integrative Action of the Nervous System.* Yale University Press, New Haven, 1961.
12. Simeons, A. T. W.: *Man's Presumptuous Brain.* Dutton, New York, 1961.
13. Skinner, B. F.: *The Behavior of Organisms.* Appleton-Century-Crofts, New York, 1938.

14. ———: *Verbal Behavior.* Appleton-Century-Crofts, New York, 1957.
15. Wells, M. J.: What the Octopus Makes of It, in *Scientific American, 49*:215, 1961.

CHAPTER 12

1. *Collected Papers of Charles Sanders Peirce.* 8 Vols. Harvard University Press, Cambridge, 1931-58.
2. Sherrington, Sir C.: *The Integrative Action of the Nervous System.* Yale University Press, New Haven, 1961.

CHAPTER 13

1. Hebb, D. O.: *Textbook of Psychology.* Saunders, Philadelphia, 1958.
2. Skinner, B. F.: *The Behavior of Organisms.* Appleton-Century-Crofts, New York, 1938.

CHAPTER 14

1. Fitch, F. B.: *Symbolic Logic.* Ronald Press, New York, 1952.
2. Freud, S.: *The Interpretation of Dreams.* Macmillan, New York, 1933.
3. Hegel, G. F. W.: *The Phenomenology of Mind.* J. B. Baillie, trans., Macmillan, New York, 1931.
4. Kierkegaard, S.: *The Sickness Unto Death.* N. Lowrie, trans., University Press, Princeton, 1947.
5. Pavlov, I. P.: *Conditioned Reflexes.* G. V. Anrep, trans., Dover, New York, 1960.
6. Sartre, J. P.: *Existentialism.* B. Frechtman, trans., Philosophical Library, New York, 1947.
7. Skinner, B. F.: *Science and Human Behavior.* Macmillan, New York, 1960.

CHAPTER 15

1. Aristotle: *Metaphysics.* 5 and 7.
2. Bellman, R.: *Adaptive Control Processes.* University Press, Princeton, 1961.
3. Boas, G.: *Some Assumptions of Aristotle.* American Philosophical Society, Philadelphia, 1959.

3a. *Collected Papers of Charles Sanders Peirce,* 8 vols. Harvard University Press, Cambridge, 1931-58.

4. Gheerbrant, A.: *Journey to the Far Amazon.* E. Fitzgeral, trans., Simon and Schuster, New York, 1954.
5. Levi-Strauss, C.: *Tristes Tropiques.* Criterion, New York, 1961.
6. Skinner, B. F.: *Science and Human Behavior.* Macmillan, New York, 1960.

INDEX OF PROPER NAMES

INDEX OF TOPICS

B

E

K

L

M

N

O

P

Q

R

S

T

U

V

W

Z